REGINA

Regina, c. 1930.

The History of Canadian Cities

REGINA

An Illustrated History

J. William Brennan

James Lorimer & Company, Publishers
and
Canadian Museum of Civilization
In Collaboration with the Secretary of State

Toronto, 1989

Copyright © 1989 by the Canadian Museum of Civilization. Crown copyright reserved. No part of this book may be reproduced or transmitted by any form or by any means, electronic or mechanical, including photocopying, or by any information storage or retrieval system, without permission in writing from the publisher.

Cartography: George Duff

Canadian Cataloguing in Publication Data
Brennan, J. William
Regina, an illustrated history

(The History of Canadian Cities)
Co-published by the Canadian Museum of Civilization
Bibliography: p.
Includes index.
ISBN 1-55028-250-6

1. Regina (Sask.) - History.   2. Regina (Sask.) - Description - Views. I. Canadian Museum of Civilization. II. Title. III. Series.

FC3546.4.B74 1989   971.24′4   C89-093891-1
F1074.5.R3B74 1989

This book has been published with the help of a grant from the Social Science Federation of Canada, using funds provided by the Social Sciences and Humanities Research Council of Canada, and from the Canadian Museum of Civilization.

James Lorimer & Company, Publishers
Egerton Ryerson Memorial Building
35 Britain Street
Toronto, Ontario M5A 1R7.

Printed and bound in Canada
5 4 3 2 1 89 90 91 92 93

Illustration Credits

National Archives of Canada: (back cover, top right, PA57766), frontispiece (PA119931), 13 (Topley, 72357), 32 top (C-1879); *Manitoba Archives*: 19, 56 top; *RCMP Museum*: 27 bottom, 28 top, 29, 30 top and bottom, 112 top; *RCMP Headquarters*: 28 bottom; *Provincial Archives of Alberta*: 34 bottom; *City of Regina Archives*: 76, 166 top (City of Regina Public Affairs Department); *University of Regina Archives*: 81, 148; *Browarny Photographers*: 156 top; *Regina Public Library*: 90; *Saskatchewan Sports Hall of Fame*: 144 top; *The Leader-Post*: 170 bottom; *Glenbow Archives*: 98, 103 top; *The Globe Theatre*: 184 (Richard Gustin, Bill Dow, Michael Caruana, Gordon Milroy); *Saskatchewan Archives Board*: Back cover top left, bottom left and bottom right, 10, 15, 20, 24 top and bottom, 25, 26 top and bottom, 27 top, 32 bottom, 34 top, 38 top and bottom, 40 top and bottom, 41, 42 top and bottom, 44 top and bottom, 45 top and bottom, 46 left and right, 48 top and bottom, 49, 50 top and bottom, 51 top and bottom, 53, 54, 56 bottom, 59 top and bottom, 60, 62, 63 top and bottom, 64 top and bottom, 66, 67, 68, 69, 70 top and bottom (Ed Rossie), 75 top (West's Studio Collection) and bottom, 77, 78 top (West's Studio Collection) and bottom, 80 top and bottom, 82 top and bottom, 85 top and bottom, 88 (West's Studio Collection), 89, 92, 93, 94, 96, 100, 103 bottom, 105 (Saskatchewan Wheat Pool Collection), 106, 108, 109 (West's Studio Collection), 112 top, 114, 116, 117, 118, 120 top and bottom (Ed Rossie), 121 top and bottom, 124, 127, 128 top and bottom, 130 top and bottom, 132 top and bottom, 134, 136, 137, 138 top and bottom (West's Studio Collection), 140, 144 bottom, 150, 152, 156 bottom, 157, 158 top and bottom, 160 top and bottom, 161 top (Richard Gustin) and bottom, 162, 163, 164 top and bottom, 166 bottom (West's Studio Collection), 170 top, 171 top and bottom, 172 top and bottom, 174 top and bottom, 176 top and bottom, 178, 179, 180, 182 top and bottom, 183 top and bottom.

Table of Contents

Foreword: The History of Canadian Cities Series 7

Acknowledgements 8

Introduction: The Origins and Incorporation of Regina, 1882-84 11

Chapter One: Town to City, 1885-1905 21

Chapter Two: Capital of a Booming Province, 1906-13 55

Chapter Three: Depression and Readjustment, 1914-39 99

Chapter Four: *Floreat Regina*, 1939-79 151

Appendix: Statistical Tables 190

Endnotes 198

Suggestions for Further Reading and Research 212

Index 217

List of Maps

1. Regina in 1883 16

2. The Provisional Districts of Assiniboia and Saskatchewan, 1903 22

3. Regina in 1905 36

4. Regina in 1913 72

5. Regina Wards, 1906-1910 and 1911-1913 86

6. Regina in 1939 122

7. Regina Wards, 1935-36 142

8. Regina's Geographic Position 154

9. Land Use in Regina, 1978 168

10. Regina Wards, 1979 186

Appendix

Statistical Tables

I   The Growth of Manufacturing in Regina, 1891-1981

II   Numbers of Males Per 1,000 Females in Regina, 1901-1981

III   Urban Population Growth and Distribution in Saskatchewan, 1906-81

IV   Population Growth in Saskatchewan and Prairie Cities, 1901-81

V   Population Growth in Regina, 1901-81

VI   Birthplace of Regina's Canadian-Born Population, 1911-81

VII   Birthplace of Regina's Foreign-Born Population, 1911-1981

VIII Ethnic Origins of Regina's Population, 1901-81

IX   Major Religious Affiliations of Regina's Population, 1901-81

X   Age Composition of Regina's Population, 1921-1981

XI   Value of Building Permits Issued in Regina, 1904-1979

XII   The Labour Force of Regina by Industry, 1911-81

XIII Wheat Acreage, Production and Value in Saskatchewan, 1905-76

To my wife, Judy

Foreword
The History of Canadian Cities Series

The History of Canadian Cities Series is a project of the History Division, Canadian Museum of Civilization (National Museums of Canada). The project was begun in 1977 to respond to a growing demand for more popular publications to complement the already well-established scholarly publications programs of the Museum. The purpose of this series is to offer the general public a stimulating insight into Canada's urban past.

It is the hope of the Canadian Museum of Civilization that the publication of these books will provide the public with information on Canadian cities in a visually attractive and highly readable form. At the same time, the plan of the series is to have authors follow a similar format. The result, it is anticipated, will be a systematic, interpretative and comprehensive account of the urban experience in many Canadian communities. Eventually, as new volumes are completed, *The History of Canadian Cities* will be a major step along the path to a general and comparative study of Canada's urban development.

The form for this series — the individual urban biography — is based on a desire to examine all aspects of community development and to relate the parts to a larger context. The series is also based on the belief that, while each city has a distinct personality that deserves to be discovered, the volumes must also provide analysis that will lift the narrative of a city's experience to the level where it will elucidate questions that are of concern to Canadians generally. These questions include such issues as ethnic relationships, regionalism, provincial-municipal interaction, social mobility, labour-management relationships, urban planning and general economic development.

In this volume, J. William Brennan presents the fascinating story of a city that has two wonderfully contrasting nicknames: "Queen City of the Plains" and "Pile of Bones." Like other prairie cities — and unlike most cities in central and eastern Canada — Regina did not rise to city status as a result of a particularly fortuitous location. In fact, in terms of natural fea-

tures, the site of Regina was not at all suitable to urban development. Thus the story told here is one of people overcoming geography and location to build a proud, tenacious urban community. While it is true that over one hundred years after its birth Regina has not rivalled Winnipeg or Calgary, the Saskatchewan capital is nevertheless a major success story. The residents of Regina have transformed a bleak patch of prairie landscape into a remarkable city of trees, parks and waterways. Indeed, in many respects Regina has amenities that would surprise visitors.

The author of this volume is a well-known prairie historian. A long-time member of the history department at the University of Regina, Professor Brennan — and his students — have been responsible for a wide variety of articles and books on this prairie city. Professor Brennan has also been an active member of Canada's urban history group and has served as a member of the editorial advisory board of the *Urban History Review/Revue d'histoire urbaine* and the editorial board of *Prairie Forum*.

Dr. Brennan's lively text is enriched by an excellent collection of illustrations and specially prepared maps. This illustrative material is not only visually enjoyable, it plays a critical role in recreating the past in all its dimensions. While photographs and maps do not by themselves replace the written word, they do have a major role to play as primary sources in any historical analysis. The fine collection of illustrations in this volume capture images of a wide variety of situations in Regina, allowing our generation to understand better the forms, structures, fashions and group interactions of earlier periods of our history.

Alan F. J. Artibise
General Editor

Acknowledgements

Historical research and writing are solitary tasks, but in the course of preparing a book such as this an author incurs many debts. I certainly have. One is to the staffs of archives, libraries and museums. None proved more helpful than the Regina office of the Saskatchewan Archives Board. I particularly wish to acknowledge the assistance of Don Richan, Margaret Hutchison, Ivan Saunders, Jean Goldie and Tim Novak. Duane Mombourquette of the City of Regina Archives was also a great help. When I began the research for the book, there was no City of Regina Archives; the council minutes and by-laws of the town and city of Regina were still located in the City Clerk's Office at City Hall. There, George Day and Roger Hamelin took time from their own busy schedules to offer assistance. Similarly, Eva Lukomski facilitated my research in the Urban Planning Department Library at City Hall.

Other archives and museums in Regina welcomed me in my search for photographs. I wish especially to thank Bill Mackay at the Royal Canadian Mounted Police Museum, David R. Allen at the Saskatchewan Sports Hall of Fame, Shelley Sweeney at the University of Regina Archives and Frances Lapointe at the Regina Plains Museum.

I am indebted as well to Alan Artibise, general editor of the *History of Canadian Cities Series*, who first approached me to write this book and who has supported and encouraged the project through the years it has taken to complete it. Edmund H. Dale, formerly of the geography department at the University of Regina and now retired, has been a source of encouragement too. Bruce Yeo helped to clarify my understanding of the early history of Interprovincial Steel and Pipe Corporation Limited. Some of my students have written papers and theses which have made my task easier; their contributions are acknowledged in the endnotes.

Marilyn Bickford typed and retyped the manuscript with her usual alacrity and good humour. George Duff prepared the maps with great skill and under a tight deadline. Paula Rein helped with the final proofreading. Curtis Fahey's editorial pen improved the narrative in countless ways. Any errors that remain are of course my responsibility.

Through all of this my sons, Shaun and Ryan, and particularly my wife, Judy, have had to put up with a too-busy father and husband. Patient and understanding, Judy has been my greatest source of encouragement. This book is dedicated to her.

J. W. Brennan
August 1989

Edgar Dewdney, lieutenant governor of the North-West Territories and co-founder (with the Canadian Pacific Railway) of Regina.

Introduction

The Origins and Incorporation of Regina, 1882-84

Permanent white settlement came relatively late to what is now southern Saskatchewan. Even after the Indian title was extinguished with the signing of Treaty No. 4 at Fort Qu'Appelle in 1874, the region had little attraction for the potential landseeker. With the exception of a few North-West Mounted Police (NWMP) forts and Hudson's Bay Company (HBC) trading posts and missions, there were still no significant settlements south of the North Saskatchewan River at the end of the decade. Prevailing opinion regarded the valley of the North Saskatchewan as the most fertile part of the vast empire acquired from the HBC, and viewed the southern prairies as part of the "Great American Desert." Not only was the northern region deemed more suitable for agriculture, it was also more accessible. The main trail led overland from Winnipeg to the HBC post at Fort Ellice, through the Touchwood Hills to Fort Carlton and then westward to Battleford, Fort Pitt and Edmonton. This advantage was bound to be reinforced once the transcontinental railway was completed, it was thought, for the line was projected to follow the North Saskatchewan to the Yellowhead Pass. The prospect of imminent rail service fuelled a minor boom in the district. Settlers flocked in and Prince Albert grew rapidly as the leading town in the North-West Territories.

But the pattern and pace of western settlement was dramatically altered by the decision of the Canadian Pacific Railway (CPR) to abandon the originally surveyed route in favour of one straight west from Winnipeg through the Kicking Horse Pass. The traditional view has it that more optimistic assessments of the agricultural potential of the southern prairies, and more especially a desire to forestall competition by rival American lines, were the principal reasons for the change. It has also been argued that the CPR recognized that by driving the line through virgin territory that had never known a settler, it would create its own traffic and avoid potential difficulties with established business interests, particularly real-estate interests. Some settle-

ment already existed along the North Saskatchewan, and many of those who had established themselves at Prince Albert, Battleford (named the territorial capital in 1876) and Edmonton had an eye to the profits that could be made from land adjacent to the right-of-way. Whatever the CPR's motives, moving the line did give the railway a clear field and enabled it to decide arbitrarily where its yards and stations would be located — as well as the towns that grew up around them.

In this task the CPR enjoyed the complete cooperation of the federal government. In March 1882 the Department of the Interior temporarily withdrew from homestead settlement all even-numbered sections next to and along both sides of the main line. These sections were to be withheld until town or station sites had been determined, thereby preventing rival speculators from reaping any benefit from lands so advantageously situated. The Canada North-West Land Company (CNWLC), a consortium of British and Canadian capitalists, also played a role in the promotion of new townsites in cooperation with the CPR. In June of 1982 the CPR, faced with a shortage of working capital, sold to the CNWLC 2.2 million acres of its land grant and all of the townsites to be laid out along the main line west from Brandon to the Rockies. The CPR was to receive half the net proceeds from future sales, and four trustees were subsequently appointed to take responsibility for advertising and selling the lots. Donald A. Smith and R. B. Angus represented the CPR; E. B. Osler and W. B. Scarth, the CNWLC.

The assistance of a cooperative federal government and of the CPR's new business ally did not completely eliminate the problem of the speculator. During the spring and early summer of 1882, squatters were busily taking up land at every likely townsite on the surveyed route of the railway, including a spot where the railway was to cross Pile of Bones (Wascana) Creek, some five or six miles north of the present site of Regina. A last-minute change in the survey outflanked those who had taken up land there; at the point where the survey was run across the creek on May 18, 1882, only three settlers could be found.

Another group of speculators who had interests in the vicinity were less easily dealt with, for among their number was Edgar Dewdney, lieutenant-governor of the North-West Territories and a close friend of the prime minister, John A. Macdonald. A transfer of the seat of government from Battleford to a more southerly location followed naturally from the CPR's abandonment of the North Saskatchewan valley. The choice of a capital fell to Dewdney and to W. C. Van Horne, general manager of the line. Ostensibly for engineering reasons the railway had skirted the valley of the Qu'Appelle, eliminating what would have been the most attractive setting for the capital. Instead Dewdney and Van Horne chose the place where the line crossed Wascana Creek. On June 30, 1882, Dewdney reserved to the government township 17, range 20, west of the second meridian, later enlarged to include half of the adjoining township 17, range 19 (this became known as the Regina Reserve). The matter of the capital was settled, in Winnipeg, on August 12. The townsite proper, consisting of sections 19 and 30 in range 19, and 24 and 25 in range 20, was christened Regina, in honour of Queen Victoria, when the first train arrived on August 23.[1] The official transfer of the capital from Battleford to Regina took place the following March.

Dewdney's official justification for the choice rested upon the fact that Regina occupied "a central position within the Provisional District of Assiniboia, and also on account of its being the natural centre of a vast and rich agricultural country." Others disagreed, and a storm of controversy erupted. There was much objection in the press and in Parliament, both over the fact that Regina had been chosen instead of some other site and over the actual sections on which the town was located. As to the first, the *Saskatchewan Herald* (Battleford) declared:

The choice of this capital has but one thing to recommend it — it lies on the line of railway; but that advantage is also enjoyed by hundreds of other places which have in addition both wood and water. Pile of Bones has little of the latter and none of the former, standing as it does in the midst of a bleak and treeless plain. However rich the soil may be, the lack of wood and water in the vicinity must militate against its becoming a place of very great importance.[2]

There was more than a little truth in comments such as these. Regina did possess few natural advantages as a townsite, situated as it was on a vast treeless plain with a meandering creek its only nearby source of water. Nevertheless, these same shortcomings were also shared by Indian Head, Troy (later renamed Qu'Appelle) and Moose Jaw — other clusters of shacks and tents along the line that were suggested as alternatives. None had possessed any commercial importance before the coming of the railway; like Regina, all were creatures of the CPR.

It was also alleged that Dewdney's interest in a section of land adjacent to the four comprising the townsite had influenced the selection of Regina as the capital (see Map 1). He readily admitted that he had an interest in the Regina section (which had been acquired from the HBC), but claimed that he had more extensive interests near other possible sites that had been rejected.

Speculation in land was certainly common enough during the early 1880s, but if this was a factor influencing Dewdney's choice he proved no match for the CPR. Dewdney and Van Horne had recommended a site for the town on Wascana Creek, within the original reserve in township 17, range 20, but the CPR subsequently located its station on section 19, one-half mile east of the two original townsite sections. Dewdney himself was not without influence. He managed to persuade the federal government to locate the lieutenant-governor's residence and the chambers of the Territorial Council on or near Wascana Creek, adjacent to the section in which he had an interest. Simultaneous with the removal of the capital from Battleford to Regina, it had also been decided that the headquarters of the NWMP should be transferred from Fort Walsh to a point on the CPR main line. Regina was selected, the choice again being Dewdney's. It was his decision, too, that the new barracks be built immediately west of the creek, two and a half miles from the railway station.[3]

William Bain Scarth, general manager of the Canada North-West Land Company, supervised the sale of Regina lots to the mutual benefit of the CNWLC and its business ally, the CPR.

Thus, for a time there were two rival settlements along the track. A Toronto *Globe* reporter who visited Regina in late August found two tent stores near the site of the station and "two fairly stocked stores, two temperance saloons, and one large livery stable (all in tents)" where the railway line crossed the creek. As it turned out, the placement of the station proved to be decisive. Businesses that had located near the creek soon moved east to section 19, and it is here that the centre of Regina remains to the present day. Within a month another visitor to Regina could report finding "102 tents, three frame buildings in course of construction, and ... seven lumber yards" adjacent to the station.[4]

Before lots could be sold, an official plan had to be prepared. As in most western American and Canadian cities, Regina's streets were laid out in a basic, if unimaginative, rectangular grid pattern. Its monotony was relieved only by a few crescents and ovals located on the periphery of the townsite. The two-block Victoria Square was one of three public reserves laid out south of the CPR main line, which ran diagonally through the middle of the townsite. Five blocks were set aside for public purposes north of the tracks. The town's promoters' oft-repeated claim that Regina was "laid out on a grand scale" was hardly borne out by reality. Nearly half the lots in the townsite, and all of those in the then-settled area near the station, were only twenty-five feet wide. Four of the thoroughfares (Dewdney and Victoria avenues, and Broad and Albert streets) were one hundred feet wide, the remainder only sixty-six. The inescapable conclusion seems to be that the prime motive in the preparation of this plan was a desire to squeeze as many saleable lots as possible from the four sections of land embraced within the townsite.

The Regina townsite was put on the market in late October, and total sales exceeded $800,000 during the first three weeks alone.[5] Yet the relationship between the government and the CPR did not prove to be a completely harmonious one. The sale of Regina lots was entrusted to a Winnipeg real-estate firm, Brandon and McFee, whose advertisements boldly declared that "Regina will be the end of the CPR Division, which involves the employment of thousands of men, and the ... junction of

branch lines to the Great Peace River District in the North-West, and the Wood Mountain region to the South." The CPR did initially lay down sidings there, but then subsequently refused to build any branch lines from that point. When pressed by Macdonald to explain this apparent change of heart, the CPR president, George Stephen, replied that he could not

> imagine how it ever came to pass that you thought there was any *agreement* to build a branch from it. We want to do all we can to make Regina a great success and anything and everything we can do to make it a success will be done, and I hope you will not allow anyone to even suggest to you, that the fact of the Govt. having a half interest in the site is going to make us any less eager for its success than if it all belonged to the Coy [*sic*]. Far better, if any feeling of this kind should arise, to dissolve the partnership between the Govt. and the Coy.

Relations were further strained when rumours began to circulate that the CPR intended to locate its repair shops in Moose Jaw, forty miles west of the territorial capital. This time it was Macdonald who expressed reservations about continuing the joint arrangement between the government and the CPR. Moose Jaw did in fact become the divisional point, much to the chagrin of Reginans, and particularly those who had bought lots in the capital on speculation, but the partnership was not dissolved. Indeed, early in 1883 Moose Jaw, like Regina, became a joint enterprise of the government and the railway.[6]

The winter of 1882-83 was filled with uncertainty for Regina. There were rumours flying that the capital would be moved, and the precarious state of the community's water supply gave these rumours some credibility. During the summer the CPR had constructed a temporary dam on Wascana Creek, but the reservoir thus created provided sufficient water for the railway's locomotives only until freeze-up. Thereafter the CPR was obliged to haul water. In an attempt to solve the problem, the company began digging a well near the station. In December water was struck at a depth of 218 feet, but another well adjacent to Dewdney's residence struck water at only 70 feet. Again doubt was cast on the wisdom of locating the centre of the town on section 19.[7]

THE GOVERNOR-GENERAL TRANSFORMING PILE OF BONES INTO REGINA, CAPITAL OF ASSINOBIA.

The selection of Regina as the territorial capital brought much criticism in the press and in Parliament. This cartoon, by celebrated nineteenth-century cartoonist J.W. Bengough, appeared in Grip, a satirical Toronto weekly.

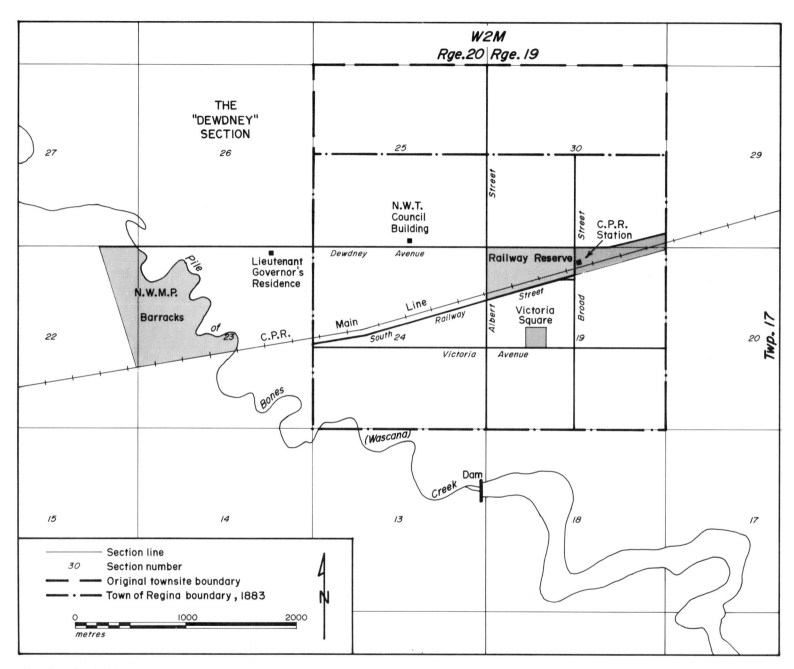

1 Regina in 1883: Regina was a product of competing real-estate interests. Edgar Dewdney sought to shift the town to the west through the placement of various public buildings and the North-West Mounted Police barracks, but the Canadian Pacific Railway's choice of a site for its station in section 19 proved decisive. Regina grew out from the station.

Furthermore, although Regina could claim 900-odd residents by year's end, the town had not yet assumed any degree of permanence. Some wooden frame buildings stood across from the CPR's small portable station, but many Reginans spent the winter in tents. Prefabricated structures, built in eastern Canada and shipped west by rail, housed the NWMP and the lieutenant-governor. The streets were neither laid out nor graded, and tents and houses alike had been erected without any regard to the survey. Indeed, nearly three-quarters of the buildings were located on the streets or on the Railway Reserve immediately south of the station. Uncertainty over the location of some public buildings, notably the post office, only created further confusion. Dewdney favoured a site north of the main line for the post office, while the CPR and the land company urged that it be placed near Victoria Square.[8]

Reginans themselves were powerless to resolve these issues, for there was as yet no effective local government. In December 1882 a group of Regina's more prominent citizens began circulating a petition requesting incorporation as a city under federal legislation. Nothing came of this, and for a time Regina was obliged to improvise. The ever-present danger of fire was the catalyst that led to the creation of an informal seven-member town council, and this new body also sought to bring some order to the generally confused state of affairs in Regina. To this latter end, it sponsored a public meeting in February 1883. A number of resolutions were arrived at: first, that the post office be located on Victoria Square so as to put an end to the uncertainty hindering building operations; second, that a larger and more reliable water supply be found; and third, that Regina be incorporated as a city. Others called for the construction of suitable accommodations for the flood of immigrants expected in the spring, the laying out of a trail to Prince Albert and assurance from the federal government that Regina would remain the capital.

This demonstration of public indignation met an immediate response. W. B. Scarth addressed the meeting and declared that the consortium that controlled the townsite would build a permanent dam across the creek, grade the principal streets and donate $500 for the sinking of a well and two lots for a fire hall.

Scarth proved as good as his word. During 1883 the consortium expended more than $14,000 on the digging of a public well, the construction of a new dam and the grading of five streets. In the last endeavour Scarth's efforts were frustrated for a time by the refusal of some of the squatters to vacate the streets and the Railway Reserve. The result was another public meeting and the appointment of a delegation of "persons having large interests in the town" to interview the squatters. The strategy worked. By mid-July forty buildings had been moved off South Railway Street and the triangular strip of land to the north. For its part the CPR moved its coal sheds north of the tracks and ordered the lumberyards moved likewise, further improving the appearance of the town.[9]

In addition, the consortium granted free lots for churches and for a right-of-way into Regina for the Qu'Appelle, Long Lake and Saskatchewan Railway, which was chartered by Parliament in 1883 to build a line from the capital north to Prince Albert. There was more than a little self-interest involved in the apparent generosity of the Townsite Trustees, as the consortium controlling Regina was known after October 1883. Their expenditures for public improvements enhanced the desirability and the value of Regina lots. Scarth's public announcement in February gave a considerable fillip to sales in the new town; the trustees sold a total of $462,194 worth of Regina lots during 1883.

They also offered a bonus of town lots to Nicholas Flood Davin to found Regina's first newspaper. Davin had been by turns an ironmonger's apprentice, barrister, newspaper reporter and war correspondent (he covered the Franco-Prussian War for the *Irish Times* and the London *Standard*) before coming to Toronto in 1872. Increasingly attracted to politics, he failed to gain an Ontario seat in Parliament in 1878 and came west in search of new opportunities. As much by accident as by design, Davin was to find them in Regina. He became a leading figure in the town, and his Regina *Leader* promoted the town as aggressively as the trustees themselves did.[10]

While the informal town council could rightly take credit for bringing public pressure to bear on the CPR and the federal government, in most other respects it proved to be an ineffective means of local government. It lacked the power to levy taxes, borrow money or enforce by-laws. As well, the council's efforts to raise funds by voluntary subscription to augment the water supply foundered. Most of the contributors refused to honour their pledges, and the council felt obliged to resign on July 12, 1883. Its larger and more elaborate successor, the so-called Citizens' Committee, laboured under the same handicaps and increasingly directed its energies towards securing the incorporation of Regina as a city. The Citizens' Committee took the lead in preparing a draft bill and in securing signatures for a petition to the North-West Council. The desired objective was realized, though Regina was incorporated as a town, not a city, and under the provisions of a general municipal ordinance, not a special charter. One change from the original draft bill caused some misgivings among members of the Citizens' Committee. The committee's bill had included the dam and the reservoir within the civic boundaries, but when Regina was proclaimed a town on December 8, 1883, not even all of the four original townsite sections were included (see Map 1). In other respects, however, Regina businessmen could have little objection to the ordinance. Borrowed largely from Ontario municipal law, it defined the nature of the franchise, set out the powers of the town council and fixed the town's borrowing limits. The property tax would be the principal source of revenue, and only those who owned property could vote or run for office.[11] Civic politics, in Regina as elsewhere, was to be very much a businessman's preserve.

Regina's first municipal election proved to be a quiet affair. There was no contest for the mayoralty. D. L. Scott, a lawyer who had had previous municipal experience in Ontario and as a member of both of Regina's informal town governments, was elected by acclamation. Two of the four successful aldermanic candidates had also served on the Citizens' Committee.[12]

The spirit of local initiative that had resulted in the incorporation of Regina manifested itself in other areas as the citizens began to lay the basis for the town's institutional growth. A variety of public buildings were erected in the settled portion of the town, thus satisfying Regina's political leaders and nascent business community. Methodist, Presbyterian, Anglican and Roman Catholic churches were built within two years of Regina's founding. A musical club that appeared in 1882 lost its original character the following year and became the private Assiniboia Club. Over the years the club's membership rolls would contain the names of many prominent territorial politicians and senior officers of the NWMP. Reginans were among the first to organize a public school district under the enabling legislation approved by the Territorial Council in 1884. A rudimentary telephone system linking the barracks and the town station in 1882 was soon extended to accommodate other subscribers.[13]

Regina was beginning by 1884 to acquire some of the amenities of an urban community, but there was as yet little evidence that the town was becoming much of a marketing and distributing centre. Almost all of its businesses, including the two brothels north of the tracks, catered to the everyday needs of a local, and predominantly male, population. Regina's future economic growth was predicated upon the expansion of agricultural settlement. Here there were some promising beginnings. A Dominion Lands Office was opened in Regina in March 1883, and at the end of the year the even-numbered sections in the "Mile Belt" and the Regina Reserve were reopened for settlement. By 1884 a total of 4,148 homestead entries had been recorded in the district around Regina, more than at any other land office in the territories.[14]

The boom proved to be short-lived. Financial difficulties beset the CPR; climatic ones, the settlers who arrived to take up land. Crops were poor in 1884. Trade slackened and the bottom fell out of the once-brisk sale of Regina lots. The town's population dropped from 613 at the beginning of the year to 400 in June, according to local estimates. All of this cast further doubt on the CPR's already vague plans to construct branch lines from Regina. The matter was aired at a public meeting in February 1884, and a delegation was despatched to interview the railway management. George Stephen offered no promise of immediate construction, but did produce a map showing two branch lines the CPR proposed to build at some future date. One was to run north from Regina to Prince Albert, the other southeast to connect with a projected extension of the Manitoba and Southwestern Railway. With this the delegation, and the town, had to be satisfied.[15]

There were few certainties about Regina at the end of 1884, save for the fact that it was the seat of government. Its future rested in the hands of the CPR, whose transcontinental line still lay unfinished, and of the federal government, whose efforts to populate the territories had not yet begun to bear fruit.

One of the earliest known photographs of Regina, taken in the fall of 1882. Regina was still little more than a cluster of shacks and tents.

Construction of the Qu'Appelle, Long Lake and Saskatchewan Railway began with a flourish in 1885. A year later, when this photograph was taken, trains were running only to Craven, twenty miles north of Regina. The line was finally completed to Prince Albert in 1890.

Chapter One
Town to City, 1885-1905

The two decades following incorporation were on the whole a period of sluggish economic and population growth for Regina. It could not have been otherwise, for the town's fortunes were closely tied to the agricultural development of the region and settlement lagged badly after 1885. In these circumstances the presence of the North-West Mounted Police barracks west of the town and Regina's role as the territorial capital proved to be considerable economic assets. The town was by 1901 the largest in the eastern half of the North-West Territories, but it was by no means clear that it would become a major urban centre. Only after the turn of the century did better crops and an influx of landseekers begin to renew confidence and inspire a successful campaign to secure for Regina both city and provincial capital status. Awkward and unpretentious, Regina also began during these years to acquire some of the social and cultural amenities that would make it a more urban, and urbane, community. Much that was accomplished here was the result of local initiative, but outside forces and agencies, notably the NWMP, also influenced the patterns of social, cultural and sporting life in early Regina.

ECONOMIC GROWTH AND METROPOLITAN DEVELOPMENT

Railways were crucial to Regina's economic development. Its location on the CPR main line gave it an initial advantage over rivals (such as Prince Albert) not so fortunately positioned, but the construction of branch lines was essential if Regina was to become the dominant commercial centre in the eastern half of the North-West Territories. While the CPR's initial reluctance to build any branch lines left a legacy bitterness, this was mitigated by the prospect that another line would soon provide the town with additional rail connections. The Qu'Appelle, Long Lake and Saskatchewan Railway and Steamboat Company proposed to build a rail and steamboat line north from Regina via Long Lake to the North Saskatchewan River near Battleford. This company's directors, who included Edgar Dewdney and W. B. Scarth, obtained the standard federal land grant of 6,400 acres per mile available to colonization railways. With the land grant in hand, the company was able to raise funds for construction in London, and work on the line began with a flourish in 1885.[1] The progress of construction was followed with great interest, but by 1886 only twenty miles of track had been laid. Remaining unfinished for want of funds until 1889, the line was then leased to the CPR and completed to Prince Albert the following year (see Map 2). The prospect of a railway link with the north was welcomed as Regina's "golden opportunity." But in fact few settlers took up land along the line, for the country between Regina and Saskatoon was deemed unsuitable for cereal agriculture.[2]

Hopes were raised again when the CPR began construction of its "Soo Line" north from Portal, at the American border, in 1892. The local press and the business community regarded George Stephen's undertaking of 1884 as a "sacred pledge" that Regina would be the northern terminus of the line. The CPR itself was more equivocal. Van Horne, now president of the company, was said to favour Regina, though it was rumoured that others had reservations about the town's uncertain water supply. Another delegation was despatched to press Regina's claims, only to be informed that the board of directors did not regard the Soo Line as the branch that George Stephen had promised the town eight years earlier. Moose Jaw was also eyeing the prize, and in the end the terminus was put at Pasqua, seven miles east of Moose Jaw. Distance, not water, seems to

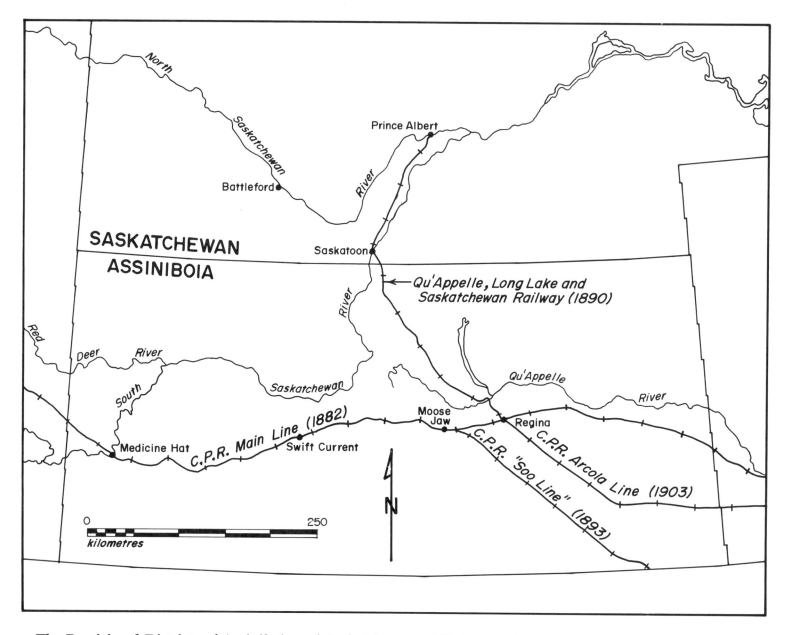

2 The Provisional Districts of Assiniboia and Saskatchewan, 1903: Regina's location on the Canadian Pacific Railway main line gave the town an initial advantage, and branch lines slowly extended its hinterland. But at the turn of the century it was not yet clear which urban centres in the provisional districts of Assiniboia and Saskatchewan would become the dominant ones.

have been the deciding factor. Ten or twelve miles were saved by building the line to Pasqua rather than to some other point.[3] It was a significant victory for Moose Jaw. The completion of the Soo Line in 1893 made it the most important rail and transportation centre in the eastern half of the North-West Territories.

Regina's business community proved no more successful in combatting the efforts of its Winnipeg counterpart to secure preferential freight rates. The CPR's existing freight rate structure, introduced in 1883, discriminated against Winnipeg as a centre of distribution. The cost of shipping goods direct from Montreal to such centres as Brandon and Regina was as much as twenty-eight cents per hundred pounds cheaper than shipping to Winnipeg and then on to more westerly points. The reaction of Winnipeg's aggressive Board of Trade was to demand a special rate for goods shipped to local points from that city so that wholesalers in the Manitoba capital might compete more effectively with wholesalers in eastern Canada. The agitation for lower rates did not go unnoticed in Regina. The town council promptly passed a resolution objecting to any change in the existing freight rate structure, and local businessmen mobilized in their own defence by organizing the Board of Trade in 1886.[4]

In its immediate purpose the board proved helpless, as might have been expected. The CPR succumbed to the pressures of the Winnipeg merchants, granting a 15 per cent discount on goods shipped west from there in 1886 and extending the same concession on agricultural machinery, dry goods and other commodities brought from the east in 1890. These concessions strengthened Winnipeg's position as a major wholesaling centre on the prairies and prevented the growth of competing large-scale wholesale firms in other prairie towns. In Regina, for example, a business directory published in 1888 listed only two wholesale houses, a drug firm and a grocery establishment.[5]

This turn of events failed to dim the optimism of Regina businessmen. Through the Board of Trade, which received a federal charter of incorporation in 1888, they lost no opportunity to promote the town's interests and their own. In 1886 the board took the initiative of marking and grading trails to the Wood Mountain country southwest of Regina, where ranching was gaining a foothold, and to Saskatoon. It published a series of maps and pamphlets, the first of the series in 1888, and petitioned the federal government to build an immigrant shed in Regina (to provide temporary accommodation for new settlers) and to facilitate the construction of a railway to Hudson Bay. It also placed exhibits of locally grown agricultural produce at fairs in Winnipeg and several eastern Canadian centres. In 1893 the board despatched one George Brown to Ontario as a special immigration agent for the Regina district "so as to bring the locality to the attention of such persons as may be intending to come to the North-West."[6]

The objective in all of this was to expand the market for local merchants. However, the area surrounding Regina did not fill up rapidly in the 1880s and 1890s. There had been some promising beginnings in 1883 and 1884, to be sure, but these were cut short by the North-West Rebellion. While Louis Riel's trial and execution in Regina drew the attention of the English-speaking world to the little prairie town, the publicity surrounding this abortive Métis and Indian uprising discouraged immigration to the Canadian prairies. The superior drawing power of the American West and a succession of dry years and poor crops in the territories further retarded settlement. The population of the district of Assiniboia, in which Regina was situated, increased from 22,083 in 1885 to 30,372 in 1891, but at the turn of the century had reached only 67,385. Although the Dominion Lands Office in Regina continued to be one of the busiest in the territories, cancellations actually outnumbered homestead entries in 1885 and 1886. In 1887 the number of cancellations nearly equalled the number of entries, and during the decade that followed, more than a third as many homesteads were abandoned as were entered for in the area tributary to Regina.[7]

The town council was no less anxious than the Board of Trade to promote Regina's economic development. Under territorial legislation towns could offer cash bonuses and exemption from municipal taxation as a means of attracting industry. Regina employed both techniques. In 1885 it granted a bonus of $2,500 to three local entrepreneurs wishing to construct a flour mill. Six years later it offered a ten-year tax exemption to

Farmers delivering grain at Regina.

Daniel Mowat arrived in Regina in 1882, the first merchant to conduct business there (in a tent). He and his brother Alex subsequently opened this store on Broad Street and developed a flourishing trade as far north as Saskatoon.

the Western Milling Company, another local firm, to assist it in building the town's second flour mill. In 1892 the council offered the same inducement to attract a 60,000-bushel elevator.[8]

A similar desire to "boost" Regina was behind the town council's involvement in the Territorial Exhibition of 1895. The idea of holding such an event to advertise the agricultural possibilities of the North-West Territories originated with Senator William D. Perley of Wolseley. He suggested in 1891 that the Assiniboia Agricultural Society of Regina provide the buildings and that the cost be borne by the thirty-four agricultural societies then scattered across the territories. Nothing came of Perley's suggestion at the time, but it acquired new life in 1893 when Charles H. Mackintosh arrived in Regina to begin his duties as lieutenant-governor. Mackintosh became the driving force behind the scheme, and he found a ready ally in the Regina town council. In 1894 the council agreed to provide $10,000 for a site and exhibition buildings. The magnitude of the town's generosity becomes more apparent when that sum is compared with the $25,000 pledged by the federal government and the $10,000 by the territorial to meet the expenses of the proposed exhibition and fair.

The construction of a main building of two storeys and three other smaller structures to house exhibits was carried forward with great speed. By the time the exhibition opened on July 30, 1895 (on a site donated by the Townsite Trustees), it also boasted a grandstand with seating for 1,000 people, a half-mile track for horse racing and extensive stables. The number of visitors far exceeded the available accommodation. The town hall and curling rink were both pressed into service, and countless tents were put up near the fair grounds to handle the throng. As a promotional venture the exhibition was a decided success, providing Regina with a good deal of publicity. It was far less successful from a financial point of view, incurring losses of $14,000. Much of this was owed to local people. Not until Parliament voted additional funds in 1897 was the management able to satisfy its creditors. However, the Territorial Exhibition did give Regina a permanent legacy. In 1896 the town purchased the site from the Townsite Trustees, and it is on these grounds that all subsequent summer fairs have been held.[9]

Richard Harry Willliams, prominent Regina retailer and successful politician. He served as mayor twice and alderman on three occasions between 1888 and 1910.

The federal government provided a more imposing residence for the lieutenant governor in 1891. Thomas Fuller, the dominion architect, designed Government House and a local contractor, William Henderson, built it.

Some of the original portable buildings and the turreted riding stable (right) at the North-West Mounted Police barracks, c. 1890.

Church parade at the NWMP barracks, 1895. The Sergeants' Mess (with verandah) is at the rear of the parade square. "B" Block is to the left.

Lawrence William Herchmer (seated in centre), commissioner of the North-West Mounted Police, 1886-1900. He was a capable administrator, but a quick temper and an overbearing nature created enemies within the force and outside it.

Members of the NWMP stationed at Regina founded Lodge No. 61 of the Ancient Free and Accepted Masons.

NWMP band at the Regina barracks, c.1896.

The results of these efforts to boost Regina were meagre at best. At the turn of the century Regina was the largest town in the eastern half of the North-West Territories, but it was little more than an agricultural service centre and still very much within the economic orbit of Winnipeg. Nevertheless, an American reporter's offhand description of Regina as a town "living off the Dominion Government, and possessing little or no enterprise" was wide of the mark. Regina businessmen did show energy and enterprise in the fields that were open to them, such as retail trade. Daniel Mowat was one example. He had come west from Ottawa in 1879, opening a store at Shoal Lake, Manitoba, and another at Fort Qu'Appelle the following year. He was attracted to Regina in 1882 and, working out of a tent, he was the first merchant to conduct business there. In partnership with his brother, Alex, he constructed a substantial retail establishment which by 1887 enjoyed a flourishing trade as far north as Saskatoon. No less successful were R. H. Williams and his family. He, too, arrived in Regina in 1882, engaging in the lumber and construction business for a time. His son, J. K. R. Williams, worked in, and subsequently acquired an interest in, a local general store. In 1888 the family bought complete control of this store and renamed the establishment the "Glasgow House." The Glasgow House prospered, necessitating the construction of a second and larger store in 1889. The firm remained an integral part of Regina's business community for nearly sixty years. Two other local men, John M. Young and J. F. Bole, founded the town's first department store, the Regina Trading Company, in 1898.[10]

The development of manufacturing in Regina was retarded by the absence of any substantial pool of local capital, such as the ranching community was able to provide in Calgary during this period, for example. Local markets were limited, the local labour force was small, and so was the water supply. For all these reasons, Regina's manufacturing establishments were not only few in number, but modest in size. In 1901 not a single firm in Regina employed even five persons (Appendix, Table I). Some firms aggressively sought outside markets for the surplus that could not be absorbed locally. The Regina Milling Company was one, shipping flour to British Columbia by 1888. The

The social life of Regina was much influenced by the presence of the NWMP. Members of the force took an active part in community affairs, staging musical concerts, dramatic evenings and balls, all events in which the townspeople shared.

A NWMP cricket match at Regina.

This NWMP team from Regina won the Manitoba and North-West Territories Rugby Union Cup in 1894.

Regina Creamery Company, founded in 1896 by several prominent local businessmen, including Daniel Mowat and R. H. Williams, was another. British Columbia customers took more than half of the company's butter production in 1898, some 16,800 pounds.[11]

Regina's role as an administrative centre enabled it to better withstand the depressed agricultural circumstances of the 1880s and 1890s. Yet the importance of its status as territorial capital should not be exaggerated. The annual influx of legislators to the unpretentious legislative building on Dewdney Avenue proved a boon to local hotels, but the territorial government had only limited responsibilities and a modest budget. The extent of its responsibilities and finances was reflected in the size of the civil service. By 1898 the "inside service," that portion of the territorial bureaucracy that lived and worked in Regina, numbered only thirty-four. There was little construction of government buildings to provide employment for local contractors and labourers. The original Territorial Council building was enlarged and veneered with locally manufactured brick in 1885. A larger "administration building," completed in 1891, sufficed to house the offices of the territorial government until provincial status was achieved in 1905.[12] Ottawa bore the cost of constructing these buildings, as well as a new and more imposing residence for the lieutenant-governor, also completed in 1891.

The federal government had a great many more favours to bestow upon Regina merchants. Until 1897 the commissioner for Indian peoples and his staff of sixteen were located in Regina, and there were lucrative contracts to supply provisions for nearby Indian reserves.[13] The economic impact of the North-West Mounted Police, however, was far greater. It had long been the desire of the force that once a permanent headquarters was established, it would be made a centre of instruction as well. The training of new recruits became an integral part of life at the barracks as early as 1885, when Parliament doubled the authorized strength of the force to 1,000 on the eve of the North-West Rebellion. Tents were hastily pitched to accommodate the men, who began arriving in early May. Additional blankets, clothing and other supplies had to be purchased in Regina. As the officer in charge of Depot Division later remarked, the whole affair proved a "godsend to the local storekeepers."[14]

In other respects, however, Regina derived little economic benefit from the North-West Rebellion. Some local teamsters were engaged to haul supplies for the NWMP, but the force played a relatively small part in suppressing the rebellion. It was the militia that did most of the fighting, and its main base of operations was east of Regina, at Qu'Appelle. Troop trains did pass through Regina on their way to Swift Current and Calgary, but scarcely paused long enough for local merchants to hand out free cigars. Winnipeg, Qu'Appelle, Moose Jaw, Swift Current, Calgary and Edmonton firms accounted for most of the $2,300,000 spent by the federal government on provisions and supplies in 1885.[15]

The number of police stationed at the Regina barracks or in training varied from year to year. It fell below 100 only twice between 1885 and 1905, and averaged 156. Their presence made Regina something of a garrison town, "a little Kingston," as one visitor remarked.[16] The portable barracks gave way in time to more permanent structures, some of which were designed by a local architect. A large covered riding stable constructed in 1886 was destroyed by fire a year later but was promptly rebuilt. This proved to be the last major building constructed at the barracks until after the turn of the century. Indeed, a number of the original portable buildings were still being used as officers' quarters as late as 1905, despite repeated pleas from the commissioner of the force that these dilapidated structures be replaced.[17]

It was police policy to purchase supplies locally wherever possible. Regina merchants quickly seized the opportunity to provide the barracks with meat and other provisions. Not a few members of the force frequented the town's bars, even though this necessitated a two-and-a-half-mile trip across the open prairie. That Regina merchants came to regard the barracks as a captive market can be seen from an incident in 1888. A canteen had been operating at the barracks for some time, though with indifferent financial success. In November 1888 the commissioner of the force, L. W. Herchmer, entered into an agreement with a Winnipeg merchant, W. F. Buchanan, to establish

Louis Riel in the prisoner's dock, 1885. His trial drew the attention of the English-speaking world to a town barely three years old, but among Reginans there was no sympathy for his cause.

A British town celebrates Queen Victoria's Diamond Jubilee, 1897. Charles H. Mackintosh, lieutenant governor of the North-West Territories, is addressing the crowd.

a permanent canteen. This did not long escape the notice of the Regina Board of Trade. It promptly passed a resolution declaring that the arrangement with Buchanan would be detrimental to the business interests of the town. Supplies for this "trading post," as it was termed, would be shipped direct from Winnipeg, thus depriving local merchants of trade to which they considered themselves entitled and for which they could not compete, owing to the favourable concessions Buchanan had secured. The board found an ally in the *Leader*, whose editor, Nicholas Flood Davin, had been engaged in an acrimonious vendetta with Herchmer for some time.[18]

Herchmer himself was unmoved. "The Police have been robbed by the Regina people all along and it is about time it was stopped," Herchmer informed the comptroller of the force in Ottawa. It was dissatisfaction with the high prices charged by local merchants that had led to the arrangement with Buchanan. He was authorized to operate a canteen for the use of the men only; no general store was contemplated and no civilians would be allowed to patronize it. After its opening, Davin and the Board of Trade continued to press for the closure of the new canteen, the latter claiming in April 1890 that local merchants had lost $5,000 worth of business during its first year of operation. They were only partly successful. The contract with Buchanan was terminated, but the canteen became a permanent, and profitable, fixture at the barracks. It was run cooperatively by the men, and supplies were purchased locally when prices were competitive. A fire subsequently destroyed part of the building in 1895. When it was rebuilt, it was converted into a chapel at the suggestion of Mrs. Herchmer.[19]

By the turn of the century, hard times began to give way to unprecedented prosperity across the West. The price of wheat rose, and cheaper transportation rates on land and sea made the export of this commodity more profitable. At the same time, sophisticated techniques for farming in a semi-arid region brought good harvests to the prairies. With the free land of the American West nearly exhausted, the "Last, Best West" of the immigration literature came into its own, as thousands of settlers arrived each year. In 1901 the population of the North-West Territories stood at 158,940; five years later the newly formed province of Saskatchewan alone had a population nearly twice that (Appendix, Table III).

Regina shared in the boom. Its population increased threefold between 1901 and 1906 (Appendix, Table V). This rapid growth was due largely to the upswing in the Canadian economy, but the removal of two handicaps of an earlier age was also a contributing factor. In 1902 the Board of Trade successfully lobbied the CPR to grant Regina local distributing freight rates and special rates on farm machinery. These special traders' rates substantially reduced the cost of shipping from Regina, whereas formerly it had been more advantageous for wholesalers to ship directly from Winnipeg to points in the territories. This, coupled with the designation of Regina as a port of entry for customs purposes later the same year, gave a considerable fillip to the agricultural machinery business. Six implement firms had established local agencies in Regina by this time and were doing a thriving retail business. After 1902 they began to build distributing warehouses to serve their rural customers, and wholesale firms showed a new interest in locating in Regina.[20]

The construction of a new CPR branch line in 1903 and the prospect of railway competition also served as a stimulus to economic activity in Regina. Reginans regarded the CPR line, which ran southeast to the towns of Stoughton, Carlyle and Arcola (see Map 2), as the fulfillment of the pledge made by George Stephen nearly twenty years earlier. Word in 1904 that the rival Canadian Northern Railway was about to begin construction of a line from Brandon or Hartney, in western Manitoba, to Regina, sparked even greater interest. "Another line of railway," a local newspaper declared, "will make Regina's position as the distribution and wholesale centre of the Territories secure and permanent." The Board of Trade lost no time in pressing the federal government to provide the necessary bond guarantees and urging the municipal authorities to deal fairly and generously with the company in the matter of a site for station, yards and terminal facilities.[21] The bond guarantees were the key, and though the federal government moved more slowly than local businessmen would have wished, there seemed no doubt as 1904 gave way to 1905 that better times lay ahead for Regina.

Regina looking north from Victoria Avenue, 1887. Hamilton Street is to the left of the Leader building.

Regina looking northwest from Victoria Avenue, 1891.

POPULATION GROWTH AND ETHNIC RELATIONSHIPS

The absence of exact statistics concerning age composition, birthplace and, until 1901, even population makes it difficult to sketch a collective portrait of Reginans during this period. Although a population of 1,400 was claimed in 1888, and of "about 2,500" in 1892,[22] it seems clear that these figures were exaggerated. Regina in fact probably experienced only a modest increase in population during the late 1880s and 1890s, when immigration to the North-West Territories was slight. Sustained growth did not come until after the turn of the century. And then, immigration — not natural increase — was chiefly responsible for Regina's population growth. This was only to be expected, since, as in most new communities, there was a preponderance of males. In 1901 men formed 54 per cent of the population (Appendix, Table II). If reliable statistics were available for earlier years, they would probably show an even greater disparity between the sexes.

Regina's small population was fairly homogeneous in terms of ethnic origin. In 1901 well over 70 per cent of the population gave their ethnicity as "British." Most were eastern Canadians or immigrants from Great Britain. They were readily absorbed into Regina society — indeed they set its tone — and moved easily into positions of prominence in local politics and in the great variety of fraternal, religious and athletic associations that appeared in the town. From the outset they were Regina's dominant or charter group, united by a common language and their British heritage, as well as by their Protestant religion. Seventy per cent of Regina's population professed an adherence to the Presbyterian, Anglican, Methodist or Baptist faiths in 1901 (Appendix, Table IX). The presence of the NWMP served to reinforce the essentially Anglo-Canadian character of early Regina. Most of its officers, perhaps 80 per cent, were Canadian-born, drawn from the governing elite of eastern Canada. Roughly half of the enlisted men were also Canadian-born during the nineteenth century, and most of the rest, at all ranks, were British-born.[23]

The only other ethnic group of any size in early Regina was its German community, which comprised 18 per cent of the population by 1901 (Appendix, Tabl VIII). A few German Catholics migrated from southern Russia to Regina as early as 1886, but those of the Lutheran faith did not begin to arrive until 1894. Larger numbers came after the turn of the century. Regina's brighter economic prospects also proved attractive to German tradesmen and labourers who had originally settled north of the town, at Balgonie, Kronau, Vibank or Strasbourg, for example, but had found the rigours of homesteading too demanding. A German weekly newspaper, *Rundschau*, appeared in Regina in 1900. Three years later a German Mutual Improvement Society was founded there, largely through the efforts of two men who were to play a significant role in the local German community, L. L. Kramer and Paul Bredt. The German population was still too small, however, to support other ethnic or religious institutions.[24]

The Ukrainians, who in recent decades have become the second-largest non-British ethnic group in Regina, were far less numerous at the turn of the century. The first Ukrainian immigrants arrived in Regina perhaps as early as 1890, certainly by 1894. It is difficult to determine with certainty how many took up permanent residence there, though an informal census in 1905 put the number at several hundred.[25] Employed chiefly as unskilled labourers, Regina's early Ukrainian population remains largely invisible to the historian. The same must be said, unfortunately, of the other European minorities present in Regina at this time.

The town's few Chinese residents, and those of Native ancestry, occupied the lowest position on the social scale. Thousands of Chinese had been brought to British Columbia during the construction of the CPR, but its completion forced them to seek other employment. A few came as far east as Regina and opened a hand laundry in 1885. Because of a lack of economic opportunity, Regina's Chinese population remained small and posed no threat to the Anglo-Saxon charter group. It was this fact, and not a spirit of tolerance and "British fair play," that explains why Regina was free of the blatant anti-

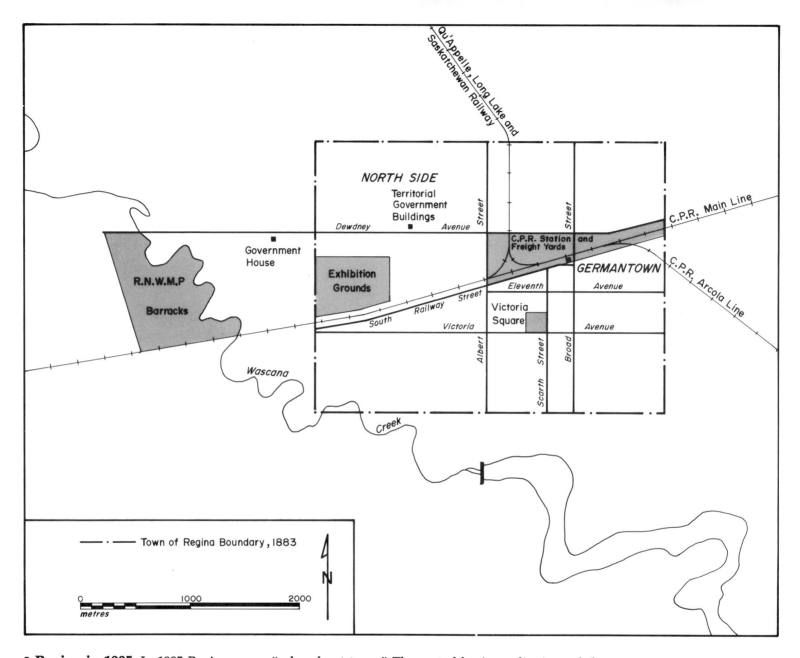

3 Regina in 1905: In 1905 Regina was a "splayed-out town." The central business district and the most desirable residential area lay south of the Canadian Pacific Railway yards, but to the west the Territorial government buildings, Government House and the Royal North-West Mounted Police barracks still stood more or less in splendid isolation.

Oriental hysteria that periodically erupted in other prairie towns during the nineteenth century.[26]

Reginans of Native ancestry were scarcely more numerous. If there was little overt discrimination against them, neither was there much sympathy for the plight of these original inhabitants of the plains. This was forcefully illustrated in 1885. The prospect of a large-scale Native uprising prompted some of Regina's more prominent citizens to organize a home guard. Once the uprising had been put down and its Métis leader condemned to hang for treason, many of these same citizens signed a petition demanding that the Macdonald government stand firm in carrying out the death sentence imposed on Riel.[27] Thereafter the Native people, like the Chinese, became an increasingly marginal element in an ever more cosmopolitan urban society.

What was true of Regina was true also of the North-West Territories as a whole: the population was becoming more ethnically diversified. To Regina's Anglo-Protestant majority the swelling tide of immigration became an object of intense interest and concern. Those who came from Great Britain and the United States were welcomed, of course. In broad cultural terms, to be British was to be acceptable, for Canada was, after all, a "British" nation. The social and cultural background of most of the Americans who made their homes in the provisional districts of Assiniboia and Saskatchewan made it relatively easy for them to be accepted. The same could not be said of Central and Eastern Europeans. While it was admitted that they would contribute to the economic development of the West by clearing its vacant lands and making them productive, some Reginans had reservations about whether they would, or could, be assimilated. Apprehension about this increasingly cosmopolitan population manifested itself when Prime Minister Wilfrid Laurier sought to reintroduce confessional schools at the time of the province of Saskatchewan's creation. The opposition of Regina's Anglo-Protestant majority to separate schools arose not only from traditional anti-Catholicism, but also from a conviction that the children of the various nationalities settling in their midst ought to be educated together. The "national" school was regarded as the ideal instrument with which to mould the various ethnic minorities in the territories into responsible British subjects and Canadian citizens.[28]

THE URBAN LANDSCAPE

Although Regina's physical growth was contained within the boundaries established at the time of its incorporation in 1883, basic land-use patterns were clearly established during this period. The direction of town expansion ceased to be a contentious issue after 1884, but the short-lived struggle between Dewdney and the CPR had a lasting impact. As late as 1905 an English visitor could remark with some truth that Regina was a "splayed-out town." The territorial government buildings and the residence of the lieutenant-governor on Dewdney Avenue were situated on the open prairie a mile or more west of the built-up portion of Regina. The NWMP barracks were even more distant, a fact that prompted the suggestion in 1885 that they be moved to the government reserve north of the reservoir as a means of consolidating the town.[29]

The pattern for Regina's physical growth had been fixed when the CPR chose its station site and offered the first sale of townsite lots. Businessmen erected their establishments south of the tracks along South Railway and Broad streets so as to be near the station. This became the town's central business district (see Map 3), though for several years the *Leader* office and the Bank of Montreal were located in splendid isolation on Victoria Avenue. Early photographs show a preponderance of wooden structures, complete with the false fronts so suggestive of frontier optimism. That they also constituted a serious fire hazard was brought home in March 1890, when an entire block of stores and offices along South Railway Street burned to the ground. New buildings, some of brick, soon began to rise in their place, but the town proved reluctant to establish fire limits — within which wooden buildings would not be permitted — to reduce the possibility of such a conflagration occurring again. This would be a financial hardship to local merchants, it was argued, and would "have the effect of driving business outside the limit and further scattering an already too much scattered town."[30] The town soon had second thoughts. In 1891 the town

Regina looking southeast from South Railway and Cornwall streets, c. 1898.

Scarth Street looking southwest toward Eleventh Avenue, 1905. By this time the original wooden buildings, with the false fronts so suggestive of frontier optimism, were giving way to more substantial structures.

council specified that all new buildings within the area bounded by South Railway, Broad and Scarth streets and Eleventh Avenue be built of brick or stone. In time the fire limits were extended, and by 1905 most of the buildings, along South Railway Street at least, were of more substantial construction and two and even three storeys in height. By this time heavy rains no longer transformed South Railway Street into a sea of mud, perhaps Regina's best-known physical feature during its early history. The town embarked on a program of street improvements in 1902. In a small way this helped to transform Regina from a rude prairie town into a city.[31]

The location of the CPR main line and freight yards influenced general land-use patterns in other ways. The CPR had early persuaded the owners of the lumberyards to move them north of the tracks, and the area adjacent to the main line proved attractive to other firms that depended on access to the railway. The town's flour mills and grain elevators were located near the tracks, as were the implement warehouses constructed after 1902 by Massey-Harris and J. I. Case. The various lines of the CPR and the Qu'Appelle, Long Lake and Saskatchewan Railway (which entered Regina from the north along Smith Street) also influenced traffic patterns within the town. This was particularly true of the CPR main line, which cut the originally surveyed townsite nearly in half. Bumpy level crossings, chosen arbitrarily by the railway company, provided the only access from the business district to the area north of the tracks. These crossings were a frequent cause of friction between the town and the CPR, and so was the increasing congestion of the railway's freight yards.[32]

Regina was still very much a "walking city" in 1905. In the centre of the city, commercial and residential buildings were intermingled, as owners erected houses near their places of business. The area south and west of Victoria Square became the favoured location of the well-to-do. Their handsome residences, typically of wood construction with wide verandahs, long marked this as Regina's best residential neighbourhood. Less desirable was the area north of the CPR main line, the "North Side." Some of Regina's most prominent citizens lived there, but its twenty-five-foot lots were beginning to prove at-

tractive to those of more modest means. Much of the North Side was still vacant at the close of this period, however, and major residential development would not occur there until later. The third discernible residential area lay east of the central business district along Tenth and Eleventh avenues, adjacent to the public market established in 1892. The earliest residents there were predominantly German, and the area became popularly known as Germantown. The construction of a Romanian Greek Orthodox Church on St. John Street in 1902 was proof of its increasingly cosmopolitan character.[33]

Regina possessed few natural amenities as a townsite, but its residents early turned their attention to remedying some of the more obvious defects. Unfortunately efforts to plant trees in Victoria Square and along some of the main thoroughfares met with indifferent success, mainly because of the town's lack of water. In 1905 Victoria Square, and indeed most of Regina, remained treeless. Moreover, the town's attitude towards parks and park development was ambivalent. In 1887 it sought to acquire a fifty-acre tract of land south of Sixteenth Avenue near the reservoir for park purposes, but the Department of the Interior refused to part with any portion of what was still a government reserve. What the town was anxious to acquire with one hand — park land — it almost gave away with the other. In 1892 it was prepared to offer a portion of Victoria Square as a site for a new court house.[34] At the turn of the century Regina boasted only one park in which its citizens could take any pride. Named Stanley Park in 1889, it was located immediately south of the CPR station and was developed jointly by the railway company and the town.[35]

THE URBAN COMMUNITY: SOCIAL AND POLITICAL LIFE

Local government was the preserve of businessmen during this period. Successive town and city councils were controlled by Regina's foremost businessmen, while the vast majority of the town's citizens were effectively excluded from the decision-making process. Only men, unmarried women and widows who owned property assessed at a value of at least $200 were

South Railway Street, Regina's commercial hub, looking east toward Broad Street, 1905.

Residence of R.H. Williams, 1827 Rose Street, 1898. At the time, this was becoming Regina's most desirable residential area.

eligible to vote; in 1901, when the population exceeded 2,000, only 330 names appeared on the voters' list. Even among those who were eligible to vote, a general apathy seems to have prevailed. With few exceptions, municipal elections, and the annual ratepayers' meetings that preceded them, were lacklustre affairs. Twelve times between 1885 and 1905 the mayor's chair was filled by acclamation, and on four occasions the entire council was elected without opposition. In years when there were contests, voting turnouts were often embarrassingly low. The period was also marked by a substantial turnover in council membership. No less than fifteen men served as mayor of Regina, and none for more than three years. In fact, there was, as one newspaper admitted in 1898, "little visible glory in managing public affairs when the treasury is depleted and when rigid economy, bordering on penuriousness, is necessary to be observed."[36]

This preoccupation with "rigid economy" was due in part to the generally depressed economic conditions experienced by the town and region after 1885. It also arose out of the circumstances of Regina's founding. The sale of lots had been entrusted to a body of four trustees representing the CPR, the Canadian North-West Land Company and the federal government, which together owned all of the land within the original townsite. At first the trustees had shown considerable initiative in grading the streets and otherwise improving the town. But when land sales began to plummet in 1884, falling from nearly half a million to only a few thousand dollars in a single year, the trustees made no further expenditures. The whole burden of carrying out necessary public works and providing other essential services thereafter fell upon the town, and it experienced great difficulty in raising sufficient revenues for this purpose because the trustees refused to pay taxes on unsold lots. The CPR claimed exemption from municipal taxation on the strength of its charter, and the federal government likewise insisted that it could not be compelled to pay taxes. With its small population and lack of power or influence, Regina was in no position to dictate to its powerful benefactors.

Negotiations with the Townsite Trustees and representations to the territorial and federal governments finally

Interior view of R.H. Williams's residence.

The construction of St. Nicholas Romanian Orthodox Church in 1902 symbolized the increasingly cosmopolitan character of the neighbourhood east of Broad Street known popularly as "Germantown."

Victoria Hospital, with beds for twenty-five patients, opened in 1901.

brought some relief in 1889, when the trustees agreed to make a lump-sum payment of $14,000 to clear up arrears of taxes, and henceforth to pay one-quarter of the taxes due on all unsold properties. This was a modest victory. The trustees admitted only that the town had the right to collect taxes on the one-quarter interest of the CNWLC, since it could claim no exemption under law. The CPR and its business ally refused to give up more in Regina than they were prepared to give up in Calgary, where an agreement ending a lengthy dispute over that town's right to tax the half interest of the CNWLC was reached that same year. With the trustees refusing to budge on the question of taxing the interests of the CPR or the federal government, Regina grudgingly accepted the terms offered. J. W. Smith, mayor of Regina in 1889, was later to admit that the total arrears of taxes assessed against the Townsite Trustees had been four times the amount offered and that the town had regarded the agreement only as the best that could be obtained under the circumstances. Although the agreement did ease the town's financial burden somewhat in subsequent years, Regina continued to suffer a substantial revenue loss, amounting to more than $30,000 between 1890 and 1899 alone.[37]

It was this limited tax base, as much as the faltering economy of Regina and the caution of the town council, that prompted the many unfavourable descriptions of Regina that abound in travellers' accounts of the period. The absence of indoor plumbing and sewers made the town unsanitary and unsightly. The town began laying sewer lines in 1891, but much of Regina continued to be served by a single "scavenger" who dumped the contents of his cart at the edge of town. Not surprisingly, Regina was periodically ravaged by epidemics of typhoid fever, scarlet fever and diphtheria. At first there was only a small private hospital, which functioned from 1889 until 1897. The Regina Local Council of Women took the initiative in establishing a more permanent institution, raising the necessary funds through public subscription and a grant from the Cottage Hospital Fund of the newly established Victorian Order of Nurses. Regina's "Cottage Hospital" opened in rented quarters in 1898. It had beds for only a half-dozen patients, but the larger Victoria Hospital, constructed in 1901, could accommodate twenty-five.[38]

For many years there was no constable, the town finding it simpler and cheaper to leave local law enforcement in the hands of the NWMP. While the police did have a detachment permanently stationed in the town, they were reluctant to patrol the streets and enforce local by-laws.[39] On occasion this necessitated some improvisation on the part of the town. In 1889, for example, it hired a private detective to investigate rumours that a brothel was operating on Lorne Street. The offending establishment was in fact uncovered, and charges were laid against its proprietor, a Mrs. Turner. The case was subsequently thrown out, however, on account of the sudden disappearance of several witnesses. The town detachment did show more zeal in arresting the inmates of another brothel in 1890. But for the more mundane duties expected of a local policeman, such as rounding up stray cattle and pigs or compelling town residents to remove garbage and manure from their backyards, it showed no enthusiasm at all. Eventually a compromise of sorts was reached. The commissioner of the force suggested that if Regina would appoint a local constable, the services of the town detachment would be made available in cases of emergency. With this the town had to be content, and in 1892 it appointed a policeman.[40]

Fire protection was a more serious matter. In the early years the efforts of the volunteer fire brigade were hampered by inadequate equipment and an oftimes insufficient water supply. In 1888, in fact, it threatened to disband unless the town provided more equipment. The disastrous blaze of 1890 demonstrated the inadequacy of Regina's fire-fighting equipment, but ratepayers subsequently turned down a proposal to purchase a steam fire engine by a margin of two to one. This was interpreted as proof that Reginans desired a system of waterworks instead. The town proceeded to engage H. N. Ruttan, Winnipeg's city engineer, to examine the feasibility of such a scheme. Ruttan rejected as too expensive the construction of a pipeline to bring water from springs near Boggy Creek, several miles northeast of the town. Instead he recommended that the existing source of supply be augmented by sinking more wells. This brought some improvement, though no real

The North-West Territories Council in session, 1884.

reduction in fire insurance rates.[41] In later years the town spent more money on fire protection. Its "modern fire hall and ... complete outfit of fire fighting apparatus" accounted for one-quarter of Regina's outstanding debenture indebtedness by the end of the century.[42]

Some of the other amenities of older, more-established urban centres also appeared in Regina during this period. The town's rudimentary telephone system, established in 1883, was absorbed by the Bell Telephone Company four years later. Initially the change was welcomed, but in time the local business community came to object to what it regarded as inferior service and high rates. While there was some sentiment favouring municipal ownership of this essential utility, financial constraints and the Bell Company's federal charter of incorporation precluded any effective action in this direction.[43]

A locally owned company also took the lead in providing Regina with electricity in 1890. However, in this case private operation proved inadequate and unprofitable, and in 1893 the Regina Electric Light and Power Company offered to sell its plant to the town. The offer was rebuffed, but in 1902, when the company demanded a twenty-year monopoly before it would undertake a badly needed expansion, the town decided to acquire the plant.[44] This change of heart is easily explained. With the territories clearly entering a period of renewed economic prosperity, the town's businessmen began to realize that Regina was approaching an important juncture in its development. Although many communities displayed the potential for spectacular growth, the experience of the nineteenth century and the rise of Winnipeg persuaded them that the benefits of this prosperity would be distributed unevenly. The extent of a town's growth would be determined not only by its railway connections, but also by the number of industries it could attract. Regina was clearly handicapped in this regard by the state of its public utilities. It did not possess a source of electric power sufficient for industrial purposes; neither did it have a modern sewer and waterworks system. Municipal ownership of electric power became part of a larger strategy worked out by the business community to make certain that Regina obtained its share of the new prosperity.

Nich⁵ Flood Davin

Nicholas Flood Davin, founder of two Regina newspapers, the Regina Leader and the West, and Member of Parliament for Assiniboia West, 1887-1900.

Walter Scott acquired the Regina Leader from Nicholas Flood Davin in 1895 and his seat in Parliament five years later. Called upon to head the first Saskatchewan government in 1905, Scott was determined that Regina should be the capital of the new province. Although there was considerable support for Saskatoon within his caucus, he got his way.

Amédée Emmanuel Forget had a long career in public service in the North-West Territories as clerk of the Territorial Council (1876-1888), assistant commissioner and then commissioner of Indian affairs (1888-1898), and lieutenant governor of the Territories (1898-1905). He was also the first lieutenant governor of Saskatchewan.

Henriette Forget was regarded as "bright, clever, an excellent conversationalist." During the thirteen years the Forgets occupied Government House they became renowned for their lavish dinner parties.

To finance the improvement of its public utilities, and thereby enhance its attractiveness to outside capital, an expansion of the town's borrowing powers was deemed necessary. It was these pragmatic considerations that prompted the council to apply for a city charter in 1903. The appropriate legislation elevating Regina to city status and increasing its borrowing powers to 20 per cent of its assessment won easy approval in the territorial legislature.[45] Regina at once proceeded to acquire the electric light plant, and the new city engaged a Toronto consulting engineer, John Galt, to draw up plans for a waterworks system. Galt recommended that the city utilize the underground springs at Boggy Creek as a source of supply. Construction of a pipeline to Regina began in June 1904. The new waterworks system, completed early in 1905, was hailed as an important step in "making Regina a city in reality as well as in name."[46]

No less important was the resolution of the controversy over the tax-exempt status of the lots owned by the Townsite Trustees. It again became a live issue in municipal politics with the discovery in 1900 that the title to all the lots comprising the townsite had been vested absolutely in the trustees from the beginning. This was taken to mean that the trustees could claim no exemption from taxation and in future would have no choice but to pay the full amount of taxes due. The territorial government promised to initiate a test case, but did not immediately do so, and the town was obliged to meekly accept the one-quarter of the trustees' taxes due in 1901 and again in 1902. The question soon became irrelevant, at least insofar as the tax-exempt status of the federal government was concerned. In 1898 the Laurier government had decided to withdraw from the Regina consortium, and by 1900 the CPR was anxious to see it dissolved as well. Early in 1902 they began the task of dividing up the unsold lots still held by the trustees in Regina. The federal government received half the lots as its share, concentrated in three large parcels. The first, and largest, embraced the area between Dewdney and Fourth avenues, and Albert and Winnipeg streets. The second was located adjacent to the CPR tracks between Albert Street and Government Road (Pasqua Street). Most of the unsold lots south of the downtown business district and east of Scarth Street also came to the federal government.

It was at this point that Regina's member in the House of Commons, Walter Scott, suggested that Ottawa hand over its share of the unsold lots as compensation for the losses the town had sustained by not being able to collect all the taxes owing from the Townsite Trustees. Clifford Sifton, the minister of the interior, refused to commit the government, but Regina was quick to endorse the suggestion. The Liberals were in fact torn between making an outright gift of the remaining lots and disposing of them by public auction, but it was the former course that was decided upon in the end. The government kept only a few lots as public reserves and transferred the remainder of its share, over 4,000 lots, to Regina in 1904.[47] The gift proved to be a valuable asset, enabling the city to undertake many schemes for the improvement and development of Regina in subsequent years.

In territorial politics a non-partisan political tradition early took root, and federal party distinctions were scrupulously avoided in contests for the local assembly at Regina. Territorial elections, in Regina at any rate, were pallid affairs compared to the federal contests, where "partyism" reigned supreme from the outset. Little is known about the men who represented Regina in the local legislature, but none played a leading role in its deliberations. Those who were politically ambitious were early attracted to the larger stage at Ottawa. In 1887 the provisional district of Assiniboia was given two seats in the House of Commons. Regina was situated in the more westerly of the two, and both men who sat for Assiniboia West during this period — Nicholas Flood Davin and Walter Scott — were Reginans.

The success of the *Leader* — one of the leading Conservative organs in the territories — had afforded Davin the opportunity to gain the seat in Parliament that had eluded him in Ontario. He managed to overcome considerable internal party feuding to carry Assiniboia West in 1887 and 1891. Davin's subsequent support of remedial legislation to restore Roman Catholic school rights in Manitoba antagonized many voters, and in the next election he won by the narrowest of margins, a single vote.

Members of the Regina Lodge of the Royal Templars of Temperance, c. 1890. It was one of many social, fraternal and religious organizations to appear in Regina by this time. Others included the Orange Lodge, Odd Fellows, Masons, Women's Christian Temperance Union and Young Men's Christian Association.

The Assiniboia Club, founded in 1882, is one of the oldest private clubs in western Canada. The club occupied these quarters from 1893 until 1912.

Even so, Davin was the only Conservative elected in the territories in 1896. (The deciding vote was cast by the returning officer whose name was Dixie Watson, earning for Davin the sobriquet "the Honourable Member for Dixie.") Davin's stand on Manitoba schools also alienated his business associate, Walter Scott, to whom he had sold the *Leader* in 1895. An Ontario farm boy who had learned the printer's trade in Portage la Prairie, Scott had arrived in Regina in 1886. Like Davin, he found a congenial home for his talents in this small prairie town, and eventually a political career as well.

In 1900 the Liberal tide engulfed even Davin. He lost to Walter Scott, who had thrown in his lot with the party of Laurier after briefly flirting with the Patrons of Industry. There was a tragic postscript to that contest. Increasingly despondent following his defeat, Nicholas Flood Davin ended his life with a revolver in a Winnipeg hotel room in 1901. Walter Scott's star, meanwhile, continued to rise. His personal popularity in Regina was, by all accounts, greater than Davin's had been, and in 1904 he again carried Assiniboia West easily for the Liberals.[48]

By this time provincial autonomy had become the dominant issue in both territorial and federal politics. As early as 1896 the creation of a separate province of Alberta (embracing the provisional districts of Alberta and Athabasca) had been mooted in the territorial assembly. F. W. G. Haultain, the territorial premier, favoured the creation of a single province, but his views were not shared by all. The idea of establishing two provinces, on an east-west or a north-south basis, became more popular as the years passed, and the ambition of rival communities to be elevated to the status of provincial capitals grew more intense. The Laurier government's decision to create two provinces was readily accepted in Regina, even by some of Haultain's staunchest supporters, doubtless because it was named the provisional capital of Saskatchewan. The final decision was to rest with the local legislature, but Regina was confident that it would be the logical choice. It had been the capital of the territories for more than twenty years, and it could count on the support of Walter Scott, soon to become the first premier of the new province.[49]

These calculations were nearly upset by the results of the

Winners of Galt Trophy, 1893.

E. McCARTHY.   J. W. SMITH (Skip).   CHAS. WILLOUGHBY.   A. S. ROSS.

Curling soon became a popular winter sport in Regina.

The Victoria hockey team, city league champions, 1904-1905.

CPR baseball team, city league champions, 1905.

first provincial election. With the constituencies north of the CPR main line solidly Liberal and those farther south evenly divided, it seemed that the government might choose a northern community as capital. The bustling town of Saskatoon proved to be the most serious rival. Regina's claim was further weakened by the fact that according to the initial election results it appeared that voters there had returned an opposition man. Even Walter Scott was forced to admit that "by giving an adverse majority they have put the Government in a mighty precarious position on this question." The final count gave the seat to the Liberal candidate by a majority of three votes, and Regina began a determined campaign to keep the capital. One alderman proposed that Victoria Square be turned over to the government as a free site for a new and larger legislative building, though no concrete offer seems in fact to have been made. Saskatoon redoubled its efforts, but in retrospect the final outcome was predictable. Once Regina was safely in Liberal hands and the danger of political embarrassment was removed, Scott was able to have his way and preserve the status quo. Regina was confirmed as the permanent capital during the first session of the provincial legislature.[50]

Regina's transformation into a more urban and urbane community was reflected in its social and cultural life. From the outset the social life of Regina's elite, in particular, was very much influenced by the presence of the police and the territorial government bureaucracy. The members of the force stationed there took an active part in community affairs, staging dramatic evenings, balls and other social events in which the townspeople shared. Rivalling the dances at the barracks, especially after Lieutenant-Governor A. E. Forget and his wife took up residence in Government House in 1898, were the dinner parties and elaborate state balls held at the opening of each session of the legislature. The dominant element in Regina society was solidly British and Protestant, and as the town grew in size the townspeople found other outlets for their energy in the establishment of a wide variety of fraternal, religious and athletic clubs and organizations. By 1890 the Orange Lodge, Odd Fellows, Masons, Royal Templars of Temperance, Women's Christian Temperance Union and Young Men's Chris-

Cast of the play Old Maid's Convention, c. 1905. Since professional touring companies generally avoided Regina, most entertainment was of the home-grown variety.

Catherine Simpson-Hayes arrived in Regina in the mid 1880s and became an accomplished author. Her literary career in Regina and Winnipeg (to which she moved in 1900) encompassed poetry, drama and fiction.

tian Association were all represented in Regina. To these were soon added a St. Andrew's Society and a Mechanics and Literary Institute.

Sports flourished, too. The Lawn Tennis Club played on cinder courts in one corner of Victoria Square, and the Regina Curling Club hosted the first territorial bonspiel in 1892. Reginans were also instrumental in organizing the Assiniboia Provincial Rifle Association in 1889, and they founded the Regina Golf Club a decade later, laying out a nine-hole course north of Wascana Creek near the reservoir. Hockey, baseball, lacrosse, polo, and soccer clubs also thrived, testimony to the popularity of those sports among Reginans and among the officers and men at the NWMP barracks west of the town. The Mounted Police made an important contribution to the development of Regina's early sporting life. Not only did they help to introduce some of these sports, but their numbers also facilitated team competitions. Challenge matches against town teams led in time to the organization of local leagues in which the men from the barracks were invariably represented. In lacrosse, soccer and hockey, competition was not confined to Regina. During the 1890s leagues began to appear that included teams from Calgary, Edmonton, Moose Jaw and other communities. A keen rivalry developed after the turn of the century, particularly between Regina and Moose Jaw hockey teams. Sports days were popular as well. The largest, sponsored by the Sons of Scotland, was held on Dominion Day. It featured lacrosse and baseball tournaments, Caledonian games, horse racing and an evening concert.

There was little professional entertainment. Most touring companies avoided Regina because of its small size, though in 1899 a troupe from the Metropolitan Opera performed *The Chimes of Normandy*. There was entertainment nonetheless, though most of it was the home-grown variety. By 1890 Regina could boast a musical and literary society, a glee club, a minstrel club and several church choirs. There were also two bands. The first, the Regina Brass Band, was founded in 1886 by local citizens who raised $400 by public subscription to purchase the necessary instruments. An official Mounted Police band was organized at the barracks three years later. A choral society, formed in 1889, held weekly rehearsals and provided free instruction in vocal music. Locally produced theatricals and concerts were community efforts, usually fulfilling the dual functions of providing entertainment and rendering financial aid for some worthy purpose. Church support was a favoured cause in the early years. Later, during the hard times of the 1890s, assistance to the needy took precedence, and a "Penny Readings" scheme was inaugurated as a sort of voluntary relief program. In 1899 the newly established Musical and Dramatic Society staged *The Pirates of Penzance*, but ran into difficulties over the non-payment of performing rights. The arrival in 1904 of Frank L. Laubach, a professional musician from Scotland, marked the beginning of a new era for the local musical community. He founded the Regina Philharmonic Society in 1905 and for seventeen years took a leading role in most musical endeavours in the city.

There were also some notable accomplishments in the literary field. In 1889 Nicolas Flood Davin published his *Eos: An Epic of the Dawn and Other Poems*. Composed over a period of twelve years, it was the first purely literary work printed and published in the territories. No less impressive was the work of Catherine Simpson-Hayes, who arrived in Regina in the mid-1880s and whose romantic relationship with Davin was for a time the subject of much gossip in that still-small community. *Prairie pot pouri*, written under the pseudonym "Mary Markwell," appeared in 1895. It marked the beginning of an impressive literary career that encompassed poetry, drama and fiction. Of a different character was J. W. Powers's breezy *History of Regina: Its Foundation and Growth*, published five years after the birth of the town.[51]

After a slow start Regina also demonstrated remarkable energy in the field of education. Classes were at first conducted in a succession of temporary quarters until the Town Hall was erected in 1886. As enrollment increased, from 119 in 1886 to 173 in 1887, overcrowding became a serious problem and pupils spilled over into the fire hall. The town finally began construction of a proper school building in 1889. The three-storey brick and stone Union School, opened in 1890, afforded adequate kindergarten (commencing in 1891), elementary and high school facilities for the first time. Its attic housed the first regular normal school (as schools for teachers were called), which opened in 1893 and served all of the North-West Territories until 1905. Enrollment continued to climb, from 230 in 1891 to 366 in 1894, necessitating the construction of a second large brick school, Alexandra School, in 1896. Manual training classes were introduced in 1901, and a third and more modest structure, Albert School, was opened on the North Side in 1905. The size of the teaching staff kept pace, increasing from 3 in 1889 to 14 in 1905. Regina's Roman Catholics organized a separate school district in 1899. Gratton Separate School opened in rented quarters the following year with 108 pupils. There was as yet no institution of higher learning established, but Reginans were confident that one would be soon located in their midst.[52]

The ambitions of Regina and its citizens were expanding, as well they might. "A steady stream of thrifty immigration is directing its footsteps this way," a local newspaper enthused in 1905, "and the eyes of the whole English-speaking world and of the European countries are turned towards these fertile plains."[53] The West was hustling and prosperous, and so was Regina.

Kindergarten classes began in 1891 at the "White School," located on the corner of Hamilton Street and Eleventh Avenue.

Newcomers such as these American settlers came by the tens of thousands to Saskatchewan in the decade before the First World War, and wheat became king in the new province.

Chapter Two
Capital of a Booming Province, 1906-13

The signs of growth and prosperity were everywhere to be found in Saskatchewan after 1906. A flurry of railway building opened previously remote areas of the province to settlement, newcomers came by the tens of thousands to take up land, and wheat acreage and wheat production increased dramatically (Appendix, Table XIII). Saskatchewan passed Manitoba in wheat production in 1909, and by 1911 led all other provinces in Canada and states in the United States. Regina shared in this prosperity, outdistancing its rivals to become the dominant city in the province and the fourth largest in the entire prairie region by the eve of the First World War. No longer the rude prairie town of territorial days, Regina impressed one prewar visitor as "a beautiful city with parks, fine residences, magnificent public buildings, and encircled by smiling farms."[1] There were other changes as well, as Regina evolved from a small, physically compact and predominantly "British" community into a large and increasingly cosmopolitan city. Its population jumped more than fivefold between 1906 and 1913, and an extension of Regina's boundaries quadrupled its area. In this larger city, class and ethnic divisions became more pronounced. Neighbourhoods came to be identified with different social strata, a trade union movement took root (although Regina workers did not prove to be particularly militant), and ethnic clubs and societies proliferated. Theirs was a changed city, but Reginans had scarcely begun to understand or appreciate the implications of this transformation by 1913, when the shifting fortunes of the prairie economy turned again and the boom was replaced by hard times.

ECONOMIC GROWTH AND METROPOLITAN DEVELOPMENT

Wheat and railways were the key to Regina's economic growth during this period, but the collective energies of its close-knit business community must not be overlooked. As cereal agriculture quickly became the mainstay of the Saskatchewan economy, predictions that wheat would one day make it "a province of big cities, and prosperous merchants and manufacturers — a very hive of business and industry" became commonplace.[2] Although no city in Saskatchewan was in a position to challenge Winnipeg's dominant role as the regional metropolis, all vied for the more immediate provincial hinterland. Each was conscious of the progress, real or imagined, of its rivals. Thus it was that the 1906 census came as something of a shock to Regina, for it showed that Moose Jaw had surged ever so slightly ahead of the provincial capital in that all-important statistic, population (Appendix, Table IV). Spurred to new activity, Regina's business leaders were determined to place it again at the front rank among Saskatchewan cities.

The means Regina employed were not novel or unique; most indeed were borrowed from Winnipeg, whose earlier success Regina hoped to emulate. The first priority was to secure additional rail connections that would provide much-needed business for Regina and ensure its commercial domination over a wide area of the province. The westward thrust of the Canadian Northern and the Grand Trunk Pacific (GTP) across the province was viewed with particular interest, since it offered the prospect of competition for the too-complacent CPR. Luring these new railways to Regina proved to be a slow business. The Canadian Northern had announced its intentions in 1904 to build a line from Brandon to Regina, but construction was con-

Ford cars outside Saskatchewan Motor Company (1947 Rose Street), c. 1909.

In 1910, R.H. Williams opened a much larger Glasgow House on Eleventh Avenue. Three storeys initially and five by 1913, it was one of the largest department stores west of Winnipeg.

tingent on federal financial assistance. When this was not immediately forthcoming, the city found itself powerless to hurry the railway's owners. Even Premier Walter Scott was unsuccessful in his efforts to persuade the federal government to subsidize the construction of this line to his home city, despite threats on the eve of the 1905 provincial election that he would resign if prompt action was not taken.

The Canadian Northern did finally enter Regina in 1906, when it acquired the line running from the provincial capital north to Prince Albert, and completed another from Brandon to Regina in 1908. Taking advantage of provincial bond guarantees first made available the following year, the GTP built a line from Yorkton and Melville to Regina in 1911, and the city provided land for the construction of new terminal facilities for both the Canadian Northern and the GTP. In subsequent years each built additional lines, as did the CPR, and by 1913 a total of twelve railway lines radiated out of the city.[3]

Regina's business community, quick to recognize that the lots acquired from the Townsite Trustees in 1904 could be used to attract prospective wholesale and other firms, encouraged council to allocate a portion of the new property for warehouse sites. Of the more than 4,000 lots transferred to the city, the largest block was situated north of the CPR tracks in an area bounded on the west by Albert Street, on the east by Winnipeg Street and on the north by Fourth Avenue. This tract of land was as yet largely undeveloped, and the city decided to reserve it for commercial and industrial purposes.

Initially the city turned to the CPR for assistance in laying out a warehouse district and spur track system. The CPR, however, proved less than willing to build new spur tracks or even to improve conditions in its overcrowded freight yards. A threat to refer the matter to the Board of Railway Commissioners, and council's determination to collect delinquent taxes on CPR property not being utilized for railway purposes, finally brought results. In 1908 the CPR and the Canadian Northern agreed to begin laying spur tracks, and the GTP did likewise when it entered Regina three years later. With the railways' cooperation assured, the city began offering serviced warehouse sites at low cost to *bona fide* concerns.

Regina's business community was also successful in securing further freight rate concessions, though again victory did not come without a struggle. The new CPR rate schedule introduced in 1902 had enabled Regina to draw a good deal of the Soo Line trade away from Moose Jaw for the first time. The advantage proved to be short-lived. In 1907 the CPR adjusted its rates yet again, setting higher rates west and south of Regina. Businessmen in the provincial capital naturally sought to have the new schedule modified, but they also came to the realization that new firms would always be reluctant to locate in Regina as long as its freight tariffs remained so much higher than Winnipeg's. Consequently, from 1907 on they began to devote their energies to challenging the overall prairie rate structure. It was not difficult to enlist council's support in a joint appeal to the Board of Railway Commissioners in 1908, but before a decision was brought down, the city reached an independent settlement with the railways. This was the first of what proved to be a series of downward adjustments in rates as Regina continued to challenge the rate concessions that had long given Winnipeg an advantage over other prairie cities as a distribution point. In two pivotal decisions in 1909 and 1912, the Board of Railway Commissioners declared that the preferential rates accorded to Winnipeg were indeed discriminatory and extended them to other western cities.[4]

Among the first to benefit from Regina's improved rail connections and more competitive freight rate structure were its retail merchants. They eagerly seized the opportunity to serve southern Saskatchewan's burgeoning population. By 1913 it was estimated that 250 towns and villages were tributary to Regina, and that the total population within its trading area numbered 400,000. These years witnessed a marked increase in Regina's retail trade and the erection of large and imposing buildings in which to conduct it.

One of Regina's most successful retail merchants was R. H. Williams. The Glasgow House prospered under Williams's capable direction, and in 1910 the firm completed a new and much larger three-storey building on Eleventh Avenue. It boasted 50,000 square feet of floor space, far surpassing its main local rival, the Regina Trading Company, and the addition of two additional storeys in 1913 made it one of the largest department stores west of Winnipeg. The new store also featured a mail order and home delivery service, the latter partially motorized by 1913. While Williams and his sons devoted all of their energies to merchandizing, other merchants of this era began to dabble in real estate. Frank Darke was probably one of the most successful. Darke had arrived in Regina ten years after Williams and had made his money in the wholesale and retail meat business. By 1907 Darke's real-estate holdings, which included a five-storey office building on Eleventh Avenue, were substantial enough to enable him to retire from active business life.[5]

The considerable building boom Regina experienced during these hectic years also served as a stimulus to economic growth. The boom proved particularly beneficial to real-estate firms, contractors, lumber and other building supply companies, and the variety of businesses engaged in the provision of financial services. In 1908 there were 17 building contractors in Regina and 37 real-estate firms; at the height of the boom, in 1912, the respective totals were 74 and 157. Here Regina derived no little benefit from its status as the capital of Saskatchewan. The provincial government constructed several public buildings after 1906. The largest, of course, was the Legislative Building, completed in 1912, which cost $2,350,000; among the others was a telephone exchange, a normal school and the Land Titles Building. There was also much construction activity at the Mounted Police barracks, as most of the original wooden buildings were replaced by more substantial brick structures.[6]

The achievements of E. A. and E. D. McCallum demonstrate how rapidly new fortunes were made in real estate. Shortly after forming a real-estate partnership with W. H. A. Hill in 1903, the McCallums used funds provided by relatives in Ontario to purchase all of the CPR townsite lots west of Albert Street and south of Victoria Avenue. In 1904 they accomplished an even greater coup with the acquisition of 14,000 acres of farm land south of the city. They in turn sold part of this property to the provincial government as a site for the Legislative Building. The remainder they began to develop as choice residential lots. "Lakeview" was advertised as Regina's finest residential

district, and W. H. A. Hill, E. D. McCallum and other prominent Reginans erected substantial homes there. Sales were so brisk that by 1912 the firm could begin construction of Regina's first skyscraper. Ten storeys high when it was completed in 1914, the McCallum Hill Building was the tallest in Saskatchewan.[7]

By the eve of the First World War Regina had come to perform a number of other specialized functions. It was a major shipping and distribution point, particularly for farm implements. Nearly 1,000 men were estimated to work in the city's agricultural implement warehouses, and over 500 members of the North-West Commercial Travellers' Association worked out of Regina. Thirty of the sixty-seven wholesale firms in the province were located in Regina, and in 1913 they handled more than half of Saskatchewan's general wholesale business.[8] Most major banks and trust and insurance companies also established their provincial head offices in the capital. Regina provided as well a wide range of professional and commercial services, and its unskilled and even many of its skilled labourers worked part of the year for local farmers. Further strengthening the link between Regina and agricultural Saskatchewan was the city's role in frequently hosting the annual convention of the powerful Saskatchewan Grain Growers' Association, whose "farmers' parliament" came to rival the legislature as the most important public forum in the province. The headquarters of the Saskatchewan Co-operative Elevator Company, a farmer-owned grain concern founded in 1911, was also located in Regina.

Local boosters claimed for Regina the title of "The Undisputed Business Centre of the Wheat Fields of Canada," but their ambitions did not end there. Their ultimate goal was to attract new industries to Regina, and they reserved their greatest effort for this task. The Board of Trade proved an aggressive propagandist, and the city a willing ally. A new booster organization, the Greater Regina Club, appeared in 1909. Its first priority was to pursue a vigorous industrial policy. The Board of Trade and the Greater Regina Club envisaged the city's industrial destiny in terms of the success of Winnipeg and midwestern American cities that had become major meat-packing or flour-milling centres. Believing that Regina shared certain attributes with those cities, notably a central position in the wheat

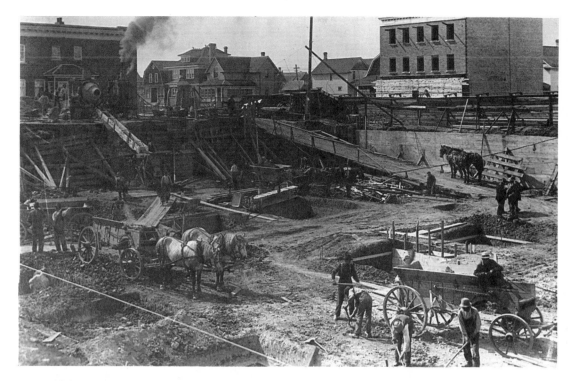

Excavating the basement for the Sherwood department store, 1913. The building boom which Regina experienced during these years served as an important stimulus to economic growth.

A group of construction workers pose for a photograph in front of the Regina Collegiate Institute (later Central Collegiate), 1908.

Pomp and ceremony: Canada's governor general, the Duke of Connaught, visits Regina in 1912 and the City Hall is decorated for the occasion.

belt and good rail connections, they actively sought out such industries and offered them a variety of inducements to locate there.[9]

Regina was not the only Saskatchewan city which fancied itself becoming a great flour-milling or meat-packing centre. Moose Jaw, with its sprawling CPR shops and marshalling yards, had similar ambitions and was prepared to offer similar concessions. So also was Saskatoon, fast becoming the most important distribution centre in central Saskatchewan. Even Prince Albert, which lacked the extensive rail connections of its southern rivals and benefited least from the agricultural prosperity the rest of the province was enjoying, dreamed of exploiting the natural wealth of Saskatchewan's northern hinterland. In 1910 that city embarked on an ill-fated scheme to harness the nearby LaColle Falls to provide the cheap power that would make it a major manufacturing centre.

Regina took a modest step towards the development of a meat-packing industry in 1905, offering a cheap site and a special water rate to a local man, Hugh Armour, to establish a small abattoir. Moose Jaw gained a bigger prize in 1910, when a Winnipeg firm, Gordon, Ironside and Fares, agreed to construct a much larger meat-packing plant there. It was indeed the largest in the province, but most of the cattle, sheep and hogs in Saskatchewan were still exported live to meat-packing plants in Alberta and Manitoba.[10]

Moose Jaw and Saskatoon also proved more successful than Regina in attracting flour-milling concerns. Robin Hood Mills built a large facility in Moose Jaw in 1911. When it was completely destroyed by fire within a few months, Regina's hopes were raised but then quickly dashed as Moose Jaw offered more generous concessions to the company to rebuild there. Regina also courted the Quaker Oats Company, offering a free site and tax exemptions. Quaker Oats decided instead to acquire an existing facility in Saskatoon and accept the more generous concessions that city was prepared to offer. When the federal government announced its intention to construct a number of large grain storage elevators on the prairies in 1913, there was another scramble. Regina offered a fifty-acre site, but lost out to Moose Jaw, Saskatoon and Calgary.[11]

The ambitious schemes of Regina's most ardent boosters were not realized. Indeed, they were unrealistic. Geography and economics raised formidable barriers to its becoming a major industrial centre. Regina was far from major markets, and in the smaller provincial market it faced stiff competition from Moose Jaw and Saskatoon. The cost of electric power was another handicap. Regina businessmen had of course been quick to recognize that cheap power was necessary for industrial and commercial development. It was they, after all, who had been the driving force behind the city's acquisition of the Regina Electric Light and Power Company plant in 1904. This coal-fired plant was subsequently expanded, but increases in power consumption continued to tax its capacity to the limit. The cost of power also remained high, on account of the absence of any local supply of bituminous coal and the high cost of imported fuel.[12] Thus, any scheme for generating cheaper power in the province was bound to be regarded with great interest.

Such a scheme was in fact mooted in 1912, when the provincial government appointed a royal commission to investigate the feasibility of utilizing the immense deposits of lignite coal in southern Saskatchewan to generate electric power. Impressed with the success that Germany and other countries had experienced in using lignite coal for this purpose, the royal commission concluded that the generation of electric power at the Souris coalfields was "both a practicable and commercial possibility." Power could be distributed from a central generating station to Regina, Moose Jaw and other communities at a much lower rate (roughly half in the case of Regina, it was estimated) if the cities cooperated by taking current in bulk. The commission recommended that the provincial government build an experimental plant to determine the best method of converting Saskatchewan lignite into a fuel suitable for heating and power generation purposes.[13]

The reaction in Regina was predictable. "Cheap power," one newspaper enthused, "would solve one of the biggest problems which confronts [Regina] at the present time." Within a few months the provincial government did begin construction of such a plant near Estevan, but it soon became obvious that the royal commission's calculations had been overly optimistic.

A printer by trade, Thomas M. Molloy was the first president of the Regina Trades and Labour Council. His most important contribution to Regina's and Saskatchewan's fledgeling union movement, however, was as commissioner of the provincial Bureau of Labour, a post he held for nearly thirty years.

Cheap power was not to come so easily to the cities of southern Saskatchewan, and Regina began construction of a new and larger power plant on Wascana Lake in 1913.[14]

Notwithstanding these handicaps, Regina did succeed in becoming something of an industrial centre (Appendix, Table I). By 1911 Regina in fact had more manufacturing establishments and a larger industrial work force and payroll than any other city in the province. The value of goods produced in Regina was nearly double that of its nearest rivals, Prince Albert and Moose Jaw, and more than double that of Saskatoon. Fully 25 per cent of the province's industrial labour force worked in Regina, and the value of its manufacturing output amounted to 30 per cent of the provincial total. Most of Regina's industries served only the city and its immediate trading area. Some supplied materials for the construction boom. A survey published in 1913 listed three sash and door factories, two brick plants and two foundries. One firm made cement blocks, another woven wire fencing and another corrugated metal products. Several processed agricultural products: Hugh Armour's abattoir, a flour and grist mill, a brewery, a cold storage plant and a tannery. Regina also produced a few consumer goods, notably soap, cigars and mattresses, and there were five printing and book-binding establishments.[15]

It is doubtful if "bonusing" contributed much to Regina's modest industrial growth. Bonusing was self-destructive, as cities competed with and outbid each other in the race for metropolitan stature. While Saskatchewan cities publicly decried the evils of bonusing, they quietly went about the task of wooing industries by whatever means were deemed necessary. Since the cities were incapable of policing themselves, the Union of Saskatchewan Municipalities asked the province as early as 1908 to ban bonusing altogether. It took no action, however, and the competition for industries continued. By 1912 even Regina ratepayers had had enough and decisively defeated a by-law offering a free site, exemption from municipal taxation, reduced light and water rates and a $500,000 bond guarantee to a flour-milling concern. The provincial government also had a change of heart and in 1913 limited bonusing to free sites and a ten-year tax exemption. Later that same year it went further and placed a complete ban on the practice "to remove all temptation to municipal folly," as the minister of municipal affairs, George Langley, candidly put it.[16]

Although Regina had assumed a prominent place in the commercial, financial and industrial life of Saskatchewan, the predictions of unbounded growth and prosperity for Regina that had accompanied the birth of the province were beginning to dim by 1913. There was a noticeable curtailment of business expansion as the city began to feel the effects of a world-wide financial depression. The value of building permits had kept pace with Regina's frenzied real-estate boom, reaching a peak in 1912, but the 1913 total was only half that of the previous year (Appendix, Table XI). The city's own financial position became a cause for concern as well. Mayor Robert Martin probably spoke for most Reginans when he declared in July 1913 that the best remedy for the "money stringency" would be a bumper crop. These hopes were only partly realized. The harvest that year did prove to be the largest to date (Appendix, Table XIII), but the tightness of the money market and higher interest rates drove prices and farm incomes down.[17] Regina's economy was tied to the value and yield of the mammoth wheat crops for which Saskatchewan was becoming so famous, and this fact was driven painfully home as the ranks of the unemployed grew ever larger in the city during the winter of 1913-14.

POPULATION GROWTH AND ETHNIC RELATIONSHIPS

Population growth in Regina kept pace with the city's economic boom, multiplying fivefold between 1906 and 1911 alone and this due largely to immigration. As in earlier years, natural increase was a much less significant factor — which was inevitable, given the continued preponderance of men over women in the population, and the fact that in 1911 only 13 per cent of Reginans had been born in Saskatchewan (Appendix, Tables II, VI). The extension of the city's boundaries that year did not substantially increase its population, for much of the land added to the city was vacant.

The Anglo-Saxon and Protestant charter group remained the

RTLC Labour Day Committee, 1909.

Labour Day parade, 1913.

Scarth Street looking south from Eleventh Avenue, with the Post Office in the foreground, 1910. Next to it is the Northern Crown Bank.

Eleventh Avenue, looking east from Scarth Street, 1912.

dominant element in Regina (Appendix, Table VIII). The city's business and professional elite was drawn almost exclusively from this group. It is difficult to generalize, but most of its members appear to have been self-made men. Like the Mc-Callum brothers, they came from relatively modest circumstances and acquired wealth and social prestige in Regina through real-estate investment, merchandizing or the provision of professional services of one sort or another. Some of the businessmen in their ranks operated their own enterprises, while others managed the local branch of a regional or national firm. Collectively they were the city's dominant force, the men who shaped its economic growth, made its political decisions and set its social standards.

Of course, not all Reginans of British ethnic origin were well-to-do. The majority were tradesmen, clerks or labourers. Although they shared the cultural and religious heritage of Regina's upper strata, they were able to participate in its wider community and social life only to the extent of their means. And these varied considerably. A survey on the eve of the First World War found that the average wages of bricklayers in Regina were 70 cents per hour; plumbers, 60 cents; carpenters, 45 cents; and ordinary labourers, 20 cents. Most workdays consisted of ten hours, the six-day week was the norm, and so was seasonal unemployment. Bricklayers were fortunate to work seven months of the year. Carpenters could work perhaps eight. Store clerks' wages at this time amounted to $20 a week, and a good stenographer earned $65 a month.[18]

The arrival of thousands of newcomers satisfied the growth ethic of Regina's leading citizens, most of whom were British in origin and outlook, but it also altered the population structure in ways that some found disturbing. For one thing, Regina's population became more cosmopolitan. Where those of German birth or extraction had constituted the only significant non-British group at the turn of the century, they were only one, albeit still the largest, of several enumerated in the 1911 census (Appendix, Table VIII).

Most Germans in Regina did not come directly from Germany, but rather from some part of the Russian or Austro-Hungarian empires. The proportion from Germany proper was higher in the city than in the rural districts. Finding employment as labourers, tradesmen or businessmen, they were regarded as thrifty, hard-working people; many owned their own homes by 1913. Anxious to transmit their language to their children, Germans in Regina were the first in to city to take advantage of an ammendment to the School Act permitting instruction in German during the last hour of the school day. In 1912 German Catholics engaged a teacher from Ottawa for this purpose and collected funds to meet his salary by a special levy as the law required.[19]

The German community in Regina became large enough during these years to support a variety of ethnic and religious institutions: Lutheran and Roman Catholic churches (founded in 1906 and 1912 respectively) and a German Catholic men's club (also established in 1906). Secular clubs and associations appeared too. Some thrived briefly and then collapsed, but the Teutonia Club (1908) was still holding regular meetings at the outbreak of the First World War. Regina's Germans also played a leading role in the Volksverein Deutsch Canadischer Katholiken, a provincial German Catholic association that appeared in 1909, and founded a lay organization, the Deutschcanadischer Provinzialverband von Saskatchewan, in 1913. The *Saskatchewan Courier*, a German newspaper that superseded the *Rundschau*, was another important initiative. It commenced publication in 1907 under the direction of a prominent local German, and Liberal, Paul Bredt. The initial capital came from the Liberal party, and by 1911 circulation stood at 7,000.[20]

Central and eastern European immigrants suffered a much more inferior status in prewar Regina. A German visitor remarked in 1909 that even his countrymen in the city regarded these "Galicians" with contempt. They found employment where they could, as day labourers or on adjacent farms, and most were citizens in name only — the property qualification prohibited all but a few from reaching the municipal voters' list.[21] The bulk of them gravitated to Germantown, an area encompassing thirty-three full city blocks which in 1913 contained 607 homes and 697 families. In fact most of these "houses" were shacks, averaging barely three rooms, situated on twenty-five-foot lots. Water and sewer lines were being extended as far east

An outing in Wascana Park, c. 1910.

as Winnipeg Street by 1913, yet 60 per cent of the homes in Germantown were so poorly constructed as to make the necessary connections impossible. Poor ventilation, overcrowding, outdoor toilets and the absence of any regular system of garbage removal gave Germantown a proportionately higher number of cases of infectious diseases than other areas of the city.

Like the Germans, these newcomers also sought to preserve and perpetuate their language and culture, but their small numbers often proved a severe handicap. Thus, the traditional Ukrainian religious organizations were slow to appear in Regina; those of the Orthodox persuasion worshipped at the Romanian Orthodox Church throughout this period, while Ukrainian Catholics attended St. Mary's Church south of Victoria Park. Nevertheless, Ukrainian social and cultural life did begin to flourish. One important stimulus was provided by the provincial government. It decided in 1909 to establish a school in Regina that would provide teachers for those areas of Saskatchewan where Ukrainian and other ethnic groups were beginning to press for bilingual instruction. The majority of the pupils enrolled at the Training School for Teachers for Foreign Speaking Communities, as it was called, were Ukrainian. It was they who took the lead in organizing a Shevchenko concert in 1911 and in founding the Association of Ukrainian-English Teachers in Saskatchewan the following year.

Numbers proved to be an even more serious obstacle for other ethnic groups in the city. Polish Catholics sought to have a separate parish established as early as 1912, but it was judged premature. There were also efforts to create a provincial federation of Polish Catholics. Such a body was founded in Regina in 1912, but it experienced great difficulty in maintaining contact among the province's scattered Polish parishes.[22]

What impact these "New Canadians" would have on the future character of the city and the province was a matter of much speculation in Protestant pulpits and in the editorial pages of Regina's daily newspapers, among other places. Indeed, there were few political or social issues in prewar Regina that did not in some way involve the "foreigner." Prohibition can serve as a case in point. The prohibition movement in Regina was not without some supporters among Roman

Catholics (notably Bishop O. E. Mathieu) and European-born immigrants, but its leadership was essentially Protestant and Anglo-Saxon. To these people it was absolutely clear that the "foreigner" had too great a fondness for alcohol. When a local option vote failed to carry in Regina by less than a hundred votes in 1910, some supporters of prohibition were quick to lament that "Germantown rules Regina in the matter of the sale of liquor."[23] Germans, for their part, condemned prohibition as an "aggressive and unscrupulous agitation which aims to ruin financially a great number of our fellow citizens and to restrict personal liberty."[24]

Some Reginans were as bitterly opposed to the separate school as to the hotel bar. What especially roused their ire was a 1913 amendment to the School Act that explicitly required that ratepayers of the religious minority support their separate schools. Premier Walter Scott's own pastor, Murdoch MacKinnon, publicly rebuked the government from the pulpit of Knox Presbyterian Church in May 1914. MacKinnon objected to the cumpulsory feature of the measure. It would deprive Roman Catholics of the "right" to send their children to the public school (though the law had always implied that the minority would be obliged to support a separate school if one was established). His real concern, however, was that the government was fostering separate schools that would only perpetuate divisions in a province where assimilation was the highest priority. Other Presbyterian and Baptist clergymen took up the crusade against "The Crime of Coercion," as MacKinnon was to label it, and so did the Orange Lodge.

The fulminations of MacKinnon and other Protestant zealots did not represent the views of all Reginans of Anglo-Saxon background. Some exhibited a concern for the welfare and well-being of the European immigrant struggling to make a new home in a new and unfamiliar land. The local press began to draw attention to the "disgraceful" sanitary conditions in Germantown, and in 1913 the Social Service boards of Regina's Methodist and Presbyterian churches sponsored a social survey of the city. It was carried out by J. S. Woodsworth, then the director of All Peoples' Mission in Winnipeg. Woodsworth described living conditions in Germantown in graphic detail

Architect Edward Maxwell, one of the designers of the Saskatchewan Legislative Building.

Together with his brother Edward Maxwell, William Sutherland Maxwell submitted the winning design for the legislative building.

and recommended the establishment of an institution modelled on All Peoples' Mission as a first priority.[25]

Woodsworth's report did have some impact. Protestant clergymen called for immediate action in dealing with the "New Canadians" who had come to live in Regina. The city's medical health officer, Dr. Malcolm Bow, announced that henceforth his department would publish its public health bulletin in at least two languages other than English. There was also talk of establishing a centre for settlement work in the "East End," but nothing concrete had been accomplished by the time war broke out in August 1914.[26]

The Chinese remained Regina's most visible minority group, and attitudes towards them were much more uniformly negative. Reginans regarded Oriental immigration as undesirable, and tolerated the few Chinese in their midst only because they posed no real economic threat. Indeed the Greater Regina Club boasted in 1910 that the city was "well provided with modern laundries equipped with the latest sanitary appliances ... thus minimizing the employment of Chinese labor which goes on unchecked in other cities, not always to the benefit of the community." Restricted by Canada's increasingly stringent immigration laws and by a lack of economic opportunity, Regina's Chinese population grew slowly (Appendix, Table VIII).

One of the few instances of overt hostility towards the Chinese occurred in 1907. Two patrons of a city restaurant died of arsenic poisoning, and the Chinese proprietor of a rival establishment next door and his cook were charged with murder. The cook, Mack Sing, was arrested at once, but the other man managed to evade the police. Feelings ran high. One local newspaper, the *Daily Standard*, pronounced the two guilty even before they had appeared in court. An American recently arrived in Regina expressed surprise that his fellow citizens did not take matters into their own hands. At least one hotel discharged its Chinese cooks. The *Morning Leader* adopted a more moderate view, reminding its readers that "mob law has no place in our Canadian national life" and calling for "fair play for the Chinaman." Fair play he received. F. W. G. Haultain, a prominent Regina lawyer and leader of the Provincial Rights party, defended him, and successfully convinced a jury that

A nearly completed Legislative Building dominates the south shore of Wascana Lake.

Victoria Square, still treeless, looking south. In 1907, the city would hire a Montreal landscape architect, Frederick G. Todd, and his plan would form the basis for an attractive downtown park.

Regina's best-known photographer of the day, Edgar Charlotte Rossie, took this photograph of Lorne Street, looking south from Twelfth Avenue. Knox Presbyterian Church is in the foreground, First Baptist Church (with the dome) is farther south.

Mack Sing had been an innocent party in the scheme concocted by his employer (who, as it turned out, was never apprehended).[27]

Passions were also aroused for a time over the employment of white women in restaurants and laundries owned by Chinese or other Orientals. The city's nascent trade union movement, which joined the Vancouver-based Asiatic Exclusion League in 1907, was in the forefront in pressing the provincial government to legislate an end to the practice. It obliged in 1912, but Regina's Chinese community at first refused to comply with the law. Although the legislation was in fact challenged in the courts, the Supreme Court of Canada at length ruled that it fell within provincial jurisdiction. Only then did the Chinese in Regina begin to discharge their white female help.[28]

As Regina's population grew after 1906 and the range of its economic activities widened, class distinctions became more sharply drawn. The beginnings of the city's trade union movement, which can be traced back to the turn of the century, marked an important change in the character of the city. The railway brotherhoods were among the first to appear in most prairie towns, and Regina was no exception. There was a lodge of the International Brotherhood of Maintenance of Way Employees there by 1900, but other groups of skilled workers were still too small to establish formal unions. That soon changed with the upswing in Regina's economic fortunes. In quick succession locals of the United Brotherhood of Carpenters and Joiners and the International Typographical Union appeared in 1904 and 1905 respectively, although the first soon disappeared. It was revived in 1906, and the other building trades were organized as well when four organizers were despatched from Winnipeg to establish the trade union movement in Saskatchewan on a firmer footing. The founding of the Regina Trades and Labour Council (RTLC) that same year was also due largely to their efforts.

Union membership in Regina increased from 677 in 1911, when statistics were first compiled, to 1,079 in 1913, and local men such as Thomas M. Molloy and Hugh Peat assumed prominent roles in provincial labour circles. Molloy served as the first president of the RTLC. He joined the provincial government in 1909 as fair wage officer and was named commissioner of its newly created Bureau of Labour two years later. Molloy headed the bureau for nearly three decades until ill health forced his retirement in 1939. Hugh Peat, who belonged to the printers' union, became the editor of *Saskatchewan Labor's Realm* when that short-lived journal began publication in the provincial capital in 1907 (it lasted only until 1910).

In Regina it was the men in the building trades who proved to be the most militant in a union movement notable for its conservatism. They went on strike six times between 1907 and 1910 alone. The largest walkout lasted six weeks and involved all but two of the city's building trades. This early militancy resulted in part from the seasonal nature of employment in the building trades and from the workers' consequent determination to secure high wages that would tide them over the winter months. One of their targets was the government. Public works such as the new buildings erected at the Mounted Police barracks, the Legislative Building and the new city hall loomed large in the eyes of the city's unions, for such projects provided employment for their members. The unions looked to the three levels of government to set an example by insisting that contractors on these projects pay the going rate for all trades. The provincial government was easily won over. It inserted a fair wage clause in its contract with P. Lyall and Sons of Montreal for the construction of the Legislative Building, the largest public works project undertaken in the city to that time. More significantly, it sided with labour in the disputes that arose with the contractor over the interpretation of the clause. Regina also adopted a fair wage clause for all municipal projects in 1909. There appears to have been some backsliding, since the RTLC had to urge again in 1912 that such a step be taken, and it was.[29] In a government town such as Regina, the recognition of this principle was perhaps labour's most important accomplishment during these prewar years.

THE URBAN LANDSCAPE

As the population of Regina grew to 30,000 and more, the physical character and appearance of the city changed. Neigh-

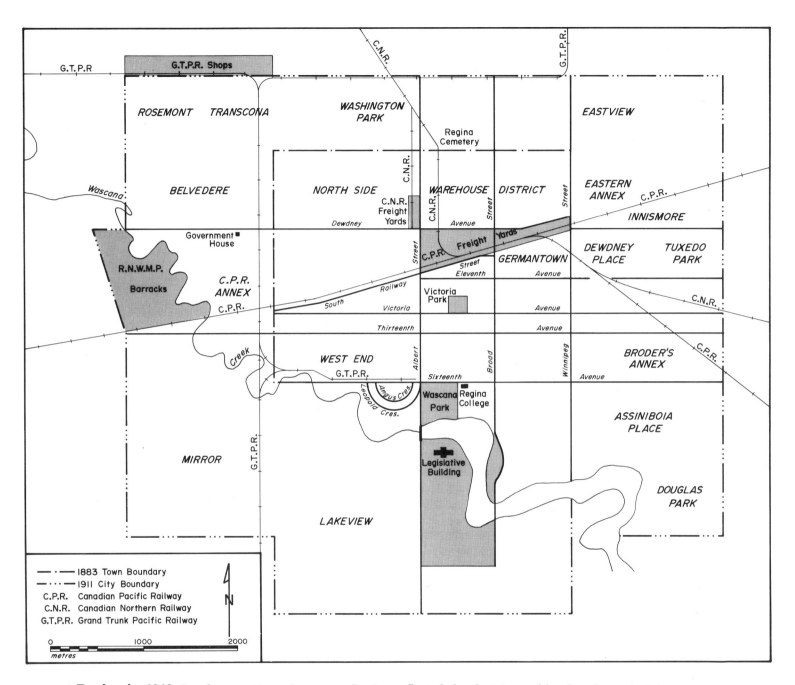

4 Regina in 1913: Land-use patterns in prewar Regina reflected the decisions of local and provincial governments and of the railways (and particularly the Grand Trunk Pacific). The character of Regina's neighbourhoods became more clearly defined as well. Those located north and east of the downtown core were working class. The better-off lived south of Victoria Park, in the West End, on Angus and Leopold crescents and in Lakeview.

bourhoods increasingly became identified with different social strata. New homes, churches and office buildings gave Regina an air of modernity and permanence, and the thousands of trees Reginans planted during these years began to soften the harsh landscape. Here, in the proliferation of trees in prewar Regina, can be found one of the city's distinguishing characteristics. Regina was, and in some respects still is, a uniquely man-made city. People, not nature, have decisively shaped its form.

Municipal authorities early saw the desirability of directing the physical growth of Regina to avoid haphazard development. In arguing for the adoption of a system of building permits in 1904, Mayor H. W. Laird noted that it would "protect the residential portions of the city from the incursions of objectionable buildings, or enterprises calculated to disturb the peace or mar the appearance of the neighborhood." The gift of some 167 blocks of land from the federal government in 1904 provided an opportunity to influence directly the location of wholesale firms that were then beginning to appear in the city. Now one of the largest property owners in Regina, the city decided to reserve a large tract as a warehouse district (see Map 4).

The timing could not have been better. While a number of businesses dependent on the railway, such as coal and lumberyards, were already located on CPR property immediately adjacent to the main line, the railway had no additional land, apart from its right-of-way, to make available for this purpose. Thus, the city found itself in the position of having a virtual monopoly of land suitable for warehouses and industrial enterprises in the area. The city and the railways cooperated to provide spur track facilities, and this further consolidated the former's control over land use there.

The city also placed a considerable number of residential lots on the market, selling them by public auction at intervals rather than disposing of them in large blocks to speculators. City-owned land was sold for residential purposes in three areas: in the warehouse district, particularly on or near Hamilton Street; in the west-central area of Regina, adjacent to the CPR main line; and south and east of the downtown business district. Successive city councils followed a conscious policy of selling first those serviced lots closest to the central core. Sales in subsequent years generally followed the extension of utilities. The city also sought first to regulate, and then after 1912 to prohibit, the location of incompatible commercial or manufacturing enterprises in residential areas.[30]

Of course, the city never exercised as much control over the sale of residential lots as it did over warehouse sites. Private interests were far more influential in determining patterns of residential development. In their zeal to provide accommodation for the thousands of newcomers drawn to Regina, real-estate speculators halved most of the existing fifty-foot lots on the fringes of the city. They also laid out new suburbs outside its boundaries. It was simple enough to purchase nearby farm land, subdivide it into lots and register the subdivision plan with the provincial government. Aggressive advertising campaigns sang the praises of Washington Park, Mirror and Rosemont, among others, and assured prospective purchasers that each would soon be incorporated into the city. Some of these subdivisions were located immediately adjacent to the city, but others were many miles distant. Most were uninspired in design, with streets laid out in the same monotonous rectangular grid and lots seldom wider than twenty-five feet. They lacked any parks, playgrounds or other open spaces, since provincial legislation did not require developers to provide these amenities.[31]

The city proved somewhat more far-sighted in this regard. In 1906, through an exchange of lots with the federal government, it acquired a forty-four-acre site located between the southern limits of the city and the reservoir, and sponsored a competition to prepare plans for the beautification of Wascana Park, as the area came to be known.[32] But what the city set out to create with one hand, it almost gave away with the other. In 1906 the provincial government began to review possible sites for a new and more impressive legislative building. In all it considered seven possibilities, including Victoria Square, Wascana Park and a 168-acre parcel of land south of the reservoir that was then owned by McCallum Hill and Company and was in the process of being subdivided into residential lots.[33] The choice of the McCallum Hill property proved to be a wise one, for it provided an opportunity to set the building in spacious grounds, but it was not universally applauded at the time. Critics, particularly Regina's city council, argued that the site was too far from the downtown business district (indeed, it was then outside the incorporated limits of the city). In the hope of inducing a change of heart, council offered to donate Wascana Park instead. Premier Walter Scott declined the offer but suggested that the park land on both sides of the reservoir be developed as a single entity. This proposal was accepted,[34] and the ground was laid for what has become one of the most attractive urban parks in Canada.

The Scott government then engaged a Montreal landscape architect, Frederick G. Todd, to begin laying out the grounds and select a site for the new legislature. His principal recommendation was that it should face north, with its centre on the axis of Smith Street, and be set well back from the water. A firm of Montreal architects, Edward and W. S. Maxwell, prepared the winning design in a competition held for the purpose in 1907. The following year a magnificent structure of Manitoba Tyndal stone began to arise on the open prairie south of Regina. The province took considerable pains to place it in a park-like setting, building a new concrete bridge and dam across Wascana Creek at Albert Street in 1908. The need to drain the reservoir during construction permitted the deepening of the creek's shallower portions to make it a more attractive "lake." The province also began landscaping the grounds surrounding the Legislative Building even before the structure was completed.[35]

Taken together, these decisions had a lasting impact upon patterns of residential development. By the turn of the century it was already well established that the better residential districts lay south of Regina's downtown core. The location of the Legislative Building on the banks of Wascana Lake, and subsequent efforts to transform the site into a spacious and attractive park, reinforced this attitude. The principal beneficiary was of course McCallum Hill and Company, which made Lakeview's proximity to Wascana Lake and the Legislative Building a central feature of its advertising campaign. Angus and Leopold crescents, situated immediately north of Wascana Creek and west of Albert Street, also became a more desirable residential area.

Real-estate interests were not the only private bodies to have an impact on the landscape of prewar Regina. Railways were important, too. The CPR had early divided Regina along north-south lines and had restricted internal traffic movement until underpasses were constructed at Albert Street in 1911 and Broad Street in 1913. The entrance of new lines into the city brought the prospect of further congestion, and from 1907 on there was considerable support for a union station for all three railways. The city was even prepared to turn over Stanley Park to achieve that objective. Only the CPR and the Canadian Northern could reach an agreement to share such a joint facility, and then only after protracted negotiations and the sacrificing of a portion of Stanley Park to provide access to it.[36]

The Grand Trunk Pacific was bent on a different course. Seeking to avoid high land prices, its Melville-Regina line skirted the northern and western boundaries of the city, leading some to assume that it would enter Regina from the west along Sixteenth Avenue. The uncertainty concerning the GTP's plans prompted one anxious newspaper editor to urge that the city "get into a generous frame of mind" in its negotiations with the company.[37] An agreement was struck in November 1910, and generous it was. The city gave the GTP land for spur tracks and freight sheds, and agreed to close a number of streets so that the company could build a short line along Sixteenth Avenue to Albert Street, where it proposed to construct its own passenger station. The GTP also agreed to build a "first class hotel" in the vicinity of the station, to make Regina a divisional point and to erect suitable shops and other facilities on land it acquired north of McKinley Avenue (see Map 4). The agreement was acclaimed by Regina businessmen, even though it permitted the construction of a railway line adjacent to what was becoming one of Regina's most attractive residential areas. For them it was enough that Regina was to be a "large terminus" of the GTP, whose facilities would, its general manager boasted, add some 5,000 residents to the city.[38]

The building of the GTP shops on the northern outskirts of the city drew railway workers and tradesmen to the residential districts north and west of the CPR main line. As a consequence, the North Side became more and more a working-class area.

One of the few examples of row housing in Regina was to be found in the West End. The detached single-family dwelling was far more common in pre-war Regina.

The devastation wrought by the 1912 tornado can clearly be seen along Lorne Street, south of Victoria Avenue.

Mayor Peter McAra (center) built a successful real estate and insurance business in partnership with his brother James and W.L. Wallace. He held Regina's highest elected office in 1906, 1911 and 1912.

There, too, the houses were crowded together on narrow lots, and as in Germantown, the introduction of sanitary facilities lagged behind population growth. Other GTP workers built homes in the area immediately north of the railway's yards, which was incorporated as the village of North Regina in 1914.[39]

During this boom period, prairie cities indulged in massive boundary extensions. Regina was no exception: in 1911 it increased from three square miles to nearly thirteen (see Map 4). The annexation of such large tracts of land has often been attributed to the inflated expectations of local boosters. While this was a factor in Regina's case, it was not the only one. The anticipation of the early construction of a street railway, and the belief it only could be profitable if Regina's boundaries were extended, were additional reasons for the annexation of 1911. Yet another was the city's desire to reassert its control over the pace and direction of urban growth. Within the boundaries marked out at the time of its incorporation as a town, Regina had been able to exercise some control over land use. Outside those limits it had not. The city had not been able to influence the selection of the site for the Legislative Building or the right-of-way of the GTP line from Melville, and it could not control the new subdivisions that were flooding the real-estate market. Still, expanding Regina's boundaries proved only a partial solution. New subdivisions continued to appear outside the city. At the peak of the prewar real-estate boom, lots were being offered for sale in twenty-one subdivisions within the city and in at least thirty-nine outside.[40]

The Regina Municipal Railway influenced the direction of the city's physical growth and patterns of residential differentiation. The initial street railway routes laid out in 1911 were designed to serve the built-up area of the city. In the downtown the streetcars travelled along Eleventh Avenue, not South Railway Street, a sign of the latter's decline as Regina's commercial and financial hub. The Albert Street underpass provided access to the warehouses and residences north of the CPR tracks. As a consequence, that street became the main north-south link in the system, with lines running west along Thirteenth Avenue and east and west along Dewdney Avenue. Only one line extended past the limits of the city as they had existed prior to

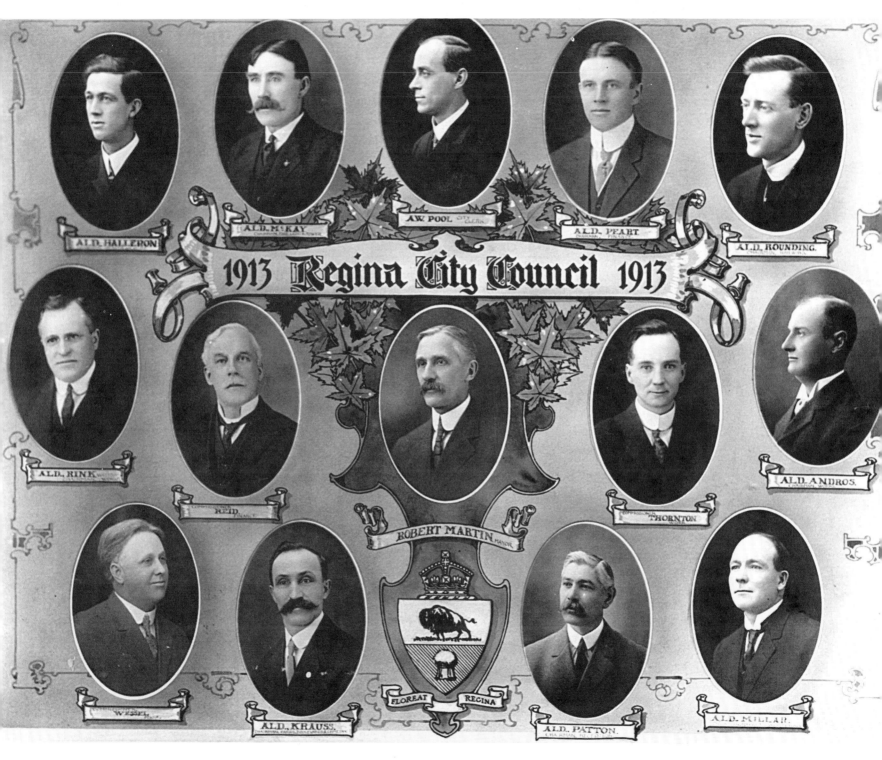

Mayor Robert Martin and the members of Regina City Council, 1913.

A new City Hall (foreground, left) was completed in 1908. It cost half again as much as had been originally estimated, but served Regina well for more than fifty years until it was demolished to make way for a shopping mall.

Regina's Police Department, 1911. Chief of Police Theodore Zeats subsequently became embroiled in a controversy with city council over the suppression of prostitution, and in 1914 left Regina for Yorkton.

annexation; it ran south along Albert Street across the creek to the Legislative Building.

In 1912, and more particularly in 1913, the system was greatly expanded to keep pace with Regina's burgeoning population and to generate more tax revenue in newly annexed areas. The terms of the 1911 annexation had stipulated that taxes would increase in new subdivisions on an escalating scale over ten years, but property within three blocks of a streetcar line would immediately be taxed at the same rate as built-up areas of the city. Thus, in 1912 streetcar tracks were extended west along Dewdney Avenue nearly to the Mounted Police barracks, and east along Eleventh and Victoria avenues via Winnipeg Street to within several blocks of Regina's eastern limits. The following year still another line was extended to the GTP shops north of the city. Ten miles of track in 1911 became twenty-eight by 1913.

In outlying areas the street railway was often little more than a tool of land speculators. In some cases they offered to construct a line at their own expense and turn it over to the city to operate once completed. Council usually proved receptive. One streetcar line was extended along Albert Street to the city's northern limits in this fashion, another south along the same street to Twenty-fifth Avenue. Here streetcars ran well past the limits of heavy settlement where little and often no housing existed. Not only was Regina's street railway system overbuilt by 1913, it had also become a substantial financial burden. City authorities asserted in 1913 that streetcar extensions had brought $40,000 in new tax revenue and that an additional $45,000 would be realized in 1914 as other new areas were brought within three blocks of a streetcar line. But the Regina Municipal Railway's own financial statements presented a rather different picture, recording deficits of $6,595 in 1912 and $64,684 in 1913.[41]

Economics aside, the streetcars had a symbolic importance to Reginans, demonstrating that theirs was a modern and up-to-date city. Visitors agreed. "Everything," an English traveller remarked in 1912, "bears the imprint of newness."[42] Nowhere was this more evident than in the downtown core, where brick and stone replaced wood as the predominant building material.

The Northern Crown Bank, erected in 1906, was an early example of this trend. Regina's new city hall and post office, completed in 1908 and 1909 respectively, were others. Office buildings such as the Darke Block had reached five storeys, and the King's Hotel six. The central business district itself was moving south, to Eleventh Avenue, where R. H. Williams's new department store would stand for more than seventy years. Most of the chartered banks also constructed new and imposing branches along Eleventh Avenue or immediately adjacent on Scarth Street. The graceful six-storey Canada Life Building stood farther west on Eleventh Avenue, further enhancing its status as the financial and business centre of Regina.

The city took steps to make the downtown more attractive. The grounds adjacent to the city hall were landscaped, and Frederick Todd was engaged to prepare plans for the beautification of Victoria Square.[43] The trees planted there prior to the First World War would in time transform this barren tract into a delightful downtown park. The area immediately surrounding the park also began to lose its exclusively residential character. By 1912 the First Baptist, Metropolitan Methodist and Knox Presbyterian churches all fronted on Victoria Park, as did the Land Titles Building, the YMCA and YWCA, and the public library. McCallum Hill and Company also chose a site across from the park for its new office building in 1912. It was designed by Stan E. Storey and William G. Van Egmond, who had themselves come to Regina six years earlier. Storey and Van Egmond were among the most prolific of Regina's architects during this period, and the McCallum Hill Building was one of the finest examples of their work.

Brick and stone also supplanted wood in the homes of Regina's business and professional elite south of Victoria Park, along Angus and Leopold crescents and in Lakeview. Architectural styles were often eclectic. W. H. A. Hill was so impressed with the style of a country estate he encountered on a trip to Great Britain that he engaged a local architectural firm, Clemesha and Portnall, to design a duplicate in three-quarter scale. The home cost $18,000 to build and was constructed of brick with stone trimmings. It featured solid oak panelling in the living room, a spacious billiard room in the attic and a cir-

Inaugural run of the Regina Municipal Railway down Eleventh Avenue, July 28, 1911. To mark the occasion no fares were charged, and some children rode the streetcars all day.

HOLDING IT OVER THEM

The question of the university location continues to be a cause for controversy in some quarters.

The contest for the University of Saskatchewan reached a peak early in 1909, when this cartoon appeared in the The Daily Standard. It was not Premier Walter Scott and his cabinet who made the final choice but a non-partisan body, the University's Board of Governors. Smug Regina lost to Saskatoon.

Music soon became a part of Regina College's educational program. Musical instruction began in 1911 and the Conservatory of Music was established the following year.

The Regina College student body, 1913. Most of the students were from rural Saskatchewan, drawn to Regina by the opportunity to obtain a high school education.

Albert School teachers and pupils, 1907 (not 1909 as photo suggests). This was one of seven public schools built in Regina prior to the First World War.

cular carriage drive. E. D. McCallum's three-story residence was even more pretentious and expensive, costing $30,000.

Reginans of more moderate means also lived south of Victoria Park. The "West End" became a popular middle-class residential area as well, particularly once the streetcar line was extended from Albert Street west along Thirteenth Avenue. By the eve of the war, two- and three-storey wood frame houses lined the streets adjacent to Holy Rosary Cathedral, whose twin spires towered over the district. The homes of Regina's working-class population were smaller and uninspired in design, but far more numerous. Crowded together in Germantown or Broder's Annex east of Broad Street, or in the residential districts that lay north and west of the solid brick warehouses along Dewdney Avenue, they were the most visible element in the urban landscape. J. S. Woodsworth was moved to comment in 1913 that "the long rows of close-set houses on narrow lots makes [sic] many of the streets appear characterless and unhomelike." Even among those with modest incomes, the detached single-family dwelling was by far the most strongly preferred form of housing. Terrace or row housing was rare. As for apartments, which first began to appear in Regina in 1907, they were concentrated for the most part along Fourteenth Avenue south of Victoria Park and catered to the more affluent.[44]

Finding decent and affordable housing was a problem for many Reginans. The opening of new subdivisions after 1906 flooded the real-estate market with inexpensive land, on the periphery of the city at any rate, but the demand for housing continued to outstrip the supply. The result was overcrowding and soaring rents. A survey in 1910 showed that rents in Regina were higher than in any other prairie city save Saskatoon. By 1912 even the Board of Trade was lamenting that the city had "lost a number of first class mechanics owing to their inability to obtain housing accommodation."[45]

The devastation wrought by the tornado which swept across Regina on June 30, 1912, sparked interest (albeit only briefly) in the possibility of the city itself providing inexpensive working-class housing. As it turned out, it did construct seventeen "cyclone houses" and five "cyclone cottages" on the North Side,

but only to provide accommodation for those who had lost their homes. Relieving the city's chronic housing shortage remained the exclusive preserve of private real-estate interests.

The tornado's impact proved to be dramatic but short-lived. It caused $1,200,000 worth of property damage, claimed 28 lives and rendered 2,500 Reginans at least temporarily homeless. Sweeping across the city from south to north, the storm struck one of the city's most prestigious residential districts, and along Lorne and Smith streets south of Victoria Park the devastation was nearly complete. Many of the churches and public buildings ringing the park were also damaged, as were the CPR freight yards, some warehouses and a larger number of homes in the working-class districts north of the tracks. The property damage, while undeniably severe, was at first greatly exaggerated. In fact, most of the city was left untouched, and even Regina's newspapers soon came to see that it had not sustained a mortal blow. "The new Regina," one declared, "will rise Phoenix-like from its ruins." The CPR freight yards and sheds, repaired by a work force of five hundred men, managed to do so in four days. The rebuilding of homes, churches and businesses was not accomplished so quickly, although the provincial government provided a $500,000 loan to facilitate the task. Reconstruction in the wake of the tornado was a significant contributor to the city's record building boom in 1912, and within a year little evidence of the havoc remained.[46]

For a few Reginans, it was not enough that their city was being rebuilt. They believed that it also had to be made more attractive. Members of the Horticultural Society were among the first to express the belief that "a well planned city with beautiful boulevards and parks … is one of the best advertisements that a city can have." Malcolm Ross, the superintendent of city parks, had similar ideas. In 1912 he proposed that an elongated park and scenic drive be laid out following the course of Wascana Creek through the city to capitalize on the one natural beauty spot Regina possessed.[47]

The businessmen who dominated city council showed far less interest in town planning and civic beautification. Having acquiesced in the GTP's decision to locate its passenger station and connecting spur line in a residential area in 1910, their priorities were revealed again two years later when council agreed to lease a portion of Wascana Park and provide tax and other concessions for the construction of a lavish GTP hotel. Two Regina newspapers and some leading citizens condemned council's action, to be sure, but their objections centred around council's refusal to submit the agreement to the ratepayers for ratification. Three aldermen, Cornelius Rink, J. E. Doerr and Andrew Krauss, also opposed it, but again on the grounds that it ought to have been put to a vote.[48] Only a few agreed with N. F. Black, a prominent Regina educator, that the alienation of any park property was a "civic blunder," and construction of the Chateau Qu'Appelle began with great fanfare in October 1912. Doerr carried his opposition to the GTP agreement into the 1912 mayoralty contest. He gained the endorsation of the *Daily Standard* and the *Daily Province*, but not the voters; Doerr was soundly defeated by Robert Martin, one of the aldermen who had supported construction of the hotel in Wascana Park from the outset.[49]

For those who wished to make Regina a "City Beautiful" the fate of Wascana Park actually served as a stimulus to greater activity. The result was the founding of the Regina City Planning Association in March 1913. Its constitution was modelled on that of the British City Planning Association, and its stated objectives included the "promotion of city planning and garden suburbs … housing and [the] improvement of sanitation."[50]

Even the city had a change of heart. In 1913 Thomas Mawson, a noted British town-planning expert whom the province had engaged to prepare a more detailed landscaping scheme for the Legislative Building grounds, offered to draw up a comprehensive plan for the entire city. Council proved receptive, believing it desirable to harmonize the efforts of the two levels of government in the work of civic beautification. Mawson's proposals for landscaping the area adjacent to Wascana Lake were apparently completed by the end of summer, though few of his recommendations had been implemented by the time war broke out a year later. Some, such as the construction of a new residence for the lieutenant-governor on Broad Street overlooking the lake, never would be realized.[51] As for Mawson's detailed plan for Regina, it was virtually finished by 1914, but

the city procrastinated nearly a decade before finally accepting it.

THE URBAN COMMUNITY: SOCIAL AND POLITICAL LIFE

Businessmen continued to be the most powerful force in civic politics. They held roughly three-quarters of the aldermanic positions during these years and monopolized the city's highest elected office. Three of the four men who served as mayor between 1906 and 1913 — J. W. Smith, R. H. Williams and Robert Martin — were retail merchants whose business careers extended back to the town's earliest days. The fourth, Peter McAra, had made his money in fire insurance and real estate.[52]

The priorities of this dominant business group were reflected in the city charter which J. F. Bole, himself a long-time Regina merchant, shepherded through the legislature in 1906. Modelled on an Edmonton charter approved two years earlier, it permitted the appointment of city commissioners with broad administrative powers and sought, however imperfectly, to implement the single-tax theories of Henry George. The essence of George's single-tax philosophy was a belief that a community or a nation should raise its entire revenue from land taxes, but the objectives he sought — an end to land speculation and ultimately to private land ownership — held no appeal for Regina's business community. They wanted to shift the burden of taxation predominantly to the land for more pragmatic reasons. The 1906 charter also permitted the division of Regina into wards (something Edmonton's did not) and stipulated that property owners would be able to vote in every ward in which they met the property qualification.[53]

This charter was in some ways a curious document. Designed by and for businessmen, it satisfied their desire for efficiency and embodied some of the innovations in civic government then spreading across North America. Yet, that said, the extent of the business community's commitment to municipal reform is open to question. The appointment of city commissioners, an innovation widely thought to make municipal government more efficient, did not come until 1910.[54]

Teacher training began in Regina in 1893. This is the Regina Normal School graduating class of 1909.

Attentive pupils at Strathcona School. By 1913 public and separate elementary school enrolment stood at 3,648.

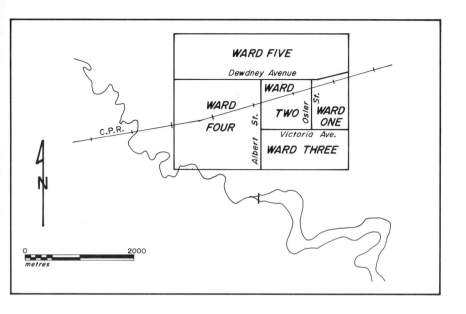

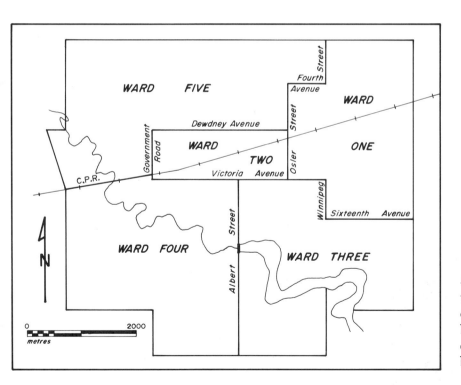

5 Regina Wards, 1906-1910 (top) and 1911-1913 (bottom): Regina adopted the ward system in 1906 and abandoned it prior to the 1914 municipal election. The ward boundaries reflected the city's existing class and ethnic divisions, and contributed to a broadening of council membership.

The city did move more quickly to adopt the single tax, since it was believed that such a step would encourage development. Its charter stipulated that land was to be assessed at its actual value, but buildings and improvements at 60 per cent. Subsequent provincial legislation permitted cities to increase the exemption by stages. By 1913 Regina was taxing buildings and improvements at only 30 per cent of their actual value. The policy proved to be almost universally popular, but its apparent success was due to the exceptional conditions of the time. A tax imposed largely on the value of land could produce adequate revenues because land values were increasing so rapidly. The assessed value of land in Regina soared from $5,377,475 in 1906 to $82,537,840 in 1913. Furthermore, the provincial government did not yet impose any property taxes in urban areas.[55] Only after 1913, when land values began to plummet and the province began to invade the property tax field, would the full implications of Regina's adoption of the single tax become apparent.

The introduction of the ward system is also curious. Among municipal reformers in Canada, the ward system was falling into disrepute, but in Regina there was considerable support for it. This was particularly true of residents of the North Side, who felt that their interests were being ignored. Their grievances found an outlet in the 1905 civic election. Several aldermanic candidates declared themselves in favour of dividing Regina into wards "so that every portion of the city would be equally represented on the Council." One was elected, and in 1906 Regina was divided into five wards, with each electing two aldermen.[56]

The ward boundaries (see Map 5) reflected the existing class and ethnic divisions in Regina, and the adoption of the ward system contributed to a broadening of council membership. In 1906 L. L. Kramer became the first Reginan of German origin to be elected to city council. He built up a strong following in Ward One, winning again in 1908 and 1910 (the second time by acclamation). The interests of the North Side were also more effectively represented. Prior to the division of the city into wards, no one residing north of the CPR tracks had ever sat on council; between 1906 and 1913 all of the aldermen but one

elected in Ward Five lived in the ward. The aldermen representing these two wards were expected to ensure that each received its share of civic improvements. Formal ratepayers' associations, the first of which was organized in Ward Five early in 1913, proved to be no less vigilant.[57]

A few of the aldermen elected in the city's two labouring-class wards also began to challenge business hegemony in civic government. The most articulate and colourful was Cornelius Rink. Born in Holland in 1871, he had emigrated first to South Africa, where he fought against the British in 1899, and then to the United States. He moved to Regina in 1907 and became interested in real estate. Rink's first foray into municipal politics was unsuccessful; he finished third in a tight aldermanic race in Ward One in 1909. He was elected to council in a by-election in the ward eighteen months later and was returned in 1911 and again in 1913. Rink proved to be a skillful ward politician, boasting in 1913 that during these years the value of civic improvements east of Osler Street had risen from $50,000 to $600,000. His energy won him the official endorsation of the Ward One Ratepayers' Association in 1913, and he polled the largest majority of any alderman that year.[58]

Rink also saw himself as the representative of ordinary citizens in every ward whose interests were being ignored by the "Big Guns" who controlled the local government. In 1912, for example, he opposed the Board of Trade's request for $25,000 for promotional advertising; he was joined by one of the North Side aldermen who declared: "We have streets and blocks crying for water and sewer connection which they will not get this year, for the want of money. Let us take care of the people whom we already have in the city, instead of striving so hard for more." A majority of the aldermen eventually agreed to provide the funds, but not before Rink demanded that the six Board of Trade members on council abstain from voting.[59]

Rink found other opportunities to challenge the business elite and their booster ethic. As already indicated, he was one of three aldermen to oppose the leasing of a portion of Wascana Park to the GTP, arguing that the agreement ought to be put to a vote of the ratepayers. The fiery alderman from Ward One took the same stand when the Wascana Country Club ap-

The Wascana Country Club was incorporated in 1912, and built this club house on the bald prairie. It laid out a fine golf course along Wascana Creek and a polo field (though the latter did not survive beyond the First World War).

proached the city in 1912 with a proposal to pay for the construction of a streetcar line from Twenty-fifth Avenue to its new facility southeast of Regina. The club even offered to cover any deficits the line incurred during its first two seasons of operation, and Rink again found himself in the minority. Council approved the agreement without submitting it to the ratepayers.[60]

The future of the ward system was cast into doubt in 1913, when the farmer-dominated legislature gave Saskatchewan cities the option of prohibiting ratepayers from voting in more than one ward. Reginans endorsed the "one man one vote" principle by a margin of 1,355 to 930 in December 1913, and in the process took the first step towards diminishing the voting power of those with large property holdings. It also raised the spectre of sectionalism reigning supreme on council at a time when the growing crisis in municipal finance dictated that the "best men" be placed at the helm. Such arguments convinced a majority in Wards Two, Three and Four to vote the ward system out in August 1914.[61]

Hand in hand with Regina's substantial physical and population growth came a dramatic expansion of municipal services. These years saw the construction of an extensive sewer and water system and a modern sewage disposal works, and the paving of Regina's main thoroughfares. Work commenced on a new city hall in 1906, but its construction was marred by controversy over its cost and design. Originally projected to cost $108,000, it was completed in 1908 for $160,000 and, for a time, it housed the public library until a new building was erected with funds provided by the Carnegie Foundation. During these years as well, the police force grew and so did the fire department. The city built a new central fire hall and three stations in outlying areas, abandoned the practice of relying on a volunteer force in favour of a paid one, and acquired its first piece of motorized firefighting equipment in 1912.[62]

As noted in chapter one, the provision of an adequate water supply was the city's greatest accomplishment, particularly in view of its unpropitious location. Lacking any large body of water nearby to draw upon, it had constructed a gathering system and pipeline to bring water from underground springs at

Boggy Creek, north of Regina. Water consumption increased so rapidly after 1906 that the city soon began to tax the capacity of the existing pipeline to the limit. The substitution of larger pipe and the addition of a pumping station overcame the immediate difficulty, but the city also took steps to augment the supply of water. It obtained the services of a consulting engineer, R. O. Wynne-Roberts, to locate additional underground springs at Boggy Creek and elsewhere, and he identified several promising sources. The city decided to concentrate first upon expanding the capacity of the Boggy Creek springs. So successful was its well-drilling program that by 1912, when Regina's daily average consumption of water had reached 2 million gallons, the Boggy Creek springs were capable of supplying 3 million gallons per day and 4.5 million gallons if further wells were sunk.[63]

There were other notable advances. In 1907 the city took over the privately funded Victoria Hospital and almost immediately began to build a new and modern facility, the Regina General Hospital. The Roman Catholic Sisters of Charity, or Grey Nuns, also opened a modest hospital in 1907, the forerunner of the much larger one erected on Dewdney Avenue in 1912. That year also saw the appointment of the city's first full-time medical health officer. These collective efforts began to make Regina a healthier city, and so did the extension of the sewer system. The number of reported typhoid cases, for example, fell from 71 per 1,000 of population in 1906 to 3 per 1,000 in 1911.[64]

Municipal ownership was very much in vogue in Canada during these years, and Regina proved to be no exception. The city had been generating its own electricity since 1904, and in 1911 it became the first in the province to operate its own streetcars. Yet the Regina Municipal Railway was not established without a struggle. Local businessmen regarded municipal ownership of a street railway as preferable, but they were prepared to offer a franchise to private interests if this would ensure that Regina led the way in acquiring this symbol of metropolitan status. Since an ambitious program of public works was already straining the city's borrowing capacity to the limit, the choice seemed to be a private franchise or no street railway. The city reached an agreement in principle with a

Scottish-trained Frank L. Laubach arrived in Regina in 1904 and left his mark on its musical life. He founded the Regina Orchestral Society, forerunner of the Regina Symphony Orchestra.

The Regina Operatic Society, established in 1909, presented such popular operettas of the day as The Toreador.

group of Winnipeg promoters early in 1910, but criticism of the twenty-year franchise appeared almost at once. Trade unionists joined with clergymen and prominent Reginans such as W. D. Cowan in opposing its terms.

J. R. Peverett, the lone alderman who had voted against the franchise, suggested an alternative: use the accumulated revenue from the sale of city-owned property to finance construction. This gave the proponents of municipal ownership an effective argument, and they employed it with good effect. Regina ratepayers rejected the proposed franchise by a margin of more than two to one early in May 1910. In a second vote less than a week later they declared themselves in favour of municipal ownership. A shortfall in the property sales account discovered soon afterward proved to be only the first of several difficulties encountered in financing construction of the Regina Municipal Railway. Too rapid expansion followed, and by 1913 the street railway accounted for nearly 20 per cent of the city's total outstanding debt of $7,553,607, more indeed that the waterworks and electric light plant combined.[65]

For all of its miles of streetcar tracks and paved streets, and millions of dollars of bonded indebtedness, Regina was still a child of the province. Indeed, these years marked the beginning of a steady and continuous erosion of what little local autonomy Saskatchewan cities did enjoy. Individual city charters gave way in 1908 to the first of the general acts that have since governed all urban centres in the province. The province also created a Department of Municipal Affairs in 1908, and from that date on exercised more and more control over the activities of towns and cities. The limiting and then the outright prohibition of bonusing were early examples of this trend. Another was the creation of the Local Government Board in 1913, which gave the province wide powers to control municipal capital expenditures. Regina, proud of its strong financial position and suspicious of outside interference, sought to gain an exemption. Its efforts were in vain, and the legislation as finally passed treated the largest city in the province no differently from the smallest town or village. In future all would be required to secure the prior approval of the Local Government Board before borrowing money to finance capital works.[66]

Economically and politically, cereal agriculture and the grain grower reigned supreme in Saskatchewan. No one city rose to dominate the province, as Winnipeg had in Manitoba; indeed, Saskatchewan's few cities were themselves tributary to Winnipeg, and rural and urban society were to a large extent mutually sustaining. Regina's shops and wholesale firms served both communities, and Reginans were ever conscious of the fact that their prosperity depended upon wheat. Thus, the Regina Board of Trade endorsed the grain growers' demand for federal ownership and operation of all terminal elevators in 1908 and was equally supportive of the proposed reciprocity agreement with the United States three years later. The belief that what was good for the farmers was good for Regina was reinforced in the federal political sphere by the predominance of rural voters in the new Regina riding created in 1908. Rural voters outnumbered urban voters by more than three to one, and they sent a Liberal, W. M. Martin (who had come to Regina to practise law in 1903), to the House of Commons in 1908 and 1911.[67]

The interests of farmers also predominated in provincial politics. No party could hope to secure power at Regina or long remain in office without the support of rural voters; hence, it was their needs and wishes that were given the greatest prominence in the legislature and on the hustings at election time. The political power of Saskatchewan's cities was further diminished by an allocation of seats that favoured rural voters. Although the size of the legislature was increased from twenty-five to forty-one in 1908, each of the three largest cities continued to be represented by a single member. When the legislature was enlarged again in 1912, to fifty-four, there was a half-hearted attempt to obtain a second seat for Regina, but to no avail.[68] The Liberals' unwillingness to give Regina more equitable representation did not become a political liability. There were too many advantages to be gained by supporting the party that had done so much for the provincial capital and seemed most likely, given its strong rural base, to continue to form the government.

Even the outcome of the contest for the University of Saskatchewan caused the Liberals no permanent harm in Regina. The act creating the university authorized its Board of Governors,

A baseball game at Dominion Park. Baseball drew the largest crowds of any sport in pre-war Regina.

a non-partisan body, to choose the site, and rival communities pressed their claims with great zeal. In the end the choice lay between Saskatoon and Regina, each of which was prepared to offer a large tract of land. President Walter Murray personally favoured Regina, believing that the university ought to be located in the capital city. A majority of the board felt otherwise, however, and in April 1909 Saskatoon was selected. So disappointed was Murray that he initially considered resigning, though in the end he accepted the decision with good grace. In Regina, even among Liberals, there was disappointment for a time, but the party's hold on Regina was not seriously shaken. The seat which J. F. Bole had won by the narrowest of margins in 1905 remained safely in Liberal hands throughout this period.[69]

Regina's desire for an institution of higher learning remained strong. In 1910 a group of prominent local Methodists persuaded the Saskatchewan Conference to found Regina College and support it financially. Their ambitious plans for the new institution included a collegiate course and the first two years of university work, as well as "an academy of music." Frank Darke and five other Regina men pledged $85,000 and raised a further $40,000, and the city donated a block of land, which was subsequently sold to raise additional capital. The construction of the college's impressive main building on a tract of land purchased from the provincial government south of Sixteenth Avenue began in 1911, and the college opened the following year. A large donation from the Masseys, prominent Toronto Methodists and farm-implement manufacturers, permitted work to begin on a women's residence in 1914, but the outbreak of the war delayed its completion until 1916. At the outset Regina College was little more than a residential high school, drawing students from rural districts that did not yet have adequate secondary schools. A music program was introduced in 1911, and the Conservatory of Music was organized the following year. University work, another of the objectives of the college's founders, would not begin for another decade or more. Meanwhile, the Church of England was active, founding a theological college — St. Chad's Hostel — in 1907.[70]

Far more impressive was the expansion of Regina's educational facilities to meet the needs of its youngest residents. The

An impromptu hockey game on Wascana Lake, 1912.

R.H. Williams department store dance at City Hall, 1912.

number of public school pupils increased fourfold between 1906 and 1913, from 734 to 3,064, and seven new schools were built to accommodate them. A full-time superintendent of schools was hired in 1906, and the teaching staff grew to more than 100. School nurses were added as well, providing all children with routine medical examinations twice a year. The children of the "New Canadians" posed a special challenge. Since many of the older girls were often obliged to stay at home to take care of younger children, Earl Grey and Wetmore Schools inaugurated a "little mothers" program to provide them with practical instruction. At the same time, a growing demand for secondary schooling prompted the construction of the Regina Collegiate Institute in 1909. Regina's separate school system experienced a similar enrollment surge; a total of 574 pupils attended its two schools by 1913. A private Roman Catholic girls' school, Sacred Heart Academy, was founded in 1910.[71]

This was a period of growth and maturation in the city's social and cultural life as well. Clubs and societies proliferated, mirroring the ethnic, religious and class divisions of the population as a whole. Thus, prewar Regina could boast thriving local branches of such national bodies as the Sons of England and the Sons of Scotland, the Catholic Mutual Benefit Association and the Epworth League, to cite only a few examples. Others were indigenous to the city. The Assiniboia Club, which moved into more spacious quarters in 1912, was the chief bastion of the well-to-do. The Wascana Country Club, incorporated the same year, aspired to achieve the same air of exclusivity. It laid out a golf course and polo field (the latter did not survive beyond the First World War) and built a club house on the bald prairie south of Wascana Creek. Functions at Government House and the ceremonies associated with the annual opening of the legislature continued to loom large in the social life of Regina's elite, who also contributed their time to a variety of worthy causes. It was Regina's leading business and professional men (and their wives) who built the handsome new churches ringing Victoria Park, directed a wide range of voluntary philanthropic activities and fostered the development of musical and other forms of artistic expression in the city.

The undisputed leader of Regina's musical life during these years was Frank L. Laubach. In addition to establishing the Regina Philharmonic Society, he founded the Regina Orchestral Society, forerunner of the Regina Symphony Orchestra, in 1908 and played a leading role in establishing the annual Saskatchewan Music Festival. The latter was only the second of its kind to appear in Canada and attracted some two hundred competitors in 1909. The opening of the 1,000-seat Regina Theatre a year later made it possible for Laubach and other gifted Reginans to display their talents to better advantage. The Regina Philharmonic Society performed there, and so did the Operatic Society, presenting such popular operettas of the day as *The Mocking Bird*, *The Country Girl* and *The Toreador*. Regina also began to attract American and British professional touring companies in large numbers for the first time. (More often than not it was Winnipeg impresario C. P. Walker who arranged the bookings.) For those who preferred simpler diversions there was vaudeville, the staple fare at the Regina Theatre and its rival, the Majestic. Touring vaudeville acts and local performers provided Reginans with live entertainment six nights a week during these prewar years. Barney Groves, who managed the Regina Theatre, is also credited with introducing moving pictures to the city. His Bijou Family Theatre opened in 1908, in what had formerly been the town hall. It lasted only a year, but others soon appeared: the Unique, the Roseland, the Rex (eighth in the Allen Theatres chain, it opened in 1912), the Elite, the Princess, the Lux and the Gaiety.[72]

While class differences were evident in many social activities, recreational pursuits, particularly those that took place out-of-doors, were open to most Reginans. By 1909 there were nearly forty distinct sports organizations in the city. Prominent local businessmen gave strong financial backing to the professional baseball and lacrosse teams, and fans packed CPR Park and later Dominion Park on the North Side to watch them play. The former, located north of the CPR main line and west of Hamilton Street, had been laid out in the late 1890s. When the railway extended its freight sheds in 1909, CPR Park was lost to local sports clubs. Dominion Park was farther north, in the warehouse district. The city constructed a 600-seat grandstand and other facilities there that same year.

Provincial government employees founded the Saskatchewan Civil Service Association in 1913. Its objective was "the promotion of social intercourse and sports among the civil servants in the Parliament Buildings."

Baseball drew the largest crowds of any sport, amateur or professional, but it was in lacrosse that Regina teams enjoyed the greatest success, winning the western Canadian championship three times with imported stars from eastern Canada such as "Newsy" Lalonde. Curling and hockey also continued to enjoy a wide following, and a sailing (and later rowing and swimming) club, the Regina Boat Club, was founded in 1909. Rugby football became a popular spectator sport, too. The Regina Rugby Club, established in 1910, was comprised largely of local men, but it also recruited players from south of the border. Fred Ritter, who was both the team's quarterback and coach for a time, was the most colourful of these early "imports." Ritter claimed to be a graduate of Princeton, a "two-time All-American" no less; in fact he had dropped out in his freshman year to pursue a career in the lumber business.[73]

Recreation also took other forms. Large firms, such as R. H. Williams's Glasgow House, held summer picnics for their staff. Sometimes the employees themselves took the initiative. Such was the case with the Saskatchewan Civil Service Association. It was founded by a handful of provincial government employees in 1913, its objective being "the promotion of social intercourse and sports among the civil servants in the Parliament Buildings."[74] Nearby Last Mountain and Qu'Appelle lakes became popular summer resorts. Regina Beach and Katepwa Beach could be easily reached by train, and in 1910 a group of intrepid Reginans travelled overland to Regina Beach by automobile. Wascana Lake was more popular with those of limited means, particularly once the street railway began Sunday service in 1913. Still others were attracted to the city's numerous bars, poolrooms and dance halls. There were fifteen hotels in Regina by the eve of the First World War. In one, the King's Hotel, there was no bar (the owners having decided to operate it as a "temperance" hotel in 1910), but the others were as wide open as any on the prairies. Dance halls, in the East End particularly, also acquired a certain notoriety. J. S. Woodsworth was moved to comment in 1913:

> Beer is frequently sold or dispensed ... The young men who patronize these halls are chiefly laborers or mechanics; the girls, employees in restaurants, hotels, laundries and factories. Not in-
> frequently there is drinking and fighting so that it becomes necessary to station policemen to prevent disturbances.

Nevertheless such establishments did fill a real social need. One young man told Woodsworth:

> I like this better than to lie on my dirty bed all the time. The room where I am staying drives me mad; I am not satisfied with these people with whom I live, and my job is hard in the daytime, so I am very willing to spend my 50 cents twice a week because I have here an hour of life.[75]

Regina's transformation into an increasingly complex urban community in time compelled a reconsideration of existing attitudes towards the poor and the unemployed. Private charitable organizations such as the Salvation Army, the YMCA and the YWCA had traditionally ministered to those in need. The formation of a local Children's Aid Society in 1910 was another illustration of this reliance on a piecemeal voluntary approach.[76] In times of severe unemployment, such as that experienced in 1907-8, the city itself had to step in. It organized some temporary work to tide the men over, but gave relief only grudgingly. The much deeper recession of 1913 made caring for the unemployed a far more serious problem. Private charitable organizations again took the lead in providing assistance, but it was soon recognized that a greater coordination of effort would be required. The result was the formation of the Regina Bureau of Public Welfare under the leadership of a local police magistrate, William Trant. With a grant provided by the city, the bureau was able to hire experienced social workers and operate a labour exchange and a hostel for transients.[77]

Confident and not a little brash, Regina had come of age by 1913. If it was not quite the "Metropolis in the Making" that the Greater Regina Club claimed it to be, it was undisputably again the largest city in Saskatchewan. Yet massive economic and population growth had brought new burdens and new responsibilities whose implications for the city were still only dimly perceived, if at all, as the heady boom that had propelled Regina to the front rank began to wind down. Difficult times lay ahead for the city and its citizens.

Army camp at the Exhibition Grounds, 1918.

Chapter Three
Depression and Readjustment, 1914-39

The year 1914 demonstrated just how susceptible Regina was to the vagaries of the wheat economy. There was drought across much of southern Saskatchewan, and prospects of a good harvest quickly dimmed. Unemployment, already serious on account of the collapse of the investment boom in 1913, grew worse. In June 1914 several hundred unemployed men gathered at city hall to demand work, but there was little the city could do. Its own financial situation looked increasingly bleak. Unable to dispose of its debentures in an unreceptive market, Regina was about to embark upon a policy of retrenchment, slashing its program of sewer and water main extensions and deferring construction of a North Side fire hall. The outbreak of war in August caused more uncertainty and a further pruning of civic expenditures. In short order the city decided not to build a new police station for which debentures had been approved and to complete only the most essential public works projects. In the private sector there was an equally sharp decline in construction activity. The value of building permits in 1914 was less than half of what it had been the previous year (Appendix, Table XI). Some Reginans escaped the ranks of the unemployed by enlisting, but by the end of the year it was estimated that at least 1,400 persons were out of work in the city.[1]

All of this was a portent of the future. The weather and the price of wheat had long determined Regina's economic fortunes, but this was to be particularly true during the quarter century following the outbreak of the First World War. Through the war years and the two decades that came after, the city alternated between periods of "hard times" of increasing severity and periods of modest prosperity that never quite managed to approximate the heady boom years at the beginning of the century. There were as a consequence new challenges and new priorities for the city and for those who governed it. Unemploy-

ment, or the threat of unemployment, haunted the lives of more and more Reginans and compelled the city to expand its concern for those who found themselves in difficult circumstances. A more humane approach towards the unemployed evolved in time, in part because local government in Regina became more broadly representative of those areas of the city inhabited by working-class families and lower-status ethnic groups. The climax came in the 1930s when Regina's disadvantaged were able to mobilize their votes behind a labour party loosely allied with the Co-operative Commonwealth Federation (CCF) and seize control of the mayoralty and council.

The years 1914-39 were a period of readjustment for Regina in other ways. No swelling tide of immigration doubled and redoubled the city's population; indeed, for part of this period it actually declined. But there were new challenges here, too. The absorption of a cosmopolitan population, a task only barely begun, took on a new urgency when Canada was plunged into war and ethnic differences became more sharply drawn. At the same time, Regina, like the nation as a whole, adopted a more North American outlook; this was reflected in the evolving patterns of recreation and social and cultural life in the city.

ECONOMIC GROWTH AND METROPOLITAN DEVELOPMENT

In 1915 Saskatchewan's economic prospects improved dramatically. The rains returned, and farmers harvested the largest wheat crop in the history of the province to that time (Appendix, Table XIII). The demand for foodstuffs in Great Britain and other allied nations drove prices up. For the duration of the war and beyond, this brought general prosperity to an overwhelmingly agricultural province. The bumper crop of 1915 revived

1938 Chevrolets roll off the assembly line at the General Motors plant on Winnipeg Street. A year later automobile production would be suspended. It would never resume.

the service and especially the merchandizing sectors. Regina began to feel the effects of more money in farmers' pockets. In addition, Regina's position as an important wholesale and distribution point was strengthened. Both the Robert Simpson Company and the T. Eaton Company established large mail-order facilities in the city during the war. Still, the level of business activity did not match that of the earlier boom, and not all local retailers did as well as the R. H. Williams firm (it was able to double its capital stock to one million dollars in 1919).[2]

The automobile, no longer a curiosity even by 1914, also broadened the base of Regina's economy and enhanced its role as a distribution centre. Motor vehicle registrations in Saskatchewan stood at 4,659 on the eve of the war. In Regina alone there were twelve automobile dealers whose sales in 1913 amounted to $1.5 million. It was after 1914, however, that the most dramatic increase in automobile ownership occurred, in large part because the war-induced prosperity enabled more and more farmers to buy one. Motor vehicle registrations reached 55,010 by 1918, and Saskatchewan ranked second only to Ontario in automobile ownership. By this time most automobile firms doing business in Saskatchewan had made Regina their central distribution centre for the entire province, or at least for its southern half. Their capital investment in the city was estimated in 1918 to be nearly half a million dollars, and their annual contribution to the local economy in salaries and wages only slightly less.[3]

Wheat prices remained high until 1920 and then collapsed. Farmers were unable to satisfy their obligations to implement companies, lumberyards and country merchants. Some abandoned their farms or lost them through foreclosure. There was in fact an actual decrease in the number of farms in Saskatchewan between 1921 and 1926. Saskatchewan was still dangerously dependent on a single staple crop, and the whole province was bound to suffer until conditions improved for the people on the land.

The remedy came from the farmers themselves. In 1923 they began organizing a voluntary pool to handle western grain. Aaron Sapiro, an American lawyer who had set up produce pools in the Midwest and California, was brought to Sas-katchewan to popularize the pooling concept. His speeches in Saskatoon, Regina and Moose Jaw spurred farmers to a frenzy of activity without parallel in the history of the province. By the summer of 1924 more than half of the crop acreage in Saskatchewan was committed to the five-year delivery contracts, and the Saskatchewan Co-operative Wheat Producers Limited was formally organized. Its head office, like that of the older Saskatchewan Co-operative Elevator Company whose facilities the Wheat Pool acquired in 1926, has from the outset been located in Regina.[4]

The organization of the Wheat Pool coincided with the revival of the Saskatchewan economy. There was a marked improvement in prices in 1925, and crops were good. The best year proved to be 1928, when Saskatchewan farmers harvested 321.2 million bushels of wheat, a record which would not be surpassed until 1951. The return of prosperity and a renewed influx of immigrant farmers also stimulated railway construction in the province. It had slowed almost to a standstill after 1914, but in the late 1920s the CPR and the newly formed Canadian National Railways built additional lines to serve new settlements, particularly in central and northern Saskatchewan. By 1928 branch-line construction had returned to a level almost equal to that of prewar years.

There was a sharp rise in the trade volume of Regina businesses, too, particularly those that served the agricultural community. In 1926 the T. Eaton Company transformed part of its mail-order warehouse north of the CPR tracks into a retail store and hired one hundred additional employees. Another major retailer, the Hudson's Bay Company, purchased a site on Twelfth Avenue for a large department store and in 1929 announced plans to begin construction within a year.[5]

Saskatchewan farmers' widespread adoption of power-driven equipment also contributed to Regina's prosperity. During the 1920s improvements in gasoline tractors and the introduction of the combine-harvester and the truck began to transform wheat growing on the prairies. The number of tractors in use on Saskatchewan farms increased from 19,243 at the beginning of the decade to 26,674 in 1926 and 43,308 in 1931. The number of cars and trucks rose from 36,098 to 76,032 during the same decade. Combines were virtually unknown in the province in 1921; by 1931 there were 6,019 on the province's 136,472 farms. Regina dealers sold $35 million worth of farm equipment in 1928 alone, and the city surpassed Winnipeg as the nation's largest distribution centre for agricultural implements.[6]

Yet, while Regina's retail and wholesale trade prospered during the late 1920s, the pace of economic activity failed to match that recorded during the prewar boom years. There were at least two reasons for this. First, agricultural growth was slowing down. Wheat acreage had increased substantially under the stimulus of wartime demand but then levelled off after 1921 (Appendix, Table XIII). Most of the good land in the province had in fact been taken up. Population density did increase somewhat in the better-settled regions of Saskatchewan during the decade, and the introduction of new and more rapidly maturing strains of wheat encouraged further expansion of agriculture north of the North Saskatchewan River. But at the same time farms were being abandoned in the drought-ravaged southwest, and it was not until late in the 1920s that settlers began to return.

Second, agriculture was not as prosperous as might have appeared at first glance. This, too, had an impact on the level of business activity in Regina. Although farms were becoming larger (the average was 354 acres in 1916 and 390 in 1926) and farmers were investing large sums in agricultural machinery (a total of $186 million by 1931 according to one later estimate), the price of wheat slowly but steadily declined after 1925 and the costs of operating a farm continued to increase. Even though yields were relatively good during these years, farmers' purchasing power was shrinking.[7]

In 1929 the cycle of boom and bust turned again, as first grain prices and then the entire economy collapsed. Saskatchewan suffered a double blow. Wheat that had been selling for more than two dollars per bushel during the late 1920s fetched a mere thirty-eight cents by 1932. Accompanying this drop in farm prices were other disasters not directly related to the Depression — drought, infestations of grasshoppers and rust. Conditions changed from year to year and from region to region. In much of central and northern Saskatchewan rainfall was close to normal, and at least hay could be grown for livestock and garden vegetables to feed farm families. In southern Saskatchewan, on the other hand, scorching summer temperatures brought as many as nine successive years of crop failure. Wheat fields that had once been fertile and productive took on the appearance of a desert as the earth was pulverized into dust and blown into rolling dunes by the wind.

The twin climatic and economic disasters of the 1930s touched all residents of the province and all sectors of the economy. In 1928 net cash income per farm had been higher in Saskatchewan than in any other province. By 1933 Saskatchewan farmers were the least prosperous of any in Canada, and by 1937 two-thirds of the farm population of the province was destitute. Saskatchewan's largest business enterprise, the Wheat Pool, also found itself in serious difficulty. In anticipation that prices would soon recover, the Pool withheld wheat from the market in 1929 and 1930. It was quickly obliged to seek financial assistance from first the provincial and then the federal government to avert bankruptcy. The Pool survived, but its marketing function was assumed by the federal government, informally in 1931 and formally in 1935, when the Wheat Board was created.

The collapse of the agricultural price structure had other repercussions in cities and towns across Saskatchewan. The value of retail trade in Saskatchewan dropped from $189 million in 1930 to $103 million in 1933, a decline of more than 45 per cent, which was greater than that experienced in any other province. It was most severe for firms selling automobiles, gasoline and accessories. Here the value of sales declined by almost 60 per cent between 1930 and 1933. Lumberyards and other firms supplying building materials, and those selling furniture, household appliances and home furnishings, were not far behind. As the farm economy crumbled, many stores, wholesale firms and other Regina businesses reduced their staffs. Some, like the Regina Trading Company, one of the city's oldest retail establishments, went out of business. An upswing in the value of retail trade became evident in 1934, but it proved to be far less robust in Saskatchewan than in other provinces.[8]

The automobile broadened Regina's economic base. There were seventeen car dealerships in the city by 1929. Gasoline filling stations were even more numerous. Their increasingly standardized design represented a new form of architecture across North America.

Saskatchewan farmers' widespread adoption of trucks, tractors and combine-harvesters during the 1920s also contributed to Regina's prosperity.

The Hudson's Bay Company had second thoughts about opening a department store in Regina. It had acquired a portion of the proposed site from the city, which had insisted as part of the purchase agreement that the building be completed by 1932, the year Regina was planning to host the World Grain Exhibition and Conference. A succession of crop failures cooled the HBC's enthusiasm, and construction of the store had still not begun by 1932. Indeed, the company sought to be relieved of its obligations altogether, and by 1938 an embittered city council was considering legal action. Lengthy negotiations finally produced a compromise in 1939. The city agreed to rescind the decade-old agreement in return for a commitment by the HBC to build a luxury apartment block on a portion of the property. The company also agreed to construct a smaller commercial block "at the earliest possible opportunity" once economic conditions improved.[9] It did eventually build a department store on the site, but not until 1965.

The Depression still hung heavy over Saskatchewan at the end of the 1930s. In other regions of the country the economy had reached its lowest point in 1933, but for Saskatchewan the worst years were 1937 and 1938. Conditions improved somewhat the following year, when the province recorded its largest crop in a decade, but it took another world war to bring real prosperity to Saskatchewan agriculture and hence to Regina.

This cycle of boom and bust was no less apparent in other sectors of Regina's economy. The level of building activity and the proportion of the city's population employed in the construction industry also fluctuated widely after 1914 (Appendix, Tables XI, XII). Both tended generally to rise and fall with the agricultural price cycle, but not always. While a bumper crop brought about a sharp recovery in retail and wholesale trade in 1915, building activity came to a virtual standstill by the middle of the war. The value of building permits did show a modest increase in 1917 and a more substantial one the following year, but in general the First World War was a period of retrenchment for the construction industry. There was a mild boom after the war, but in 1921 only a quarter as many were employed in building construction as had been a decade earlier and another slump began in 1922. At mid-decade there was a dramatic resurgence in construction activity that coincided with the return of agricultural prosperity. New apartments, churches and business blocks appeared, and there was a flurry of house building on lots that had stood empty for ten years or more. In 1929 the city issued $10 million worth of building permits, a record that would not be surpassed until 1952. With the onset of the Depression, construction activity again came almost to a complete standstill. In 1941 fewer Reginans were employed in this industry than ever before or since.

Regina continued after 1914 to be the leading manufacturing city in a province where secondary industry remained of minor economic importance. In 1928, a banner year for the Saskatchewan economy, only 6,173 residents of the province were classified as industrial workers. The total value of manufacturing amounted to $69.1 million, a far cry from the $521 million worth of grain, livestock and other agricultural commodities produced that year.[10] The abolition of bonusing in 1914 made it more difficult for the city to attract new industries, but some inducements were still permissible. Regina continued to offer fixed assessment and utility rates to large firms, subject only to later ratification by the provincial legislature. The city also possessed ample reserves of industrial land, at least until the late 1920s.

Regina did enjoy some success in broadening its economic base. In 1917 Imperial Oil Limited opened a large refinery on the northern outskirts of Regina to serve the growing market for petroleum products in western Manitoba, Saskatchewan and eastern Alberta. Described by one newspaper as "the largest manufacturing works of any kind, not only in Regina, but in the entire province," it was capable of refining 1,500 barrels of crude oil per day. The oil was initially transported by rail from fields in Wyoming, and after 1936 from Turner Valley in Alberta. Capacity was subsequently expanded to 4,000 and then 7,000 barrels per day, and in 1937 the Regina plant began to supply eastern Manitoba customers as well. A second oil refinery appeared in 1935, the culmination of the efforts of Regina, Moose Jaw and Weyburn district farmers to reduce their fuel costs. In the depths of the Depression they managed to raise $32,000 and establish the Consumers' Co-operative Refineries Limited. The

HEAD OFFICE OF SASKATCHEWAN WHEAT POOL, REGINA, SASK.

During 1926 the Saskatchewan Wheat Pool acquired this fine office building, which now houses the combined staffs of the Pool and its subsidiary—Saskatchewan Pool Elevators, Limited—on two floors.

One of the few large firms to locate its head office in Regina was the *Saskatchewan Wheat Pool*. Founded in 1924, it acquired the facilities of the *Saskatchewan Co-operative Elevator Company* two years later to become one of the largest grain-handling concerns in Canada.

first cooperatively owned refinery in the world, its initial capacity was only 500 barrels per day. By 1940 this had been increased to 1,500 barrels.[11]

The other major new manufacturing enterprise established in Regina was a General Motors assembly plant, which opened in 1928. It remains a moot point whether the concessions offered (thirty-eight acres of land, which the city sold for $1,000 per acre, and a ten-year fixed assessment on the land and improvements) or the city's central location in the prairie region was the decisive factor in influencing General Motors to choose Regina. In any case the impact was significant. Not only did the sprawling plant on Winnipeg Street provide jobs for 850 Reginans at peak production, it also helped to alleviate the city's chronic seasonal unemployment problem. General Motors' labour needs were heaviest in the spring, when farm jobs were scarce and the local labour supply plentiful, and lightest during the fall harvest period. The presence of the General Motors plant also attracted associated glass and paint industries to Regina, and was considered to mark the beginning of a new era in the economic life of the city. It was not to be. Automobile sales plummeted after 1929. General Motors began reducing staff, swelling the number of unemployed in Regina to 3,756 by August 1930, when the last men were laid off. The plant opened again briefly for a few months in 1931 and then closed for six years. When production was finally resumed in 1937, there was work for only half of the original labour force. Even this level of employment was maintained only until 1939.[12]

Regina was unable to markedly improve its position as a meat-packing centre during these years. One new firm, P. Burns and Company of Calgary, was attracted to the city in 1918. Burns acquired the Armour plant from its local owners and subsequently expanded it. But the Burns plant, like those in other Saskatchewan cities, was handicapped by the excess capacity that plagued the entire industry in the province during the interwar period. Simply put, there were too many meat-packing houses for the available supply of cattle and hogs and too many of those animals continued to be slaughtered in larger and more efficient plants in Manitoba and Alberta.[13]

In 1939, as in 1914, Regina could scarcely be said to have any commercial or industrial existence independent of agriculture. Nevertheless, Regina's business community continued to believe that a greater economic destiny awaited the city. Their "booster" rhetoric was muted somewhat by economic adversity, to be sure, but they continued to seek out new opportunities. Two of the most successful were William H. Houston and Morley Willoughby. Houston had worked for a time in Winnipeg for the Bell Telephone Company, and then for Manitoba's government telephone system, before establishing his own telephone engineering and construction business in Regina in 1912. Building telephone lines soon lost its appeal, and Houston became general manager and part owner of the Regina Brokerage and Investment Company. Founded by two prominent local businessmen, Charles H. Willoughby and William H. Duncan (who together had parlayed a small lumber supply business into a controlling interest in a much larger enterprise, Beaver Lumber), Regina Brokerage and Investment initially dabbled in real estate and sold fire insurance.

In the early 1920s the Regina firm entered into an agency agreement with Dominion Securities, a national investment house that was anxious to expand into the province. Inspired by this turn of events to strike out on his own, Houston sought and found a partner in Morley Willoughby, who was then managing his father's lumberyard in the city. Together they established Houston Willoughby and Company in 1925 and purchased Regina Brokerage and Investment's fire insurance and stock and bond business. At the time the older firm was the unrivalled leader in the sale of municipal bonds and debentures in Saskatchewan, and this long remained Houston Willoughby's stock in trade. In the following decade, the Depression took its toll on the bond and investment market. There were thirty-two bond dealers and investment companies in Regina in 1930 and only nine in 1937, but Houston Willoughby was one of the survivors. At the end of the decade it was still Saskatchewan's only locally owned and operated investment house.[14]

Other Regina businessmen were determined that the city should capitalize upon the growing tourist trade associated with the spread of the automobile. In the 1920s promotional literature began to emphasize Regina's attractiveness to tourists. The

To cater to the growing tourist trade the CPR built the Hotel Saskatchewan, fourteenth in its nationwide chain, in 1927. Much of the steel used in its construction came from the ill-fated Chateau Qu'Appelle which the Grand Trunk Pacific had begun more than a decade earlier but never finished.

An instructor in the Royal Flying Corps during the First World War, Roland John Groome became Canada's first licenced commercial pilot in 1920. He was killed in an airplane crash near Regina in 1935.

Regina's First Air Harbor. This was the First Government Registered Air Harbor in Canada. It was Operated by the Aerial Service Co Ltd. R. J. Groome, Pilot. Ed. Clarke, Manager. ~ 1920 ~

Regina's first "Air Harbour" was located on what was then open prairie southwest of the Legislative Building (near the corner of Hill Avenue and Cameron Street).

Royal Canadian Mounted Police barracks and the grounds surrounding the Legislative Building were given special prominence, as were the nearby Qu'Appelle Lakes, "one of the most charming holiday spots in the Dominion."[15] Of course, it was early recognized that simply advertising the city's attractions was not enough. Better hotel accommodation and improved roads were also essential.

With respect to the first, the situation remained uncertain as long as the future of the Grand Trunk Pacific's lavish hotel in Wascana Park remained unresolved. Work had been suspended on the Chateau Qu'Appelle at the outset of the war, and it was still unfinished in 1919 when the GTP went bankrupt. As the partially erected steel framework became more and more of an embarrassment, the city pressed first the receiver and then the government-owned Canadian National Railways (which had absorbed the GTP) to complete the hotel. Nine years after construction had halted, Canadian National finally announced its intention to do so, but the federal government refused to include the necessary funds in the railway's 1924 budget. This marked the end of that ill-fated hotel. In time the steel girders were dismantled, and the site was cleared and returned to the city.[16] But all was not lost. While the city had been negotiating with the GTP, it had also begun to make overtures to one of its rivals. Where once Regina aldermen had complained bitterly and often of the CPR's insensitivity to local needs, in 1919 they had urged this "corporation of which all Canada is justly proud" to erect a suitable hotel in the city. It did so in 1927. The opening of the Hotel Saskatchewan, the fourteenth in the company's nationwide chain, gave a boost to the local tourist and convention trade. The CPR included Regina in the series of music and folk arts festivals it inaugurated across Canada that same year. Meant to attract tourists to its hotels, they were the brainchild of John Murray Gibbon, the railway's publicity director. The Great West Canadian Folksong, Folkdance and Handicrafts Festival took place at the Hotel Saskatchewan in 1929 and featured the songs and dances of almost thirty ethnic groups.[17] For its part the city laid out an auto camp near Wascana Lake in 1926. It was "fully equipped with every modern convenience, having ladies' waiting room, shower baths and adequate kitchen facilities."[18]

Obtaining better highway access to the city proved more difficult. Automobile owners were themselves among the first to press for improved roads. An automobile club had been founded in Regina in 1910, the first in the province. Reginans also took a leading role in the formation of a provincial motor league in 1914, which among other things hoped to see an interprovincial highway built from Winnipeg to Calgary. Progress was slow. By 1926 Regina could claim to be "the junction point of three well-travelled motor highways," but those highways were passable only in good weather. Gravelling did not begin until 1929. While Regina and most of the other large centres in Saskatchewan were linked by gravel highways by 1932, the provincial government spent less and less money to maintain them as the Depression deepened and fewer and fewer motorists used them.[19]

The airplane was also revolutionizing transportation and commerce during these years. Regina was determined not to be left behind its prairie rivals, and the airplane became an integral part of the city's transportation network. At first, of course, the airplane had been little more than a novelty, introduced to Reginans by American "barnstormers" who performed at the summer fair. But two local men were quick to see its commercial application. In 1920 Roland J. Groome and Ed Clark, both Royal Flying Corps veterans, established a primitive airfield on the open prairie southwest of the Legislative Building. That field became the nation's first licensed aerodrome, and Groome, Canada's first licensed commercial pilot. Their Aerial Service Company gave flying lessons and carried passengers and freight.[20]

The inadequacy of that first airfield, and of a second and even more primitive facility which the city later established near the Imperial Oil refinery, soon became apparent. Anxious that Regina not be ignored in the laying out of commercial air routes, air enthusiasts and the Board of Trade began to press for a new and larger municipally owned airfield. Success came in 1928, when the city set aside 160 acres of vacant land west of Wascana Creek and began construction of a hangar and other facilities. The wisdom of the city's efforts quickly became apparent. Regina was included in the regular mail and passenger service that Western Canada Airways, a Winnipeg firm, initiated that same year. Other improvements were subsequently added to Regina's municipal airport, notably a new terminal building, and additional land was set aside for future expansion. By 1938, when the first Trans-Canada Airlines flight landed in Regina, the city had achieved a secure place in the new air age.[21]

These were all important initiatives, but they did not change Regina's essential economic character and function. It could still be fairly stated at the end of this period that although the city exercised a measure of commercial domination over southern Saskatchewan, it was still clearly part of Winnipeg's tributary hinterland.[22] Regina had never had much control over its own economic destiny, and what little independence it had enjoyed was slowly beginning to erode. The trend was most evident in the retailing sector. Outside interests acquired local firms; a Winnipeg group purchased the Regina Trading Company in 1928, for instance. Large Canadian and American merchandizing organizations also began to enter the city. F. W. Woolworth Company opened its first store in Regina in 1914 and enlarged it in 1936. Safeway Stores appeared in 1929, S. S. Kresge in 1930 and Metropolitan Stores in 1936. A new form of locally owned retailing enterprise did appear in 1931 — the Sherwood Cooperative Association — but the general trend was towards less and less local control over this important sector of the city's economy. The decision in 1919 to enlarge the scope of the Royal North-West Mounted Police to include all federal police work in Canada also had implications for Regina. Ottawa, being more central, became the headquarters of the RCMP.[23] Yet the loss of the headquarters had more symbolic importance than economic: Regina has remained the home of the Mounted Police training facilities down to the present day.

POPULATION GROWTH AND ETHNIC RELATIONSHIPS

Population growth in Regina during these years mirrored the shifting economic fortunes of the city. Its population almost doubled between 1911 and 1941, but the rate of growth was erratic. Indeed, at the outset of this period Regina was the only city in Saskatchewan to show a decline in population. In 1916 the census counted 4,000 fewer people in Regina than it had in 1911. The loss was probably much greater, since the city's population had not reached its prewar peak until 1912 or 1913. Nevertheless, Regina remained the largest city in the province (and Saskatoon supplanted Moose Jaw as its closest rival). The results of the first postwar census proved far more reassuring to local boosters, and during the 1920s Regina's rate of population growth exceeded that of the province as a whole. The population of the city never fell again during the interwar period, though there was scarcely any increase between 1931 and 1936 (Appendix, Tables III, IV, V).

Relating population change to fluctuations in the economy is not entirely satisfactory. During the Depression an actual decline in Regina's population might have been expected, given the severe impact of the economic downturn and the fact that the population of the province as a whole fell by nearly 26,000 between 1931 and 1941 (Appendix, Table III). Yet Regina's population actually increased by 9 per cent, in part because families from farms and small towns adjacent to Regina moved into the city hoping to obtain the more generous relief payments available there. The population of the census division in which Regina was situated fell by more than 1,000 between 1931 and 1941, and three quarters of the towns and villages experienced population losses. North Regina, the community nearest to the city, saw its population decline from 783 to 582.[24] There was also a considerable expansion of the provincial civil service during the 1930s. It grew from 3,152 in 1929 to 4,194 in 1938.[25] It is difficult to determine with precision how many of these new civil servants lived and worked in Regina, but the expansion of the provincial public service at a time when other large employers in the city were reducing their staffs probably helps to account for the modest population gains Regina experienced during the decade.

Immigration contributed little to Regina's population growth. The First World War brought an abrupt end to the swelling tide of newcomers from overseas. The influx resumed

Ottawa became the headquarters of the Royal Canadian Mounted Police in 1920, but the training depot remained in Regina. It became an increasingly popular tourist attraction, and welcomed royal visitors too. A more imposing tower was added to the front of the chapel shortly after King George VI's 1939 cross-Canada tour.

When the Sons of England Lodge posed for this photograph in 1914 Regina still thought of itself as British, even if it was not. The absorption of a cosmopolitan population took on a new urgency when Canada was plunged into war and ethnic differences became more sharply drawn.

in the mid-1920s but was slight compared to the numbers that had arrived during the prewar boom period. With the onset of the Depression in 1929 immigration again ceased. The decline in the relative importance of immigration as a factor in population growth is revealed most clearly in the size of the city's foreign-born population. Where slightly over half of all Reginans had been so classified in 1911, scarcely more than a quarter were in 1941 (Appendix, Table VII). Because fewer immigrants were coming from Great Britain, those of British racial origin began to lose their domination in Regina. Nearly three-quarters of the city's population was British in 1921, but by 1931 only two-thirds were (and in the province as a whole less than half were). Regina's German population showed the largest percentage increase during the decade 1921-31, while other European groups' share of the total remained stable or increased only slightly (Appendix, Table VIII).

Natural increase played a role of increasing importance, albeit one that is also difficult to measure precisely. The number of women in the city did increase, but Regina's birth rate slowly declined, from 28.2 per thousand in 1921 (the first year for which statistics are available) to 15.6 in 1936. It then began to rise again, to 16.8 by the eve of the Second World War. Furthermore, in every year but one (1930) during this period the city's birth rate lagged behind that of the province.[26] Regina's population remained quite young, certainly in comparison to more recent decades. In 1921 only 1.8 per cent of Reginans were sixty-five or older; two decades later they still comprised only 4.5 per cent of the total (Appendix, Table X). Even at the relatively low birth rates of the 1930s, natural increase ought to have augmented Regina's population to a greater extent than it did. However, not all of the young people born in Regina remained there. Just as there was a shift of population from the small towns and the farms to Regina, so also were Reginans seeking greater economic opportunities outside the province.

Although the immigrant tide receded after 1914, the war years were marked by a sharp increase in ethnic tensions. Regina's sizeable German community bore the brunt of wartime hostility. In August 1914 the Teutonia Society voluntarily suspended its activities, but this did not allay the suspicions of patriotic Reginans. Some firms discharged their German employees. The local carpenters' union also barred Germans from its ranks.[27] Der Courier (as the city's German newspaper was renamed in 1914) immediately became suspect as well. There were frequent complaints that the paper was publishing anti-British editorials, though no charges were laid. Der Courier in fact took pains to display its loyalty. It dismissed one editor under pressure from the paper's English-speaking shareholders and endorsed the Canadian Patriotic Fund, but as the war dragged on, hostility towards Der Courier grew more intense. In 1916 irate citizens and in 1917 a group of soldiers attacked its offices, and in September 1918 the newspaper voluntarily suspended publication in the German language. The federal government banned all newspapers published in "enemy alien" languages a few weeks later. Der Courier was not permitted to resume publication in German until January 1920.[28]

While the city's Central and Eastern European population had no indigenous ethnic press to attract the wrath of aggressive patriots, it too was victimized. Many found themselves classified as enemy aliens and were subsequently disfranchised along with those of German origin under the federal War Time Elections Act. After the war, the situation became further inflamed. Not only were veterans forced to compete with these people for jobs, but "foreigners" came to be associated in the public mind with labour radicalism.

The use of "foreign" languages in the classroom also came under attack, for the war gave a new impetus to the assimilationist cause and to the view that the school should be the major instrument of Canadianization. In Regina the seeds of the controversy were sown in 1914, when a dispute arose within the separate school board over the hiring of three German nuns. It was proposed to make room for them by dismissing three English-speaking teachers, but the English Catholic trustees, who comprised a majority on the board, objected. There was a public outcry as well, and in the end the board decided not to hire these "alien teachers." Even this did not long satisfy those Reginans who wanted to ensure the primacy of the English language in Saskatchewan schools. Local clergymen, educators and politicians assumed a leading role in the province-wide assault

Czechoslovakian dancers perform at the Great West Canadian Folksong, Folkdance and Handicrafts Festival in Regina, 1929. This was one of a series of music and folk arts festivals which the CPR sponsored across Canada to attract tourists to its hotels.

against the use of German, Ukrainian and even French. The provincial government eventually succumbed to this pressure. In December 1918 it introduced legislation stipulating that English would henceforth be the only language of instruction permitted in public and separate schools (although French could continue to be used in the first grade — and was until 1931, when it too was proscribed). There was never any doubt that the bill would pass. Indeed, there were some in the province who wished to go further and suppress even the holding of religious services in German.[29]

In Regina the impact of the new law fell most heavily upon the German community. Other ethnic groups were little affected, since they had always been too small, too poor or too poorly organized to hire teachers who could provide instruction in the mother tongue. They had been obliged to find other ways to preserve familiar traditions, language and culture. For one of these groups the war years were in fact a period of great activity and accomplishment.

The Training School for Teachers for Foreign Speaking Communities had inadvertently given an early stimulus to Ukrainian cultural activity in the city, but it was closed in February 1914. This proved to be only a temporary setback; within a few months Ukrainians founded two organizations of their own. One was an ethnic club, which soon organized a small lending library. The other was a branch of the Ukrainian Social Democratic Party. The two merged in 1917, acquired the local Romanian Hall and renamed it the Ukrainian Labour Temple. It quickly became the centre of Ukrainian social and cultural life in the city. Here classes were offered in Ukrainian for children and adults, and lectures and musical and theatrical performances were presented.

Not all Reginans of Anglo-Saxon background succumbed to the war-induced hysteria against the "foreigner." Some sought to assist the "New Canadians," as they preferred to call them, to become good and prosperous citizens. These sentiments found expression in the establishment of a centre for settlement work in the East End. This had been one of the principal recommendations of J. S. Woodsworth's 1913 social survey, but it was not until 1916 that three of the city's Methodist churches took the lead in founding Settlement House. Under the capable direction of Miss Nellie Forman, it offered night school classes in English, provided instruction in homemaking and other practical subjects, and organized a variety of social and recreational programs for immigrant children. Settlement House soon outgrew the modest quarters it occupied first on Toronto Street and then on Victoria Avenue. New and larger facilities, which included a gymnasium, were opened on Wallace Street in 1927 and continued in operation until 1956.[30]

The First World War also gave a stimulus to the campaign against alcohol, but those of European background remained largely unconvinced. Thus, in Saskatoon prohibition carried by a margin of ten to one in the 1916 referendum, but in Regina (with a German population three times as large) it carried by less than five to one. When Saskatchewan voted again, in 1920 (to re-establish a ban on the importation of liquor after Canada's brief experiment with national prohibition had ended), Regina was the only city in the province to record a "wet" majority. Opposition to the Saskatchewan Temperance Act first took organized form in Regina with the founding of the Temperance Reform League in 1922. The strength of the Moderation League, as it subsequently became known, lay in Regina and the other cities, where a "dry" majority of 11,781 in 1916 was turned into a "wet" majority of 10,009 when Saskatchewan ended prohibition in a third vote in 1924. Some rural areas, particularly those with a large concentration of European-born voters, also gave decisive majorities against prohibition.[31]

The war and immediate postwar period was also marked by great tensions between organized labour and business across the nation. Regina was certainly no Winnipeg, but even in this small city there were more strikes; labour-management conflicts began to touch the wider community as essential services were affected by walkouts. Mail service was disrupted for nine days during the first nation-wide postal strike in July 1918. For a time it appeared that the Regina Trades and Labour Council would show its support for the postal workers by staging a general strike, but the polling of member unions of the RTLC had not yet been completed when the Post Office employees returned to work. In October 1918 provincial telephone workers went

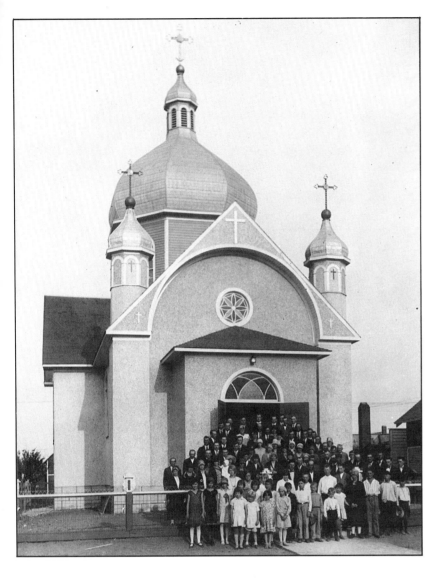

The congregation of St. Basil's Ukrainian Catholic Church. The church was built in 1928.

out, but in this case local and even long-distance service was not disrupted during the three-week strike. Regina's business and political leaders viewed these developments with apprehension. Some were quick to attribute labour's new and more aggressive stance to outside forces. When the telephone operators walked out, Charles Dunning, the minister responsible for the government telephone system, blamed the strike on "Bolshevik agitators" from the United States.[32]

Concern about "Bolshevik agitators" was further heightened in 1919. There was talk of a sympathetic strike in the spring during a dispute involving Regina's building trades, and in Calgary the foundation was laid for a mass industrial organization — the One Big Union (OBU) — espousing similar tactics. Saskatchewan, however, did not prove to be fertile soil for the OBU. Even in Regina, where radical trade unionists were thought to have great influence, the response was a cautious one. When a packed meeting of the RTLC pledged its full support to the OBU, three member unions promptly withdrew. The OBU would in fact have attracted little attention in the city had it not been for the revolutionary utterances of a local bricklayer, Joseph Sambrook, who publicly advocated the adoption of the Russian soviet form of government.[33]

The most dramatic manifestation of postwar labour discontent occurred in Winnipeg. Thirty-five thousand workers left their jobs on May 15, 1919, in what became the nation's first general strike. The RTLC at once began to canvass member unions to seek approval for a sympathetic strike. The majority in favour was two to one, with eleven of the twenty-five affiliated locals voting to walk out and nine undecided. The prospect of a crippling general strike roused Regina's business community to action. The *Morning Leader* belligerently declared that "there will be nothing even resembling a soviet created here." City council authorized Mayor Henry Black to take any steps necessary to maintain order and continue the operation of the public utilities, and Regina businessmen formed a citizens' committee patterned after a similar organization which had been set up in Winnipeg.

These preparations proved unnecessary, for the radicals rapidly lost their grip on the RTLC. Early in June it decided to take no further action in support of the strikers in Winnipeg. A renegade group did form a provisional strike committee, but less than 200 men, chiefly construction labourers, electricians and railway shopmen, left their jobs. Even they began to return to work within a few days.

It should not have been surprising that labour's flirtation with the general strike was brief and half-hearted. Comprising only a small minority of the population, Regina's trade unionists were wary of antagonizing the larger urban community and more particularly the farmers, who clearly had little sympathy for the men on strike in Winnipeg. When the RTLC voted by a wide margin in August 1919 to retain its affiliation with the international craft unions, Sambrook and the other radicals on the executive promptly resigned. They managed to recruit a few local men — there was an OBU unit in Regina as late as 1930 — but only a few.[34]

Regina remained a bastion of craft unionism and moderation through the 1920s and 1930s. Trade union membership rose and fell as Saskatchewan drifted from depression to prosperity and back again. In all of the province it exceeded 9,000 only three times during these two decades, but fell below 6,000 twice.[35] Strikes were infrequent, and many became apathetic. Those who remained determined to improve the lot of Regina's labouring classes increasingly turned to political action, challenging business hegemony at city hall and eventually winning control of the mayoralty and council during the 1930s.

Ethnic tensions also subsided after the war. Antagonism towards Germans, largely a product of wartime conditions rather than of deep-rooted prejudice, virtually disappeared. Even deep-rooted prejudice — towards the Chinese, for instance — began to soften. The province had banned the employment of white women in Chinese laundries and restaurants in 1912, but in 1919 substituted a licensing system. There was some initial resistance in Regina to the issuing of such licences, but by the late 1920s this was no longer controversial (the provincial statute, however, was not repealed until 1969).[36]

A proliferation of ethnic clubs and associations testified to Regina's increasingly cosmopolitan character. The Germans were the most active, reviving clubs and organizations that had

The Ukrainian Labour Farmer Temple Association string orchestra, 1929.

The McCallum Hill Building, designed in 1912 by Regina architects Stan E. Storey and William G. Van Egmond, would dominate the downtown skyline and the market for prime office space through the interwar years and beyond.

been dormant during the war years and founding new ones. *Der Courier* played a leading role in this work and in the process became the most widely read German newspaper in Canada by the mid-1930s. A German Baptist church was also established in Regina, along with new Catholic and Lutheran parishes and a private residential high school, Luther College. To coordinate the activities of these various clubs and societies, an umbrella organization, the Deutsch-Kanadisches Zentralkomitee, was founded in 1929. Local Germans also played a leading role in the inauguration of *Deutscher Tage* (German Days) in 1930. The first, held in Regina, drew 5,000 Germans from across the province for two days of sports competitions, folk dances, singing, speeches and displays of handicrafts.[37]

For other elements of Regina's population the pattern was similar. Ukrainians established a branch of the Prosvita Society in 1921 and distinct Ukrainian Greek Orthodox and Catholic parishes in 1924 and 1925 respectively. A branch of the Ukrainian Labour Farmer Temple Association also appeared in the early 1920s, as did a Canadian Hungarian Cultural Club and a Chinese Benevolent Society. A Scandinavian Club was founded in 1927 and Polish and Hungarian Catholic parishes at the beginning of the next decade.[38] One consequence of all of this was to measurably enrich Regina's social and cultural life.

Of course, old predjudices remained. There were some among the English-speaking charter group who feared that the influx of Central and Eastern Europeans would depress wage rates and displace British and Canadian workers. Others questioned whether these newcomers could, or would, be assimilated. The Ku Klux Klan appealed to such fears and anxieties as these when it appeared in the city in 1926. Posing as a "great Christian, benevolent, fraternal organization … that … was going to save Canada for Canadians," the Klan claimed to have recruited 1,000 Reginans by October 1927. More may have joined in 1928 and 1929, when Klan membership in the province reached 25,000 according to one reliable estimate. But the Klan's impact proved to be short-lived. Immigration all but ceased after 1930, eliminating much of its *raison d'etre*, and the Klan collapsed as quickly as it had risen to prominence.[39] The episode is significant only because it constitutes such a dramatic exception to the general trend, one of steadily improving ethnic relations in Regina.

THE URBAN LANDSCAPE

Regina's physical appearance in 1914 was a study in contrasts. While the built-up area of the city had an air of solidity and permanence, vacant lots outnumbered the few houses on many blocks in outlying districts. A quarter century later such a description of Regina would still have been apt. Land-use patterns, the location and desirability of its residential districts, the very size of the city itself did not alter appreciably during these years.

Continuity, not change, characterized the urban landscape. This was especially true of the downtown core, which looked much the same in 1939 as it had in 1914. The McCallum Hill Building continued to dominate the downtown skyline and the market for prime office space. Indeed, only two new office buildings of any consequence were constructed in the interwar period. One, the Broder Building on Eleventh Avenue, was erected in 1930. The Dominion Government Building appeared five years later. Designed by Regina architect Francis Portnall on a site overlooking Victoria Park, it contained elements of both Art Deco and Art Moderne styling. The only other notable additions in the downtown area were the Capitol Theatre (1921), the Hotel Saskatchewan (1927) and the Trianon Dance Palace (1929).

Vacant lots were another constant in the urban landscape during these years. The city had absorbed large tracts of surrounding farm land in 1911, but even the hectic pace of construction in those boom years had not begun to fill in all the empty space. Because the pace of building activity was so erratic after 1914 (Appendix, Table XI), empty lots still dotted the city at the end of this period. They were a delight to children, serving as convenient playgrounds, but a vexatious problem for successive city councils.

It was largely a matter of money. The city derived most of its revenues from property taxes, but as the real-estate boom (and land values) collapsed, the owners of many of these vacant

Scarth Street looking north from Eleventh Avenue, c. 1915.

Eleventh Avenue looking east from Scarth Street, c. 1915.

Eleventh Avenue looking west from Rose Street, c. 1920.

By the late 1920s, the T. Eaton Company was providing parking for its customers (and retailing gasoline as well).

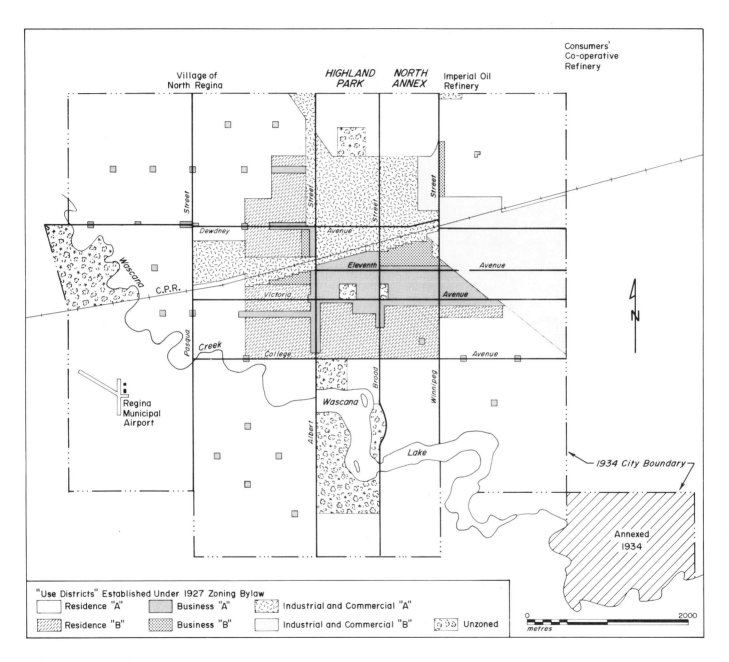

6 Regina in 1939: Continuity characterized the urban landscape in the period 1914-1939. There was only one minor annexation. Land-use patterns did not change appreciably. The zoning bylaw adopted in 1927 for the most part simply maintained the status quo.

tracts could not, or would not, meet their obligations. By the end of 1914 no fewer than 3,000 parcels of land were in arrears. The following year provincial legislation made it possible for the city to sell these lots to recover the taxes due. But the procedure was complicated, time-consuming and expensive, and the city, anxious to maintain tax revenues at as high a level as possible, gave delinquent taxpayers every opportunity to redeem their property. Even with such a lenient approach, the city began to acquire large numbers of lots, which it attempted to sell at public auction. At the first, in 1925, literally thousands were offered for sale, but bids were received on only twenty lots. It is easy to see why there were so few takers. Most of the lots acquired by the city were located in outlying areas and lacked basic services. Choicer lots were readily available; a survey in 1923 disclosed that there were 4,929 vacant lots on sewer and water lines in Regina.[40] City sales of tax-delinquent land improved somewhat later in the decade, but fell sharply after 1929. At the same time many more property owners found themselves in arrears, and the city's landholdings began to grow once again.

By the end of the 1930s the city was well on its way to becoming one of the largest landowners in Regina, as it had been at the beginning of the century. Of course, it was obliged to forego the tax revenues which these properties would otherwise have provided, but Regina's ill fortune was not without its benefits. The most important of these was the fact that the city was able to directly influence and control the pattern of physical growth in Regina more than otherwise might have been possible.

The city's success, limited though it was, in influencing residential development can serve as a case in point. Anxious to consolidate its built-up area, Regina began in 1924 to exchange city-owned lots that were located on sewer and water lines for unserviced lots in outlying districts. As a condition of the exchange, either an existing house had to be moved to the new lot or one had to be constructed. While few lots were in fact exchanged, the scheme does illustrate the city's determination to promote compact development. City policy governing the sale of residential lots, modest though such sales were in

the 1920s and 1930s, sought the same objective. The city's refusal to extend sewer and water lines to outlying areas also acted as a brake on uncontrolled suburban expansion.[41] Successive city councils showed even less enthusiasm for the annexation of suburban areas outside Regina proper, rejecting pleas from Highland Park, North Annex and the village of North Regina to be added to the city. There was only one modest annexation during these years. A parcel of land southeast of Regina was acquired for a cemetery in 1934 (see Map 6).[42]

The city was rather more successful in controlling industrial land use. It had long sought to direct industrial development to the area east of Albert Street and north of the CPR main line, where it possessed a virtual monopoly of suitable land. This policy was continued after 1914, but the sale of thirty-eight acres of land to General Motors in 1928 almost completely exhausted the tract which the city had set aside for this purpose. The acquisition of a large block of tax-delinquent lots in what had been the Innismore, Dewdney Place and Tuxedo Park subdivisions thus proved to be fortuitous. The tract was well suited for industrial purposes. It was immediately adjacent to the existing industrial area, it had good rail connections (the CPR main line and a branch line bounded the tract on the north and south), and there had as yet been little residential intrusion. The area was set aside for industrial purposes in the late 1920s, thereby ensuring that when industrial development resumed again in earnest after the Second World War, the city would still enjoy a monopoly of suitable land.[43]

In 1928 another large tract of tax-delinquent property, Mirror subdivision on the western outskirts of the city, was set aside as a site for an airport. Other parcels were reserved for park purposes in 1929. Most were located in subdivisions annexed by the city in 1911, many of which had been laid out without any provision for public open space. The largest area so designated was Douglas Park on the southeastern fringe of the city adjacent to Wascana Lake. None of these parks were developed immediately — the city had other priorities during the Depression — but Regina was for the first time making provision for open space in advance of residential development.

Regina's record with respect to parks was not always so

Early tree-planting efforts on the grounds of the Legislative Building begin to transform bald prairie, c. 1915.

praiseworthy. In its zeal to attract the T. Eaton Company, the city agreed in 1917 to sell Dominion Park, a public reserve in the warehouse district that had been developed as a sports field. The federal government promptly intervened, contending that Regina had acted illegally in selling the property, and confiscated the proceeds of the sale, some $100,000. The Exchequer Court agreed with the federal government in 1926 and dismissed the city's claim. Regina did eventually manage to recover part of the purchase price through arbitration proceedings in 1927. Ironically, one condition of the arbitration award was that the money be used for park development.

The partially erected steel framework of the Chateau Qu'-Appelle in Wascana Park served for more than a decade as another reminder of municipal folly. Not until 1924, after all hope of finishing the hotel had been abandoned, did the city take steps to reclaim this park area for future generations to enjoy. The spur track was also taken up as far west as Elphinstone Street, thereby restoring the residential character of the adjoining neighbourhoods. With the tracks gone and the site cleared, not a trace remained of that ill-fated hotel.[44]

Thomas Mawson's comprehensive plan for the future development of Regina suffered a similar fate. He had virtually completed it by 1914, but worsening economic conditions cooled his client's enthusiasm for "City Beautiful" concepts. Consequently, the city simply refused to accept the plan. A new factor was introduced in 1917, when the province passed the Town Planning and Rural Development Act. Based largely on a draft bill prepared by Thomas Adams, a British town-planning expert who was then employed by the federal Commission of Conservation, the act gave Saskatchewan cities broad powers to control land use. Under the act, cities were required to prepare a development plan by 1921 and appoint a board to implement it.

Regina was slow to comply. Even after 1917 the city still did not wish to accept Mawson's report, and it eventually agreed to do so only because of pressure from the provincial government and from local residents whose enthusiasm for town planning found expression in the formation of the Regina Town Planning Association in 1922. The Mawson plan was made public early the following year. Designed for a population of up to 120,000, its centrepiece was a grandiose civic centre consisting of a city hall, courthouse and other public buildings to be situated on Smith Street between Sixteenth Avenue and Wascana Lake. Other proposals called for a system of diagonal roadways superimposed on the existing rectangular grid layout and for the relocation of the warehouse district north of the city. Mawson's proposals were ambitious, to say the least. Most were also impractical, given economic conditions in the city and the province at the time. Only one — his recommendation that the existing park area adjacent to Wascana Lake be enhanced and extended along the creek in both directions — was not, and in 1938 the Rotary Club began to lay out a small park immediately west of Albert Street in Lakeview.[45] The rest of the Mawson plan was soon forgotten.

The city took a less ambitious and less expensive approach to town planning. In 1924 it created a town-planning board, comprised of senior municipal officials and members of the Regina Town Planning Association. These individuals then prepared a draft zoning by-law, which council adopted in 1927. It regulated the height of buildings, the proportion of a lot a building could occupy and the size of yards and other open spaces. The by-law also attempted to control land use by dividing the city into six "Use-Districts." Generally speaking, these simply confirmed existing land-use patterns. Industrial and Commercial District "A," for example, embraced the industrial area north of the CPR main line (see Map 6). Industrial and Commercial District "B" reflected the city's determination to set aside adjacent tax-delinquent lands to meet future needs. The same was true of the residential and commercial zones. Already-established patterns of growth would be continued, and contiguous undeveloped areas zoned in such a way as to facilitate expansion. The adoption of this by-law was only a first step. Three years later the city appointed a town-planning commission to prepare a comprehensive plan for Regina. The new body set to work with great enthusiasm, initiating a study of what was termed "Regina's traffic problem" in 1931. Interest in town planning soon waned, however, and would not revive until after the Second World War.[46]

The "traffic problem" studied by the commission — a product of the increasing popularity of the automobile and Regina's narrow streets — had first become apparent during the 1920s. Beginning in 1927 the city began to restrict parking in the downtown core, although some worried that this would be an inconvenience to the large numbers of country people who came into Regina to shop.[47] There was as yet no support for the idea that the city should itself provide off-street parking. That would be left to private enterprise. The T. Eaton Company was the only major firm to do so, beginning in the late 1920s. Of course, traffic congestion was not yet as serious in downtown Regina as it would become in the 1950s with the growth of the city's population and of automobile ownership. Only then would the introduction of one-way streets (first proposed but rejected in 1927) be given serious consideration as a means of improving traffic flow.

During the interwar period it was the streetcar, not the automobile, that had the more decisive impact on patterns of urban development. The street railway was responsible for the growth of commercial activity away from the downtown core. Clusters of neighbourhood shops early began to appear along streetcar lines, on Thirteenth Avenue in the West End, for instance, and on Victoria Avenue east of Winnipeg Street. The T. Eaton Company store on Broad Street provided parking for its customers, to be sure, but it was also located on a major streetcar line.

The Regina Municipal Railway also influenced patterns of residential growth. The location of its streetcar routes had from the outset begun to shape attitudes about the desirability of residential areas in Regina, and later developments only reinforced these views. There were no extensions after 1914; indeed, little-used sections of track were dismantled. Thus, residential areas that already enjoyed good streetcar connections were able to maintain that advantage for many years.[48]

The district south of Victoria Park, the Angus and Leopold Crescent area, and Lakeview remained the preserve of well-to-do Reginans. The first was the most pleasing to the eye, for the last open spaces along College Avenue (as Sixteenth Avenue was renamed in 1925) were filled in by the end of the 1920s.

The trees planted a generation earlier now provided welcome shade on hot summer days, and this too made the neighbourhood attractive. As for Lakeview, it became somewhat less exclusive than its founders had envisaged. Some of the new homes erected there in the 1920s were as imposing monuments to wealth and architectural design as those that W. H. A. Hill and E. D. McCallum had built a decade earlier. But the majority were more modest in size and were situated on narrower lots. For all its pretentiousness, Lakeview still looked unfinished. Even at the end of the 1930s, there were vacant lots along Albert Street, the trees were sparse and the bald prairie was only a few blocks away.

Of course, most Reginans could not afford to live in Lakeview, along College Avenue or even in the West End. For them accommodation remained difficult to obtain throughout most of this period. The problem was not a new one in 1914, but the virtual cessation of construction during the war exacerbated it. Only 163 homes were built in Regina between 1915 and 1918. By the end of the war the shortage of decent housing was acute, and the situation was further complicated by the return of demobilized servicemen. Regina's business elite had wooed large firms to the city but showed little interest in the construction of moderately priced homes, save to commend Imperial Oil for building houses for its employees north of the city. A short-lived federal housing loan scheme in 1919 proved to be of no benefit to Regina, since the provincial government declined to participate.

Private residential construction did revive in the 1920s. A total of 868 new homes were built in 1921 and 1922 alone, but the substantial down payments required put all but the most modest bungalows beyond the reach of ordinary wage earners. Most of the new apartment buildings that appeared during the decade also catered to middle- and high-income tenants. The Balfour Apartments was one of the most luxurious. Built in 1929 at a cost of $475,000, it boasted the first automatic elevator to be installed in an apartment building in the city, and its suites rented for more than $300 per month.[49]

With the onset of the Depression, the housing situation in Regina again became critical. Construction activity halted, but

The residential area south of Victoria Park remained the preserve of the well-to-do. Thomas Brown Patton, who made his money in lumber and coal, built this house on Scarth Street in 1914.

the city's population continued to grow. The result was serious overcrowding. Large houses were subdivided to provide accommodation for as many as a dozen families, and even basement rooms in downtown stores and offices were rented out. The Dominion Housing Act of 1935, another federal loan scheme intended to stimulate house construction, provided almost no relief, since only a few loans were made in Saskatchewan. The federal government subsequently made funds available for home repair and for low-cost housing, but Regina does not appear to have derived any benefit from these schemes. Early in 1938 a survey of local conditions could claim that Regina was "one of the most overcrowded cities in the Dominion of Canada for its size." According to the survey, 7.4 per cent of all families in Regina lived in one room, compared to the national average of 2.5 per cent. Another 9.6 per cent lived in two rooms, compared to 4.4 per cent for Canada as a whole.[50]

THE URBAN COMMUNITY: SOCIAL AND POLITICAL LIFE

During the war years there were new priorities for the men (and they were all men until Helena Walker was elected to city council in 1932) who governed Regina. One of the most pressing was the plight of the unemployed, who were turning to the city for assistance in greater numbers than ever before. Private charitable organizations took the lead in aiding those who had fallen on hard times. The work was coordinated by the Bureau of Public Welfare, established on the eve of the war. The city provided most of its operating funds; the balance came from the province and from private donations. Overall the bureau's budget amounted to some $15,000 in 1914 and 1915 and $6,000 in 1916. With 450 families on relief by 1915 it met a real need, but city officials were never inclined to view the bureau as a permanent relief agency. When improved economic conditions in 1918 appeared to make the bureau's continued existence unnecessary, the city withdrew its support and the bureau was forced to close.[51]

The repair of civic finances was another priority. Regina's financial difficulties were a legacy of the preceding boom period. Extending light, water and sidewalks, and schools and streetcar lines, had pushed Regina's debenture debt to $7,553,607 by 1913. The city sharply curtailed capital expenditures during the war, but its debt continued to grow, reaching $10,857,887 by 1918. At the same time the city found it increasingly difficult to raise sufficient revenues to meet its obligations. In part this was due to an equally sharp decline in the assessed value of land, from $82,537,840 in 1913 to $45,449,770 at war's end. Since property taxes were the main source of civic revenue, tax rates had to be substantially increased. The mill rate jumped from 13 in 1914 to 24.7 in 1915 and 30 in 1918 to meet the city's revenue needs and to satisfy the requirements of the Patriotic Revenue Tax, a wartime levy that marked the province's first intrusion into the urban property tax field. Tax arrears climbed, too, reaching a wartime peak of $817,573 in 1916. Tax collections improved during the next two years, but in 1918 arrears still amounted to $395,464.[52]

The state of Regina's finances figured prominently in the annual municipal elections of the war years. Those contests also mirrored the city's ethnic and class divisions. Cornelius Rink made a bid for the mayoralty in 1914, but his foreign birth and the fact that he had once fought against Great Britain counted against him. He lost decisively to a local lawyer, James Balfour, winning only the East End poll. There was no longer a ward system to ensure that all sections of the city were represented on council, but ratepayers' associations continued to keep a watchful eye on city hall. Those representing the North Side proved to be particularly vigilant.

Organized labour also began to take an active interest in municipal politics, putting three candidates in the field in 1914. None were elected, but in 1915 Harry Perry, vice-president of the Regina Trades and Labour Council, carried the East End and North Side to become Regina's first Labour alderman. A second was elected the following year, and Perry led the field in his bid for re-election in 1917. Some elements of the business community initially welcomed labour's entrance into municipal politics, but by 1918 attitudes became more hostile. Believing that "big men" were needed to direct postwar reconstruction in the city, a self-proclaimed Citizens' Committee recruited a half-

D.W. Houston (seated in foreground) became superintendent of the Regina Municipal Railway in 1914 and held the job for thirty-two years. He oversaw the conversion to one-man operation (in 1920) and in other ways sought to pare expenses and improve service on an overbuilt streetcar system.

Major James Coldwell and his grade VIII class at North Regina School, c. 1914. M.J. Coldwell's political career began at the municipal level, but he would go on to lead the provincial Independent Labour Party, the Saskatchewan Farmer-Labour Party and the national Co-operative Commonwealth Federation.

Civic Relief Board office, 1933. Here forms had to be filled out before a family could receive $16.00 a month in grocery vouchers.

The 1930s were a tumultuous decade in municipal politics. Cornelius Rink rose from political obscurity to defeat James McAra, then Regina's longest-serving mayor, in 1933. Rink in turn fell two years later when the Civic Labour League captured City Hall. The male monopoly on city council was broken during the decade as well, with the election of Helena Walker in 1932.

dozen business and professional men to challenge the incumbent mayor, Henry Black, and the "agitating Socialists" who were said to be bent on seizing control of city hall. Labour in fact put up only three candidates, though it did form a loose alliance with the two North Side ratepayers' associations, each of whom also nominated a candidate. Although both newspapers supported the Citizens' slate, Black easily bested fellow businessman J. F. Bole for the mayoralty. The Citizens' Committee did capture three of the five seats on council, and none of the Labour or ratepayers' candidates were successful.[53]

Labour's political fortunes improved after the war. There was less antipathy towards "agitating Socialists" as the events of 1918 and 1919 receded into memory. Labour also benefited from the widening of the municipal franchise, especially the abolition of the property qualification in 1920.[54] Harry Perry became something of a fixture at city hall, winning re-election four more times, and between 1922 and 1925 there were two Labour aldermen. Allied with the Labour group on council was M. J. Coldwell, whose victory in the 1921 municipal election marked the beginning of a long career in local and then provincial and national politics. An English-born school teacher, he had come to Saskatchewan before the war, settling first in Sedley and then in North Regina. In 1919 Coldwell became the principal of Dominion Park School on Regina's North Side and began to take an active interest in local politics and in the Regina People's Forum, which was just then getting under way. (It met on Sunday afternoons during the winter months to discuss the issues of the day and became a favoured haunt of those with left-wing sympathies.) Running in 1921 as an independent candidate with the support of the North Side Ratepayers' Association, Coldwell finished second in a field of five. The next three times Coldwell headed the poll. Although he did not officially align himself with Labour's political organization until 1930, Coldwell shared many of its concerns, among them a desire to reform the administration of relief in the city.

As for the mayoralty, it remained securely in the hands of local businessmen during the 1920s. James McAra was the most politically successful. Partner with his older brother in an insurance and real-estate business, McAra had gone overseas with the 28th Battalion in 1914 and then returned to Regina to organize a local unit of the Military Hospitals Commission. A lieutenant colonel at war's end, McAra joined the Great War Veterans' Association and served for a time on its national executive. This popular war veteran, a resident of Regina since 1883, first won the mayoralty in 1926. By the end of the decade, with his fourth triumph at the polls, James McAra had become the longest-serving mayor in the city's history.[55]

Successive city councils followed a conservative policy with regard to capital expenditures during this first postwar decade. Regina's debenture debt increased by a little over a million dollars between 1918 and 1924, fell slightly in 1925 and then began to grow again, reaching $13,492,805 by 1929. These were modest increases, certainly when compared to the prewar era. Regina continued to share the property tax field with the province, whose Patriotic Revenue Tax was renamed the public revenue tax. The tax was based on municipal assessments, which varied greatly. Predictably, complaints arose that it imposed an uneven burden on local governments, which were required to collect it. The province appointed a royal commission to study the matter, and in 1922 created a permanent agency, the Saskatchewan Assessment Commission, to equalize assessments. Its efforts were only partly successful, for complaints about discrimination (between rural and urban areas particularly) persisted throughout the decade. The cities also objected to the province's intrusion into the property tax field at all, but to no avail. The Public Revenue Tax was not abolished until 1952.[56]

Property tax rates in Regina remained high, higher than they had been even during the war years, and the city increasingly looked to its utilities to cushion the impact on property owners. As early as 1914 it had begun to use "profits" from the generation and distribution of electricity to offset the alarming losses sustained by the street railway, losses totalling nearly half a million dollars by 1918. Even with the economies made possible by the adoption of one-man operation in 1920, the Regina Municipal Railway continued to lose money until 1927. After 1930 the losses began to mount again, in spite of several attempts to cut costs through reductions in wages and service.

Thus, it was Regina's municipally owned power plant, by

One of the most celebrated events of the Depression decade was the On-to-Ottawa Trek. More than 1,000 men left Vancouver early in June 1935 to take their grievances about R.B. Bennett's relief camps directly to the prime minister. Their numbers grew to 1,400 by the time federal authorities halted the trek in Regina on June 14.

While their leaders went on to Ottawa to meet with Bennett, the trekkers were housed and fed at the Exhibition Grounds. Bennett rejected their demands and the delegation returned to Regina, but the trek did not end peacefully. On July 1 a combined RCMP-City Police attempt to arrest the trek leaders while they were addressing a rally at Market Square touched off a riot. A city detective was killed and scores of policemen, trekkers and citizens were injured.

the mid-1920s the most modern and efficient in the province, that became the darling of postwar city councils. Not only did it produce cheap power (Regina had the lowest power rates in Saskatchewan in fact), it also generated handsome surpluses which could be used to keep the tax rate down. It became a matter of civic pride that the 1924 surplus had reduced the tax rate by 6 mills and that of 1926 by nearly 4.[57]

This coloured Regina's attitude towards a 1928 proposal to link the three largest cities as the nucleus of a province-wide power scheme. In 1913 the provincial government had seriously examined, but then abandoned, the idea of producing electric power at the Souris coal fields and transmitting it across southern Saskatchewan. Improvements in the transmission of power over long distances convinced the government to take a second look, and it appointed another royal commission to study the matter in 1927. The Power Resources Commission made known to the government what were almost certainly its final recommendations in May 1928, and these formed the basis of discussions with the three cities that same month. Simply put, the provincial government proposed to build a central generating plant that would supply power to Regina, Saskatoon and Moose Jaw, and to operate the existing city plants as stand-by units. When the cities countered with a proposal that the province consider "the utilization of the present civic plants for supply of power to outside points," the Power Resources Commission promptly reversed itself. In its final report, which appeared in July, it declared that a large central generating plant would be economically impractical for years to come. Instead, it recommended that the three city plants be enlarged to form the basis of a provincial power network.[58]

The new proposals won ready approval in Saskatoon. That city needed to augment the capacity of its existing plant or construct a new one, but it had reached the limits of its borrowing power. Thus, the provincial government managed to acquire the Saskatoon plant in short order. Regina decided to retain its power plant, and Moose Jaw sold its utility to private interests in 1929. It has been argued that in following the course they did, Regina and Moose Jaw retarded the development of an integrated power grid in Saskatchewan for a generation or more. There is little doubt that both cities judged the merits of the 1928 scheme largely in terms of self-interest. Regina, for instance, was loath to give up what was thought to be its most attractive inducement to industries, its low power rates. But the provincial government cannot entirely escape criticism. Anxious to win the cities over following the abortive May conference, the province concocted a scheme that was bound to create almost as many objections as it removed. To make the scheme more attractive to Regina, the province proposed that Moose Jaw bear all of the fixed charges on the transmission line that would be constructed between the two cities. This Moose Jaw found unacceptable, and it proceeded to insist as a condition of sale that the province agree to expand its plant unit-for-unit with Regina's. Regina showed no enthusiasm for this idea, fearing that such an arrangement would limit future plant expansion there and prevent further reductions in power rates.

Regina remained aloof from the Saskatchewan Power Commission, the provincial power utility that came into existence with the purchase of the Saskatoon plant in 1928. The city showed no interest in becoming part of a private power grid either. With Regina's plant requiring new and costly equipment in the depths of the Depression, two private companies approached the city with offers to extend their transmission lines to the provincial capital. Both were rejected out of hand, as the province's proposal had been seven years earlier. Regina continued to claim the lowest power rates in Saskatchewan and to boast of the substantial surpluses returned to the city coffers from this "most valuable asset."[59]

The efforts of Regina and Moose Jaw to obtain a larger and more assured supply of water affords another example of the limits of cooperation between Saskatchewan's two levels of government during the interwar period. Here it was the cities that took the initiative, approaching the province in 1919 for assistance in constructing a pipeline from the South Saskatchewan River. A succession of unusually dry years had reduced their available supply, then drawn entirely from underground sources. Recognizing that the cost of constructing a pipeline would be beyond the means of either or both cities, they enlisted the support of adjacent towns and villages and the

Alderman J.H. Taylor

Alderman T.G. McNall

His Worship Mayor A.C. Ellison

Alderman W.J.F. Adamson

Alderman Murdo Cameron

1937 CITY COUNCIL CITY OF REGINA

Alderman C.M. Fines

Alderman A.M. Derby

Alderman S.B. East

Alderman J.M. Toothill

City Clerk George Beach

Alderman G.N. Menzies

Alderman J.A. McLeod

City Commissioner R.J. Westgate

In 1937 Labour held five of the ten council seats (Aldermen Derby, East, Fines, Menzies and Toothill). Mayor Alban C. Ellison, who had run and won as an Independent, held the balance of power.

rural municipalities through which the proposed pipeline would pass.

The province responded with a royal commission, which concluded that a pipeline would be feasible though expensive. The initial construction cost was estimated to be $5,700,000; subsequent expansion to meet anticipated increases in water needs would require the expenditure of an additional $1,300,000 within five years. To construct and manage the pipeline, the Saskatchewan Water Supply Commission recommended that a Regina-Moose Jaw Water District be established. The Water District would have the power to issue debentures to cover construction costs, and the fixed charges on that debenture debt would be met from the revenues realized from the sale of water to these communities. The royal commission also recommended that the province take no steps to implement the scheme until residents of the cities, towns and adjoining rural areas had had an opportunity to show their support for it. The vote took place in 1921. Sizeable majorities in favour of the pipeline project were recorded in Regina and Moose Jaw and in most of the towns. Farmers, on the other hand, were decidedly opposed to it, and the provincial government used this as a reason not to proceed.[60]

And so Regina augmented its existing underground water supply at Boggy Creek and began to develop another at Mallory Springs, five miles northeast of the city. In 1929 New York and Toronto consultants investigated other potential sources, including the South Saskatchewan River and two nearby lakes, Last Mountain to the north and Carlyle (now White Bear Lake) to the south. Both lakes were judged unsuitable due to the extreme hardness of the water there. While the South Saskatchewan River was recognized as Regina's ultimate source of supply, the consultants recommended that the city continue to concentrate on developing less expensive underground sources, which they deemed adequate to meet its needs until the population reached 75,000.

This Regina did, adding a larger pipeline from Boggy Creek to the city and developing a third underground source at Mound Springs further north. "When Mound Springs and other springs in the same district are developed," City Commissioner

R. J. Westgate declared in June 1931, "we will have enough water for a population of 90,000." Believing that its water needs could be met for the foreseeable future, Regina showed little interest when Moose Jaw attempted to revive the South Saskatchewan River pipeline project that year as a means of providing work for the unemployed. A substantial financial commitment from the provincial and federal governments was considered essential. When it proved impossible to secure such assistance, Moose Jaw's initiative died a quiet death. At the end of the 1930s Regina still relied entirely on an underground water supply, the second largest city in Canada (after London, Ontario) to do so.[61]

During the 1930s providing relief to the unemployed and repairing civic finances again became the chief preoccupations of those who governed Regina. Beginning with the winter of 1929-30 and continuing well into the second year of the Second World War, unemployment in the city reached unprecedented levels. By June 1931 fully 23 per cent of all adult male wage earners there were out of work. Unemployment continued to rise through the winter of 1932-33 and thereafter declined only gradually. In June 1936 male unemployment still stood at 19.7 per cent. City expenditures on relief soon dwarfed anything that had been seen during the war years, and so did the city's financial difficulties. Tax rates rose sharply (from 41 mills on the eve of the Depression to 48 in 1931). Tax arrears climbed, too, reaching the million-dollar mark by 1933; they would eventually reach a peak of $1,460,287 in 1937.[62]

In some respects, the city's initial approach to this crisis marked a sharp break with the past. To be sure, it did attempt to reduce ordinary expenditures, cutting civic salaries by 10 per cent in 1931 and encouraging the school boards, the public library and the Regina General Hospital to follow suit. But the city also initiated a series of public works relief projects in an effort to provide gainful employment for Regina's jobless men. The first job-creation scheme was a modest one: extending sewer and water lines during the winter of 1929-30. Others, more ambitious in scope, were partly financed by the provincial and federal governments in 1930 and 1931. In total, the three levels of government spent $1,907,545 on unemployment relief

As the Progressive tide swept across the west in Canada's first postwar federal election, William Richard Motherwell held the Regina seat for the Liberal party. Regina was one of only two seats the Liberals would win on the prairies in 1921.

projects in Regina.[63] The federal and provincial governments each assumed one-quarter of the cost of approved public works projects; the city was responsible for the balance.

The widening of the Albert Street Bridge alone provided employment for more than 700 men. Others were put to work deepening Wascana Lake by two feet and creating two artificial islands with the fill, and constructing a new building on the Exhibition Grounds to house the World Grain Exhibition and Conference. Extensions and improvements to Regina's waterworks system were another part of the legacy of this federal-provincial-municipal job-creation scheme. The city also proceeded on its own to construct a new police station on Market Square, and the CPR built a railway underpass at Winnipeg Street and a large addition to Union Station.

In time the city found it increasingly difficult to proceed with additional projects of this kind. After 1931 the senior governments were no longer willing to share the cost, and the deteriorating condition of the city treasury precluded independent action. The fact that work relief projects could be financed by long-term borrowing had initially made them attractive, but with Regina holding over $1,000,000 in unsold debentures by 1931 this was no longer the case. And the numbers requiring assistance continued to grow; by October 1932 nearly 20 per cent of the population of Regina was on relief.[64] Thus, from 1932 on the city was obliged to resort almost entirely to direct relief, the "dole."

The city had initially distributed relief itself but in September 1931 turned the work over to a private body, the Civic Relief Board. Grocery relief was based on an allowance of eighteen dollars per month (subsequently reduced to sixteen in 1932) for a family of four. There were other vouchers covering rent and fuel, and relief recipients were required to promise to repay the amount of their debt to the city. No provision was made for clothing, though the *Leader-Post* had established a Community Clothing Depot in 1929 that collected and distributed used clothing. That work had in turn been taken over by another new relief agency established in 1931, the Regina Welfare Bureau. Loosely modelled on the earlier Bureau of Public Welfare, its objective was essentially similar: to coordinate the work of the various private charitable organizations then engaged in relief work in the city.[65]

The cost of providing even this minimal assistance soon dwarfed the sums that had been expended on job-creation projects. In 1929, 1930 and 1931 a total of $543,505 had been spent on direct relief. Expenditures in 1932 alone added another $621,150, and by 1935 the accumulated cost of direct relief in Regina stood at $4,754,216. The senior governments assumed two-thirds of the cost of direct relief, but it should not be assumed that direct relief imposed a less severe burden on the city. The provincial and federal governments limited their contribution to the actual relief payments; the city was responsible for all of the associated administrative expenses and for the cost of providing medical care to those who were on its relief rolls. As a result, Regina was actually funding close to half of all relief expenditures. Until 1931 it met its share entirely out of current revenues, but in succeeding years it capitalized half or more of the cost of direct relief rather than add to the already heavy burden on municipal taxpayers.[66]

The distribution of relief in Regina did not long escape criticism. The Independent Labour Party (ILP), founded in 1929 to represent labour's interests, helped to mobilize the discontent. Labour aldermen — there were three by 1932 — criticized the food allowance as "entirely inadequate" and demanded that relief be paid in cash.[67] Organizations representing the unemployed also began to appear, the first in 1930. Communists dominated some and were active in most, and their tactics were more dramatic than those of the Fabian socialists in the ILP. In November 1930 the Canadian Unemployed Workers' Association attempted to have the city relief officer dismissed on account of his "discourteous and autocratic manner," but a civic inquiry exonerated him. Two years later the Regina Unemployed Workers' Council staged a "relief strike" over the city's practice of paying only one-quarter of the wages due to relief recipients employed on public works projects in cash. The Civic Relief Board intended that the remainder be provided in the form of direct relief, but when most of the men quit work in protest, the board agreed to pay the entire amount in cash. Communists also sponsored a May Day rally in 1931 which

For the first twenty years only Liberals represented Regina in the provincial legislature. Conservative Murdoch Alexander Mac-Pherson, a popular local lawyer, ended all that in 1925. He won again in 1929 and served as attorney-general in J.T.M. Anderson's Co-operative Government.

Charles Avery Dunning left the Saskatchewan premiership in 1926 for federal politics. (Some touted him as the heir apparent to William Lyon Mackenzie King, whose political star seemed to be in eclipse.) A safe seat was found for Dunning in Regina, but it did not prove safe enough. King's minister of finance was swept away by the Tory tide in 1930.

The new CCF held its first national convention in Regina, and approved a political charter which became popularly known as the "Regina Manifesto."

drew 8,000 people to Market Square (it ended in violence when some onlookers took objection to the presence of their red flag), and nominated a mayoralty candidate, Herbert Court, to contest the civic election that fall.[68]

Civic Political Parties in Regina, 1929-1939

Name	Elections Contested
Independent Labour Party	1929-1930
Co-operative Labour Party	1931-1933
Civic Government Association	1932-1934
Civic Labour League	1934-1936
Regina Home Owners' and Taxpayers' Association	1936-1937
Civic Labour Association	1936-1937
Civic Voters Association	1939

These stirrings on the left galvanized Regina's business community into action, as they had in 1918. The result was the formation of the Civic Government Association (CGA) in November 1932. Modelled on a similar body in Calgary, it purported to be concerned only with encouraging greater citizen involvement in local politics. One of its candidates came closer to the truth when he warned darkly that "the Independent Labor party had brought politics into the council chamber and this minority would be successful at the next elections unless the majority organized."[69] With 40 per cent of Regina's tax levy committed to interest and sinking fund payments, and with relief costs soaring, the CGA also called for financial retrenchment. It proved to be a potent appeal, for three of the CGA aldermanic candidates were elected in 1932. (One was Helena Walker, the first woman to be elected to city council.) The CGA was as good as its word, initiating a wide-ranging review of the city administration that resulted in further salary cuts and the merging of some civic departments.[70]

The CGA did not endorse a candidate for the mayoralty in 1932. There was no reason to, for the city's highest elected office appeared to be in safe hands during the early Depression years.

To be sure, James McAra had fallen victim in 1930 to "the desire for new blood and the dissatisfaction felt with governing bodies generally."[71] But his successor, James Balfour, was as solid and substantial a representative of Regina's business and professional elite. And McAra regained the mayoralty easily in 1931. The 1932 contest proved to be much closer; he squeaked past his nearest rival by a mere nineteen votes. The man who nearly defeated McAra in 1932 was Cornelius Rink. Long absent from city hall, save for one term as an alderman in the mid-1920s, Rink had burst upon the political stage again with the onset of the Depression. Claiming to be "an independent candidate for the poor people," Rink won a seat on council in 1931. His mayoralty campaign a year later contained more of the same populist rhetoric and a promise to give the city honest and economical government.[72]

Rink did unseat McAra in 1933. He was aided by the fact that there were no less than four "business" candidates seeking the mayoralty. Indeed the CGA clumsily sought to narrow the field, but none would agree to withdraw. As it turned out, these four divided the vote in the downtown, the West End and Lakeview among them, while Rink piled up large majorities in the traditional working-class areas to the east and north. The CGA did manage to win four of the six available aldermanic seats; one of its successful candidates was Ralph Heseltine, long active in the RTLC, who was deemed a representative of "sane Labor." The other two seats were won by the Co-operative Labour Party.[73]

Cornelius Rink's first term as mayor was a stormy one. His quest for economy brought him into conflict with the Exhibition Board over the city's guarantee of the $120,000 loss it had suffered in hosting the World Grain Exhibition and Conference. His efforts to reduce costs at the Regina General Hospital precipitated a wrangle with another independent board determined to preserve its autonomy.[74] The controversy over the distribution of clothing to families on relief also came to a head in 1934, with the Labour aldermen and the unemployed organizations demanding that the Community Clothing Depot be abolished and an "open voucher" system be implemented. (Such vouchers would be redeemable at any retail outlet in the city.) Rink also favoured the change, and in August instructed the Civic Relief Board to begin issuing vouchers for clothing upon the recommendation of the Welfare Bureau investigators. The bureau refused to cooperate, and Rink was obliged to back down. The Community Clothing Depot continued to function, and relief continued to be provided in kind.[75]

The mayor blamed his lack of real accomplishments on a hostile business-dominated council, and in 1934 he urged Reginans to elect a council more in sympathy with his own views. In this he was only partly successful. He won a second term, by a substantially reduced margin, but only two Labour aldermen were elected. One was a newcomer to civic politics, Clarence Fines. A school teacher (principal of Albert School) and like M. J. Coldwell an early participant in the Sunday-afternoon sessions of the Regina People's Forum, Fines was also to enjoy a long and successful career in municipal and later provincial politics.[76] The other three council seats went to the CGA.

Reginans also decided in 1934 to divide the city into wards for subsequent civic elections. Interest in the ward system had waned after the First World War, but revived in the early 1930s. Residents of the North Side were its most enthusiastic proponents. It was they who took the lead in pressing city council to put the matter to a vote. The ratepayers' organizations added their support, and by a margin of 6,204 to 4,191 Reginans endorsed the creation of five wards with two aldermen to be elected in each.[77]

Rink's relationship with the new council initially appeared to be more harmonious. In March, for instance, council agreed to substitute cash payments for the food vouchers issued by the Civic Relief Board. Then the mayor's political stock began to decline, particularly among the unemployed. There were two relief strikes, in March and October, to protest the introduction of "credit work." Under this scheme men were put to work on city projects but received no pay; their wages were simply credited against their entitlement to relief. Even the Labour aldermen joined in the chorus of objections to what was termed "slave labor."[78]

A much more celebrated incident occurred on July 1, 1935. Determined to publicize the plight of single unemployed men then languishing in federal camps in British Columbia, the Communist-dominated Relief Camps Workers' Union organized the On-to-Ottawa Trek. A thousand men left Vancouver early in June with the intention of taking their grievances directly to Prime Minister R. B. Bennett. Their numbers grew to 1,400 by the time the federal authorities ordered the trek halted in Regina on June 14. Mayor Rink was at least initially hostile to the trekkers, declaring on June 4 that "they had better keep away from here if they figure the city is going to feed them and look after them while they are here."[79] In fact he kept a low profile while the trekkers were in Regina. Other residents of the Saskatchewan capital showed a good deal more sympathy for these men. The Citizens' Emergency Committee was organized. It eventually included the Local Council of Women, the Ministerial Association, the RTLC and a variety of organizations representing the unemployed, as well as local branches of the Co-operative Commonwealth Federation, the Canadian Labour Defence League and the Ukrainian Labour Farmer Temple Association. They proved remarkably successful in raising funds. A tag day on June 15 raised $1,146, the largest sum any community would contribute during the trek. The trekkers themselves were housed and fed at the Exhibition Grounds for two weeks without incident while their leaders went on to Ottawa. R. B. Bennett rejected their demands and the delegation returned to Regina, but the trek did not end peacefully. On July 1 a combined force of RCMP and city police attempted to arrest the trek leaders while they were addressing a rally at Market Square. This touched off a riot in which a city police detective was killed and scores of policemen, trekkers and citizens were injured.[80]

Six months later a major political upset occurred in Regina. Alban C. Ellison, a popular English-born lawyer, war veteran and Labour alderman (since 1932), easily defeated Cornelius Rink, and Labour won half the aldermanic seats as well. Whether the Regina Riot was a significant factor in the election of the city's first Labour council is difficult to ascertain. It is worth noting that Ellison had been active in the Citizens' Emergency Committee, and so had Peter Mikkelson, T. G. McManus and John Toothill, three of the Labour aldermen elected in 1935.

Regina Collegiate Institute girls' hockey team, 1915.

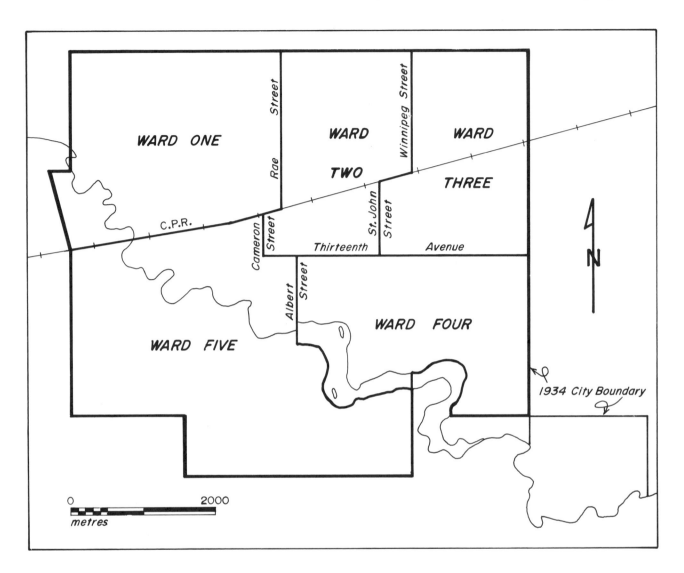

7 Regina Wards, 1935-36: Regina adopted the ward system for the 1935 and 1936 municipal elections. The ward boundaries again roughly conformed to the existing class and ethnic divisions within the city. This contributed to Labour's political success (though it was not the decisive factor, for Labour's hold on City Hall actually grew stronger in 1937 and 1938).

Still, other factors were probably more important. Labour was better organized than its perennial rival, the CGA, which inexplicably decided to disband with the advent of the ward system.[81] Labour also boasted an attractive candidate for the mayoralty in Ellison, and its call for reform of the relief system, restoration of the cuts in civic salaries, and the inauguration of a "work and wages" program and a housing rehabilitation scheme contrasted sharply with Rink's folksy appeal to preserve the status quo. "Don't throw away your old shoes," he told one audience. "Hang onto them and you'll be comfortable."[82] In 1935 Reginans ignored Rink and voted for change.

The reappearance of the ward system also benefited Labour, since the ward boundaries again roughly conformed to the existing class and ethnic divisions within the city (see Map 7). This enabled the Civic Labour League (CLL) to concentrate its efforts in those neighbourhoods where it had traditionally done well. The CLL made a clean sweep in Wards One and Three, and elected a fifth alderman in Ward Four. The same pattern was repeated in the mayoralty vote, with Ellison winning Wards One, Three and Four handily. Rink obtained a majority (and a slim one at that) in Ward Two, and Charles Dixon, a traditional "business" candidate, carried Ward Five.

"The common people have spoken with a mighty voice," declared a triumphant John Toothill when the ballots had been counted, "the banks and bondholders across Canada will tremble in their shoes tonight."[83] The prediction proved to be premature. Indeed Labour briefly lost control of city council early in 1936. The right of two of the newly elected aldermen to sit on council was challenged in the courts on the grounds that the City Act prohibited any person who was indebted to the city from holding municipal office. Peter Mikkelson and T. G. McManus were on relief and of course had been required to sign notes promising to repay. Before the court could render a verdict, Labour attempted to establish the principle that the acceptance of relief did not constitute a debt to the city, but to no avail. Mikkelson and McManus were duly convicted and unseated. By-elections followed, and two new Labour aldermen were elected in their place in May 1936. (One of the newcomers was the celebrated Reverend Samuel B. East, who in 1935 had

attempted to lead a convoy of trekkers out of Regina in defiance of the RCMP).[84] The right of the city to cancel relief debts was also successfully challenged in the courts by a new "citizens'" group that appeared early in 1936, the Regina Home Owners' and Taxpayers' Association.[85]

Labour did manage to reform the relief system in other ways. It abolished the Civic Relief Board, establishing a committee of council to carry out the work, and initiated a half-yearly cash payment for clothing. There was still a place for voluntary relief agencies after 1936, and they continued to function. The Regina Welfare Bureau coordinated their work and took the lead in initiating an annual joint fund raising campaign. Some $35,000 was raised in the first Community Chest drive in 1935, and it became an enduring institution in the city.[86]

Some of the more radical Labour aldermen also wished to reform civic finances. One, Samuel East, proposed that the city unilaterally reduce the interest paid to its bondholders, but this suggestion was criticized even by some of his Labour colleagues. Careful financial management actually permitted a modest reduction in the mill rate, which had risen to 51 mills by 1935. Labour was helped, too, by the fact that in 1936 the city's share of the cost of actual relief payments fell to 20 per cent (and would remain at that level for the remainder of the Depression) thanks to a more generous schedule of federal relief payments to the provinces.[87]

Ellison himself was no radical, but a man of moderate socialist views whose first priority was to administer the affairs of the city in a businesslike fashion. Alleging that Communists were seeking to gain control of the CLL, Ellison publicly eschewed Labour's support in 1936 and sought re-election as an independent.[88] He won handily over the CLL's own candidate and the peripatetic Cornelius Rink, who ran under the Homeowners' Association banner. Homeowners' candidates were successful in Wards Two, Four and Five, so that overall the balance of political forces at city hall remained unchanged. With city council evenly split, Mayor Ellison would again hold the deciding vote.

In 1936 Reginans also decided by a narrow margin to return to the at-large system of electing aldermen. An assault on the

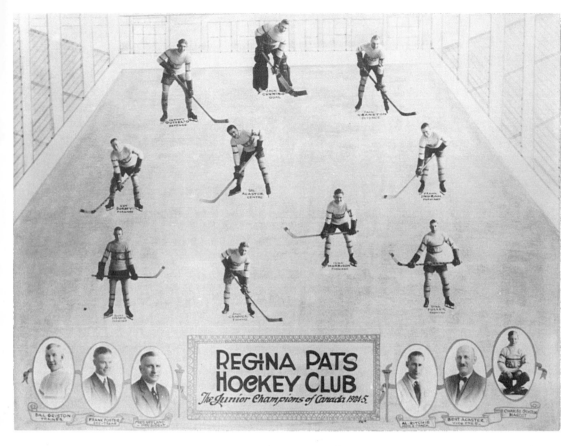

Coached by Alvin Horace (Al) Ritchie, the Regina Pats won the Memorial Cup in 1925 and again in 1930.

The Regina Little Theatre was founded in 1926. It continues to flourish, providing an outlet for the artistic talents of local performers.

ward system had begun almost as soon as the ballots had been counted the previous year. Indeed the "business" majority on the 1935 council had taken the first steps to repeal the ward by-law during its last weeks in office. The Homeowners' Association also took dead aim at the ward system, circulating a petition calling for a vote and forcing the issue before the electors. As might have been expected, sizeable majorities in favour of retaining the ward system were recorded in Wards One and Three, but Wards Two and Four narrowly rejected it and Ward Five overwhelmingly so (see Map 7).[89]

As it turned out, the abolition of the ward system had no real impact on Labour's electoral fortunes. The rift in Labour's ranks was repaired, with Ellison again accepting its official endorsation in 1937. He beat the Homeowners' candidate, former mayor Henry Black, by more than 8,000 votes. Labour gained another seat on council as well. In 1938 the Homeowners' Association, like the Civic Government Association before it, became moribund.[90] Ellison won by acclamation, and Labour also added to its majority on council, emerging from the 1938 civic election with eight of the ten seats.

Prudent fiscal management remained the hallmark of the Labour councils that governed Regina until the end of the decade. The tax rate was held at the 1936 level, and there were modest reductions in the city's debenture debt. That debt had reached a Depression-era peak of $16,870,225 in 1936; by 1939 it stood at $15,875,283. Although the number of Reginans on relief fell by roughly half between 1936 and 1939 (from 11,220 to 6,664), relief remained a serious financial burden for the city. Indeed, Regina reached something of a milestone in 1939, when the cost of direct relief surpassed $10,00,000. Even with the provincial and federal governments absorbing a larger share, civic expenditures on direct relief were substantial during the late 1930s, totalling $1,600,455. This brought Regina's share of the cost of direct relief since 1929 to $3,528,090.[91] These commitments were met only by the city continuing to forego almost all routine maintenance of streets and sidewalks and replacement of worn-out equipment, and putting off any reversal of civic wage cuts.

In 1935 Labour had promised to relieve the plight of the unemployed by providing them with jobs instead of the dole, but this pledge proved almost impossible to implement. The condition of the civic treasury dictated that a home rehabilitation scheme could not be initiated without a $400,000 federal loan, which the city was prepared to guarantee but which Ottawa declined to provide. A second appeal for financial aid (this time for either a loan or a federal guarantee of municipal debentures) to enable the city itself to construct new houses met a similar fate. Mayor Ellison then attempted to obtain a special city charter for Regina in order to give it wider powers of taxation, but the province rejected this proposal out of hand. The city did derive some benefit from two job-creation schemes the federal government introduced in 1938 and 1939. It was able to make some much-needed improvements to the power plant and to initiate a modest "work and wages" program, putting some unemployed Reginans to work gravelling streets, planting trees and laying sewer and water lines. The federal government for its part constructed a new terminal building at the airport, and this too provided some employment.[92]

Labour's political fortunes shifted dramatically in 1939. Again, as in 1936, there were accusations of undue Communist influence in the selection of the Labour slate. The accusations were well publicized by those who were opposed to Labour's continued dominance at city hall, and the fact that Canada was now at war meant that the issue could easily be linked to patriotism. "Does any rational, right-thinking Reginan want Communist influence asserting itself in Regina municipal affairs," the *Leader-Post* demanded, "particularly at a time like this, with a war on and Canada and the empire ... fighting for their very life?" The forces opposed to Labour were also better organized in 1939, having founded yet another non-partisan "citizens'" group, the Civic Voters' Association. Like its predecessors, the CVA was opposed to "class government," and in 1939 this message could be couched in patriotic rhetoric.[93] The result was a resounding defeat for Labour. Ellison lost to the CVA nominee, James Grassick, in the mayoralty contest, and all of the Labour aldermen who sought re-election also went down to defeat. Labour's brief hold on city hall had been broken, permanently as it would turn out.

In provincial and federal politics Regina was for most of this period solidly Liberal, although the party's hold did occasionally falter. The first break with tradition came in 1917, when the city elected W. D. Cowan, a supporter of the Union Government that was pledged to introduce conscription. Cowan himself was a Conservative, but he enjoyed the support of the provincial Liberal "machine" that had swung behind the Union Government and won handily. The alliance did not survive the end of hostilities in Europe, and Regina returned to the Liberal fold in the first postwar federal election. In this Regina proved to be something of an anomaly, for it was the only riding in Saskatchewan to elect a Liberal in 1921. Elsewhere in the province a new farmers' party known as the Progressive Party swept all before it, but in Regina W. R. Motherwell (himself long prominent in the farmers' movement but still an avowed Liberal) triumphed over his Conservative and Progressive rivals. The Progressives trailed the field again in 1925, and in 1926 they did not even put up a candidate.

In the mid-1920s the political pendulum began to swing with the revival of the Conservative party. The Conservatives captured one of the two Regina seats in 1925 and both in 1929, when the Liberal government that had ruled the province for a quarter century was finally defeated. Much has been made of the contribution of the Ku Klux Klan to the Conservatives' revival, but this is not a wholly satisfactory explanation for the party's success in Regina. M. A. MacPherson, who served as attorney-general in J. T. M. Anderson's short-lived Co-operative government, first won his seat in 1925, a year before the Klan appeared. Of course, it cannot be disputed that some Conservative elements, and particularly the *Regina Daily Star* (founded in 1928 with R. B. Bennett's money), did seek to profit from the Klan's gospel of racial and religious bigotry. But MacPherson and his running mate in 1929, James Grassick, were both popular in the city. There were also other issues in 1929. The Conservatives played up the excesses of the ruthless Liberal "machine" and pledged to reform the civil service if they were elected.

The momentum remained with the Conservatives into the Depression; in 1930 they captured the Regina federal seat from Charles Dunning, the minister of finance in William Lyon Mackenzie King's government. Yet the shift to the Conservatives proved to be short-lived. The Liberals won both city seats (and the provincial election) in 1934, and in 1935 they recaptured the federal riding, now wholly urban in composition for the first time.[94]

The Depression years also witnessed the emergence of a loose alliance of farm and labour political movements in Saskatchewan. Representatives of the Independent Labour Party, founded in Regina in 1929, met with the United Farmers of Canada (Saskatchewan Section) in Saskatoon in July 1932 and founded the Saskatchewan Farmer-Labour Party. M. J. Coldwell, a Regina alderman and leader of the ILP since its inception, became the leader of the new party. Later that summer it joined with other farm groups and a variety of labour and socialist parties to form the Co-operative Commonwealth Federation. The CCF held its first national convention in Regina in 1933 and approved a political charter that at once became popularly known as the "Regina Manifesto," but the city did not prove to be very receptive to the new party. Even the discredited Conservatives polled more votes there in the 1934 provincial election than M. J. Coldwell and Garnet Menzies, the two CCF candidates. In the federal election a year later the CCF fared no better, again finishing a distant third.

Disappointed with its poor showing across the province (the party had won only five seats in the provincial election, two in the federal), the CCF adopted a more moderate platform in 1936. It also sought to cooperate with the Conservatives, Social Credit and the Communists to avoid splitting the anti-Liberal vote. In the end no province-wide agreement could be reached with any of these parties, but there was considerable support for cooperation at the local level. Such was the case in Regina, where a union of "progressive" forces seemed on the verge of materializing until first the CCF and then Social Credit withdrew on the eve of the 1938 provincial election. Nine candidates eventually entered the fray. In addition to the two "unity" candidates (Alderman Samuel East and T. G. McManus), there were two Independent Labour men, a Social Crediter, two Conservatives and two Liberals. Again, as in 1934, it was the Liberals who headed the field, followed by the two Conservatives and Mayor A. C. Ellison, who ran under the Independent Labour banner.[95] Thus, Regina and Saskatchewan were both still solidly Liberal as the Depression decade drew to a close.

After 1914 Regina's social and cultural life continued to follow the patterns laid down in the earlier boom years. But there were also some significant changes as the city, like the nation as a whole, adopted a more North American (and less British) outlook. One manifestation of this new orientation occurred in 1917 with the founding of a local branch of the Rotary Club. Other American service clubs — the Kiwanis, Gyro, Lions and Kinsmen — were also represented in the city by the end of the 1930s. All stressed community service, and over the years they made important contributions to Regina in the form of parks, playgrounds, athletic facilities and annual music festivals. Reginans also flocked to local movie houses to see the latest Hollywood features and danced the fox trot at the Trianon Dance Palace or the Hotel Saskatchewan. The Capitol Theatre was the largest and most ornate of the city's "movie palaces." Constructed at the end of the vaudeville era, it was designed to permit both live performances and the showing of moving pictures and was part of the Famous Players chain.

Radio also brought postwar American popular culture to this prairie city. American stations dominated the airwaves, but local interests were also quick to see the potential of the new medium. The *Morning Leader* established the first local station, CKCK, in 1922; ironically the station's first program began with a rendition of "Rule Britannia." The R. H. Williams department store was not far behind; its station CHWC went on the air in 1925. Both carried popular American shows, but they also provided a wider audience for local musicians and musical groups. This helped to extend Regina's cultural influence more widely across southern Saskatchewan. Radio station CKCK also broadcast Sunday services from Regina churches and a regular Wheat Pool news program (beginning in 1923 and 1927 respectively). It also pioneered the broadcasting of hockey games on March 14, 1923, with L. D. "Pete" Parker calling the play-by-play from Exhibition Stadium. Foster Hewitt would accomplish the same feat nine days later in Toronto.[96]

Hockey continued to enjoy a wide following, although not wide enough to support a professional team for very long. Regina sportsman Wesley Champ obtained a franchise in the Western Canada Hockey League in 1921, but his Regina Capitals lasted only four seasons. The entire league disappeared shortly afterward, its best players sold to the rival National Hockey League, which had begun to expand into the lucrative American market. It was the amateur teams that brought glory to Regina. The senior Vics were the first city team to win a national championship, capturing the Allan Cup in 1914. When the professionals arrived after the war, senior hockey languished and despite a brief resurgence during the 1930s never really flourished again. But junior hockey, born at the end of the First World War, certainly did. The Regina Pats (founded in 1917 and named for the Princess Patricia's Canadian Light Infantry) won the Canadian junior hockey championship twice, in 1925 and 1930. Another team, the Regina Monarchs, won the Memorial Cup in 1928. These years also witnessed a greater degree of participation at the lower age levels, particularly after the Parks Hockey League was established in 1930. With the city providing the outdoor rinks, literally thousands of boys participated in this winter sport during the more than four decades of the league's existence.

Professional baseball also returned to Regina after the war but lasted only two years. "Commercial" leagues — with teams sponsored by local businesses — continued to thrive, however, and the semi-professional Regina Balmorals and Nationals compiled an impressive string of provincial championships in the 1920s and 1930s. (Swede Risberg and Hap Felsch, two members of the Chicago Black Sox who were banned from professional baseball in the United States for throwing the 1919 World Series, played for the Balmorals in 1926 and 1927.)

In the autumn, football reigned supreme in Regina. The city's senior team, known after 1924 as the Regina Roughriders, went from strength to strength while rivals in Moose Jaw and Saskatoon floundered and eventually withdrew from league play. The Roughriders managed to win the western championship fourteen times between 1914 and 1936. Playing first at

Regina College enriched the city's cultural life in many ways. Its Music and Art Building (right), built in 1929, was a gift from local businessman Frank Darke.

Dominion Park and then at Park Hughes and Park de Young (both near the Exhibition Grounds), the team drew 1,000 fans or more to its games, and 5,000 for a playoff match against arch-rival Winnipeg in 1934. Although defeated in all seven Grey Cup games, the Roughriders won respect for western football, introducing the forward pass in 1929 and scoring the West's first Grey Cup touchdown in 1930. The city's junior teams were more successful in national competition, winning twice during these years, in 1928 and 1938.

The common denominator in many of Regina's sporting accomplishments during these years was Alvin Horace Ritchie. "Al" Ritchie, who had come to Regina from Ontario in 1911, played baseball, lacrosse and football. When war came, he enlisted in the artillery, and returned to the city in 1919. A full-time employee of the federal Department of Customs and Excise, Ritchie devoted most of his spare time to coaching and managing local baseball, hockey and football teams. In the process Al Ritchie became the best-known sports figure in Regina, and certainly the most colourful (his coonskin coat and seemingly endless supply of cigars became legendary). His teams won two Memorial Cups and a national junior football championship, but the Grey Cup eluded him.[97]

Music and drama flourished as well, even in the depths of the Depression. The Regina Little Theatre was founded in 1926 and played host to the first Saskatchewan drama festival in 1933. The CPR enriched the city's musical life, staging the Great West Canadian Folksong, Folkdance and Handicrafts Festival and sponsoring a series of concerts in its hotels in the 1920s and 1930s that brought gifted British and Canadian artists to Regina. Others performed there as part of the Celebrity Concert Series, organized by Winnipeg impresario Fred M. Gee, which toured the prairies from 1934 on. Local initiative also continued to be important. Frank Laubach, long the central figure in Regina's musical community, retired in 1922, but two other men soon took his place. One was W. Knight Wilson, an accomplished violinist, who began a thirty-two-year career as conductor of the Regina Symphony Orchestra in 1923. The second was Dan Cameron. He arrived in the city that same year as head of the voice department at Regina College, and in 1939 he became director of its Conservatory of Music. He also conducted the Regina Male Voice Choir and the choir at Knox Presbyterian Church and wrote a regular music column in the *Leader-Post* until 1963.

Regina College, which became a junior college affiliated with the University of Saskatchewan in 1925, made other contributions to the city's cultural life. Its Music and Art Building, erected at the end of the decade through the generosity of local businessman Frank Darke, provided talented Reginans and touring groups with another fine facility in which to perform. The college also early added courses in art to its curriculum, inviting Inglis Sheldon-Williams, an accomplished Engish painter, to join the faculty in 1916. Despite the generous patronage and encouragement of Norman Mackenzie, a Regina lawyer and art collector, Sheldon-Williams left the College and the city within a year, but art instruction reappeared under the direction of the Conservatory of Music in the 1920s.

The Regina Local Council of Women took some important initiatives during the decade. Its Arts and Letters Committee, founded in 1920, sponsored annual exhibitions and began to purchase works by Canadian and Saskatchewan artists in the hope that these would form the nucleus of a future art gallery in the city.

Regina College also had ambitions to offer a full university program in arts. Nothing came of this in the 1920s, but Principal E. W. Stapleford approached the University of Saskatchewan again in 1930. In the end it was the Depression that decided the issue, for the college soon found itself in serious financial difficulties. In 1934 the University of Saskatchewan took it over, and the Carnegie Corporation provided a grant to pay off Regina College's indebtedness. As part of the agreement with the United Church, the university agreed to continue the emphasis in music and art which had been part of the college's program almost from its inception. A full-fledged School of Art was in fact established there in 1936 under the direction of Gus Kenderdine. The establishment of the school fulfilled part of the dream of Norman Mackenzie, who earlier that year had bequeathed his large collection to the University of Saskatchewan to help further the study and appreciation of art in the city.[98]

The Mackenzie bequest and the creation of the Regina College School of Art were both important initiatives in the artistic field, but it would take the return of prosperity for their impact to become fully apparent.

Looking at the period 1914-39, one cannot help focusing on the bust-boom-bust cycle of the wheat economy and the magnitude of Regina's economic and social difficulties, especially in the 1930s. The vagaries of the wheat economy and the problems left in their wake were the the dominant factors in the city's life during these years, overshadowing all else. Everything in Regina — even modest initiatives that would one day enrich its artistic and cultural life — depended upon the condition of the crop and the price of wheat.

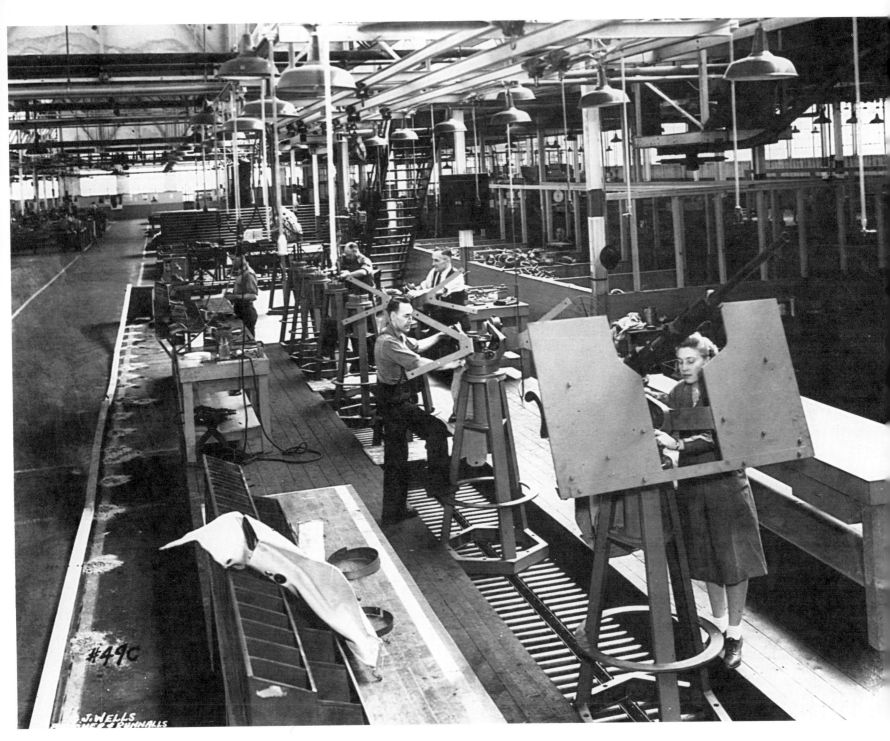

Regina Industries Limited, as the General Motors assembly plant was renamed, was Saskatchewan's largest munitions plant during the Second World War. At the peak of wartime production 1,596 men and women worked there.

Chapter Four
Floreat Regina,
1939-79

The worst of the Depression was over in Saskatchewan by 1939, and in the four decades that followed, Regina did indeed flourish. Farm prices rose sharply during the Second World War, the crops were good (indeed, that of 1942 was of near-record proportions) and prosperity returned. There were still 5,559 Reginans on relief at the beginning of 1941, but only 2,494 a year later. Buoyant revenues permitted the restoration of civic and school board salaries to their pre-Depression levels. Regina was also able to substantially reduce its outstanding debenture debt, emerging from the war in a much sounder financial position.[1] There was no postwar slump as there had been following the conflict of 1914-18, and Regina grew steadily if unspectacularly after 1945. Its fortunes remained tied to the value and yield of the annual harvest, but less so than in earlier periods thanks to extensive oil and potash discoveries that made Saskatchewan's economy one of the richest and most diversified in the country by the 1970s. Change also came in other ways. Regina was subjected to the same influences — the proliferation of the automobile, suburban sprawl, the decay of the inner city, heightened racial tensions — which reshaped the North American city in the postwar age. Regina's social and cultural life also increasingly reflected the homogenizing influences which were drawing regions and nations closer together. And yet as the 1970s gave way to the 1980s, Saskatchewan's capital city still retained something of its distinctive character.

ECONOMIC GROWTH AND METROPOLITAN DEVELOPMENT

The key to economic revival lay in rural Saskatchewan, and after 1939 farmers were prosperous again. The pace of farm mechanization accelerated during the Second World War, to the considerable benefit of Regina implement dealers. Retail sales in the province generally increased by 13 per cent during the war years, a growth rate exceeding that for Canada as a whole.[2] In other respects the Second World War had little impact upon the city's economy. The wartime demand for munitions provided Regina with little opportunity to industrialize; almost no orders were placed with local firms in the early stages of the war. While this should not have been surprising given the city's poorly developed industrial capacity, it did nevertheless become a source of grievance that both the Board of Trade and the city and provincial governments sought to have redressed. Some contracts were diverted to local firms, notably to the General Motors plant, which the federal government acquired for the duration of the war. Regina Industries Limited, as it was renamed, became the province's largest munitions plant, providing work for 1,596 men and women at the peak of wartime production in 1943. Yet in the long run this did little to broaden the base of the city's economy, for the plant shut down in 1945 and automobile production was never resumed.[3] Similarly, wartime demand also provided a stimulus to the meat-packing industry — the Burns plant was the second-largest industrial employer in Regina during the Second World War — but after 1945 the perennial problem of excess capacity returned to plague this and other meat-packing plants in Saskatchewan. Burns finally decided to close its Regina plant in 1973. Intercontinental Packers, which opened a plant in Regina after the war, sharply reduced the scale of its operations in 1976 and subsequently left the city as well.[4]

Agriculture continued to prosper after the war. Crops were generally good, and the opening of new markets for wheat in the People's Republic of China and the Soviet Union proved a godsend for country farmer and city merchant alike. Although

Reginans celebrate victory in Europe with a parade down Eleventh Avenue, May 8, 1945.

farm income continued to fluctuate year by year in response to changes in commodity prices, it remained consistently higher than during the Second World War (Appendix, Table XIII).Yet farm operating costs continued to rise steadily as well, so that while Saskatchewan agriculture flourished for most of this postwar period, farmers were not always as well off as the level of agricultural prices might have suggested.[5]

Since the war, Regina's historic role as the chief market and supply centre for southern Saskatchewan has been altered to some extent as a result of the structural changes that have occurred in agriculture. To make the most efficient use of larger tractors and combines and to support the larger capital costs that their purchase entailed, farmers acquired more land. In 1941 the average farm in Saskatchewan comprised 432 acres; over the succeeding thirty years it nearly doubled in size, to 845 acres. At the same time the number of farms fell sharply. Between 1941 and 1971 more than 61,000 farms disappeared in Saskatchewan. The trend to fewer but larger farms (76,970 by 1971) accelerated an exodus from the land that had actually first begun to manifest itself in the 1930s. It became much more pronounced during and after the Second World War. Between 1941 and 1951 the population of Saskatchewan dropped from 895,992 to 831,728, a decline of 7.2 per cent. During the same period the rural farm population fell from 513,279 to 398,279, a decline of 22.4 per cent. After 1951 the population of the province again began to increase, but its rural population continued to fall, to 44.5 per cent by 1976 (and the rural farm population to 20.9 per cent).[6]

Not only did the size of Regina's regional market begin to shrink somewhat in the 1950s and 1960s, but smaller cities in southern Saskatchewan began to assume some of the retail functions (in the general merchandizing and clothing sectors especially) that Regina had once largely monopolized within its trading area. But even so, the city's share of total provincial retail sales continued to increase as population growth within Regina created a larger internal market. In the immediate postwar period, 1951-61, Regina accounted for 18 per cent of retail sales in the province. Its share increased to 20 per cent in 1966 and 24 per cent in 1976. Wholesale trade in Regina, on the other hand, remained strongly oriented towards agriculture. This was reflected in the nature of wholesale activity in the city. In 1961, for example, the provision of food and groceries (22.6 per cent), machinery, equipment and supplies (25 per cent), petroleum and petroleum products (18.6 per cent), and lumber and building materials (9.1 per cent) together accounted for three-quarters of wholesale sales in Regina.[7]

Regina also retained and indeed enhanced its paramount role as a centre for financial services for the province. Long the headquarters of the major chartered banks operating in Saskatchewan, Regina also assumed a central place in the network of credit unions that served the province. First established in the 1930s, credit unions by 1978 claimed more than half of the population of the province as members and assets of $2 billion. Regina's Sherwood Credit Union, one of the first to appear, has also been the largest since 1946. In Regina, too, was located the credit unions' central bank, the Saskatchewan Co-operative Credit Society, founded in 1941. Four Regina-based insurance firms also appeared. One was a provincial crown corporation, the Saskatchewan Government Insurance Office. Originally created in 1944 to compete with private firms in the field of general insurance, it was in 1946 given the added responsibility of administering the compulsory automobile insurance scheme that Saskatchewan pioneered. The others were private ventures. Co-operative Life was founded in 1945 with the support of a variety of cooperative organizations, including the Saskatchewan Wheat Pool. Co-operative Fire and Casualty appeared four years later (the two were merged to form Co-operative Insurance Services in 1963), and a group of Regina businessmen established Pioneer Life in 1971. Pioneer subsequently added a trust company, but overexpansion and a downturn in the volatile Alberta real-estate market led to its collapse in 1985. Houston Willoughby also expanded its operations, opening a branch in Saskatoon in 1961 and obtaining seats on the Vancouver, Toronto and Alberta Stock Exchanges before merging with a Vancouver-based firm, Pemberton Securities.[8]

Postwar discoveries of oil and potash have had a significant impact on Regina, contributing to a modest diversification of its economy. The petroleum industry in Saskatchewan was still in

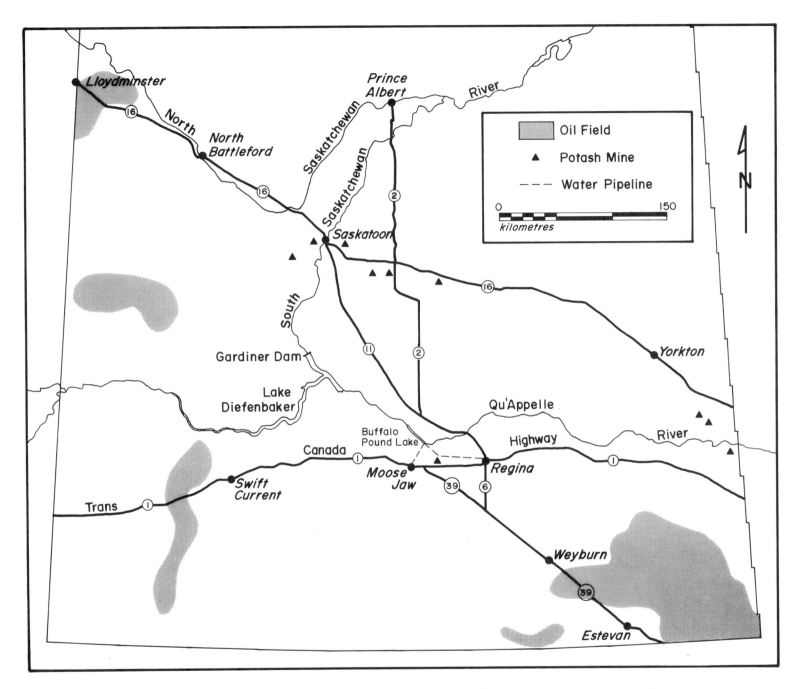

8 Regina's Geographic Position: Regina benefited more than any other Saskatchewan city from the province's oil boom, but far less from potash development. Six of the ten producing potash mines are located within seventy miles of Saskatoon.

its infancy at the beginning of this period, the major oil companies and the smaller "independents" alike having long found Alberta more attractive. Oil and natural gas had been discovered in the Lloydminster area in 1934 and at Kamsack in 1937, but not in volumes that justified commercial production. Fewer than twenty oil companies were active in Saskatchewan during the war years. The largest was Imperial Oil, but it abandoned the province in 1946 to concentrate its efforts in Alberta. Within a year it made a major discovery there, at Leduc, and Alberta became even more the darling of the industry. Oil exploration and development did continue in Saskatchewan but on a modest scale. Commercial production began in the Lloydminster field in 1945 (see Map 8). By 1948 there were seventy-seven producing wells, and Saskatchewan had become Canada's second-largest oil-producing province, albeit a very distant second. But the petroleum from the Lloydminster field was thick ("heavy" oil in the parlance of the industry) and thus difficult and expensive to refine.

The political coloration of the provincial government — CCF from 1944 to 1964 — may also have dampened the oil companies' interest in Saskatchewan. The CCF's opponents repeatedly insisted that this was so. Sensitive to these accusations and conscious of the fact that Alberta was surging ahead of Saskatchewan, Premier T. C. Douglas reassured the oil industry in 1948 that the CCF had no wish to expropriate or socialize it. These assurances had the desired effect, and in 1949 the major oil companies returned to the province. Their renewed search for petroleum in Saskatchewan was not immediately successful. It was 1951 before another new field was discovered, but it too contained the least desirable heavy oil. Socony-Vacuum finally found "medium" crude at Fosterton, north of Swift Current, early in 1952.[9]

This proved to be the watershed year for petroleum development in Saskatchewan. Exploration and production doubled each year thereafter, and within five years oil and gas wells outnumbered grain elevators in the province. There were additional discoveries in the west central and southwestern areas of Saskatchewan, chiefly of medium and heavy oil. The most dramatic oil play was in the southeast, where light gravity crude was first discovered in 1952. At the peak of the boom in the Williston Basin, in 1955 and 1956, every third well drilled turned out to be a producer. Proven oil reserves soared from 21 million barrels in 1951 to 675 million barrels in 1957, and daily production reached 100,000 barrels by the latter year. Exploration activity in the province declined after 1957, but oil production continued to rise, to a peak of 93.2 million barrels in 1966. While there were also important discoveries of natural gas during these years, beginning with the Brock field in 1951, proven reserves of gas increased more slowly. Altogether, 2.1 billion barrels of oil and 2.4 trillion cubic feet of natural gas had been discovered in Saskatchewan by 1976. This represented 19 per cent and 3 per cent respectively of oil and gas discoveries in Alberta.[10]

Although Saskatchewan's oil boom failed to match Alberta's either in duration or magnitude, its economic impact was nevertheless considerable. Regina benefited more than any other Saskatchewan city. Located astride the Interprovincial Pipe Line constructed from Edmonton across Saskatchewan and Manitoba to southern Ontario in 1950, Regina's refineries were the first in the province to gain access to oil from Alberta's new fields, and petroleum from fields in western Saskatchewan began to flow through the Interprovincial Pipe Line in 1954. Both Regina refineries increased their capacity and the city became for a time the fifth-largest oil refining centre in Canada, and second only to Edmonton on the prairies. But unfortunately the high sulphur content in much of the light and medium crude oil found in western Saskatchewan made it less attractive than oil from Alberta. In fact, most of the production from fields in western Saskatchewan was shipped to Minnesota, where a refinery specifically designed to process this "sour" crude was constructed. Saskatchewan's most desirable crude oil, light in gravity and low in sulphur, was located mainly in the southeast, downstream from the Regina refineries, and hence it too was processed elsewhere.

Successive expansions increased the capacity of the city's two refineries to 57,500 barrels per day by the early 1970s, but during that decade petroleum refining increasingly came to be centralized in Alberta, and more particularly in Edmonton.

Stock sale at the Canadian Western Agribition. Begun in 1971, the Canadian Western Agribition now ranks with Toronto's Royal Winter Fair as one of the largest livestock exhibitions in Canada. Exhibitors, visitors and buyers come to Regina from around the world.

The Regina-based Saskatchewan Government Insurance Office has strengthened the city's role as a centre for financial services for the province. Originally created to compete with private firms in the general insurance field, this crown corporation has since 1946 also administered the compulsory automobile-insurance scheme which Saskatchewan pioneered.

Smaller, older and less-efficient refineries in other prairie cities were shut down. Imperial Oil closed its Regina facility in 1975 when its 140,000-barrel-per-day refinery in Edmonton came on stream. The Consumers' Co-operative refinery, its capacity expanded to 40,000 barrels per day in 1978, was the only one still operating in Saskatchewan by the end of the decade.

During the 1950s some oil companies, such as Tidewater and Sohio, located offices and staff in the city. But they departed when the oil boom subsided, and today only one firm with substantial interests in the province has its headquarters in Regina: the Saskatchewan Oil and Gas Corporation, a crown corporation founded in 1973. A cement plant and a precast concrete firm were also established near Regina, in part to supply the petroleum industry.[11]

The oil boom's most important legacy was Interprovincial Steel and Pipe Corporation Limited (IPSCO), the largest single manufacturing enterprise in Saskatchewan. It was the demand for pipe that provided the initial stimulus for the development of a steel industry in Regina. In 1956 a group of western businessmen, with Reginan George Solomon prominent among them, founded the Prairie Pipe Manufacturing Company. Regina businessmen raised nearly three-quarters of the equity capital, and the provincial government provided a $900,000 loan. Within a year the new plant north of the city was producing small-diameter pipe for use in natural gas and oil gathering systems and the extensive gas-distribution network that the provincial power utility, the Saskatchewan Power Corporation, was then beginning to construct. Initially Prairie Pipe obtained skelp (the coils of steel plate used for making pipe) from steel firms in Ontario, but in 1958 some of the principals in the company founded the Interprovincial Steel Corporation and began construction of the West's first hot roll sheet and plate manufacturing facility. Again the province provided financial assistance, in the form of a $10,000,000 bond guarantee. The two firms merged in 1959 while construction was still under way, and steel production (using scrap iron as the basic raw material) began in 1960.

IPSCO prospered with the strong demand for pipe. It also drew other industries to the city: a plant to supply the steel

By 1954, Regina had become the fifth largest oil-refining centre in Canada, and was second only to Edmonton on the prairies.

A steelworker at the Interprovincial Steel and Pipe Corporation mill.

Manufacturing tank-trailer units at Westank Industries, 1975.

mill with oxygen; a pipe-coating plant; and a plant that manufactured coating materials. Under the leadership of founding president Bill Sharp and his successor, the flamboyant and somewhat unorthodox Jack Turvey, IPSCO subsequently acquired pipe mills in Alberta and British Columbia. It also expanded its product line to include large-diameter pipe, steel plate and structural steel, and sought out new markets in the agricultural implement manufacturing industry that was beginning to develop across the prairies for instance. (A Regina firm, Degelman Industries, was an early customer.) But despite these limited steps towards diversification, IPSCO's fortunes remained tied to the western Canadian petroleum industry.[12] So, too, were those of Westank Industries, a manufacturer of bulk storage tanks and trailer units that was established in the city in 1969. In this regard, both IPSCO and Westank were typical of the entire industrial sector in Saskatchewan, which remained largely oriented towards local markets. Regina's role as the leading manufacturing centre in Saskatchewan was not seriously challenged, but the proportion of the labour force employed in this sector steadily declined after the Second World War (Appendix, Table XII).[13]

During the 1960s Saskatchewan also became the largest North American producer of potash (used principally as fertilizer) — there were ten producing mines in the province by 1970 (see Map 8) — and this resource also brought jobs and capital investment. But potash bestowed fewer benefits upon Regina than oil did. Only one of the potash firms operating in Saskatchewan, Kalium Chemicals, located its provincial head office in the city (its mine is located at Belle Plaine, twenty-five miles west of Regina). Not even the Potash Corporation of Saskatchewan, a crown corporation established in 1975 which acquired several of the privately owned mines and now accounts for more than half of Saskatchewan's potash production, has its headquarters in the provincial capital. Instead it chose Saskatoon, as did most of its rivals, principally because six of the ten producing mines are located within seventy miles of that city.[14]

Regina did continue to benefit from its status as the provincial capital. The city secured a large part of the administrative expansion associated with the growth of the welfare state during the postwar period. Indeed, Saskatchewan was a pioneer in this field. The CCF government there introduced Canada's first province-wide hospital insurance scheme in 1947 and led the way again in establishing a comprehensive medical care insurance plan fifteen years later. It was also active in other fields, expanding the operations of the provincial telephone and electric power utilities after 1944, introducing the nation's first compulsory automobile insurance scheme, and assuming a greater share of the cost (and administration) of social aid. All of these initiatives led to a considerable expansion in the size of the provincial civil service, one which more than offset the decline in the number of federal government employees in the city after 1951, and pushed Saskatchewan's capital to the front rank among prairie cities in this occupational category (Appendix, Table XII).[15] The construction industry was one of the principal beneficiaries, for the new employees of the province's myriad government departments and crown corporations were accommodated in high-rise office towers that dramatically altered the city skyline.

POPULATION GROWTH AND ETHNIC RELATIONSHIPS

There was little if any increase in Regina's population during the Second World War, but it began to grow again after 1945. The most substantial gains came in the 1950s and early 1960s. Indeed, Regina's rate of population growth during the entire postwar period consistently exceeded that of the province as a whole. Still, Regina did not grow as fast as Saskatoon, with the result that the gap between the two narrowed considerably (Appendix, Tables III, IV).

Immigration contributed little to Regina's population growth, less even than during the interwar period. Most of the newcomers to Canada gravitated to the largest urban centres — Montreal, Toronto and Vancouver — rather than to any Saskatchewan city. The diminished role of immigration in augmenting Regina's population can be seen most clearly in the continuing decline in the proportion of foreign-born in the city.

The postwar "baby boom" sparked a school construction boom. These children were among the first to attend Marion McVeety School in Hillsdale.

Playing baseball during recess at Highland Park School, 1960.

In Regina, as elsewhere, women have been entering the labour force in greater numbers, and working in fields that traditionally were considered a male preserve.

Provincial civil servants joined the ranks of organized labour in 1945. The Saskatchewan Civil Service Association (later the Saskatchewan Government Employees' Association) became the largest single trade union in the city.

Eleventh Avenue looking west from Broad Street, 1943.

Persons born outside of Canada accounted for roughly one-quarter of the city's population in 1941, but by the early 1960s scarcely a tenth could be so classified (Appendix, Table VIII).

Natural increase was a much more significant factor, thanks to the postwar "baby boom." Although the city's birth rate lagged behind Saskatchewan's until 1954, it still increased substantially, from 16.3 per thousand in 1939 to 19.4 per thousand in 1943 and a postwar peak of 29.8 per thousand in 1959. By 1961, 35,000 Reginans (31 per cent of the population) were children aged fourteen and under, born since the end of the Second World War (Appendix, Table X). They filled the city's public and separate schools to overflowing, compelling some schools, on the North Side especially, to operate in double shifts. Neither school board had built a new school in Regina since 1930; now there was a flurry of construction that surpassed anything seen before (twenty-three new elementary schools built in the 1950s and thirty-one in the 1960s). When these children began to reach high-school age, there were new collegiates to accommodate them as well.

In the 1960s the birth rate began to fall again (Regina's stood at 18.5 in 1979, Saskatchewan's at 17.7), but the native-born and more particularly the Saskatchewan-born segments of the population continued to increase. The Saskatchewan-born comprised slightly more than half of Regina's population in 1941. Thirty years later the proportion was closer to three-quarters (Appendix, Table VI). Rural-urban migration within the province also played a significant role in augmenting the population of Regina during these years, and it too contributed to the increasing preponderance of the Saskatchewan-born in the city.[16]

With no fresh influx of newcomers from overseas, the strength and vitality of the city's German, Ukrainian and other ethnic communities began to wane. Ethnic differences became less pronounced as succeeding generations born in Canada abandoned their distinctive language in a determined effort to enter the mainstream of Canadian society. And the charter group, those of British racial origin, no longer felt so threatened by a diversity of languages and cultures in their midst. The result was a greater degree of harmony among Regina's diverse

Scarth Street looking north from Twelfth Avenue at the end of the Second World War. The block in the foreground was closed in 1974 to create a pedestrian mall; another farther north was closed at the end of the decade to permit construction of the Cornwall Centre.

Victoria Park and Scarth Street looking north in the late 1940s. Trees planted thirty years earlier now provide shade on a hot summer day.

At the beginning of this period retail trade was still concentrated in the downtown core, particularly along Eleventh Avenue. This is Simpson's department store. (The national chain purchased it from the Williams family in 1946.)

ethnic groups.

The experience of Regina's German community during the Second World War can serve as a case in point. There were some manifestations of anti-German feeling, but Regina went to war in 1939 without the distrust and discord that had poisoned ethnic relations during the 1914-18 period. Of course, by 1939 the city's Germans were well established, and many were second generation Canadian-born. Furthermore, few had shown much interest in, or sympathy for, Adolph Hitler's exploits in Europe. Only sixty Reginans belonged to the Deutscher Bund Canada, a pro-Nazi society founded in 1934 which at its peak enrolled perhaps 800 to 1,000 members in Saskatchewan, the province where the society was strongest. Indeed, the German community in Regina denounced Hitler's annexation of the Sudetenland in 1938. Some Reginans suspected of pro-Nazi sympathies were interned in 1939, and mobs attacked German clubs and businesses in the East End in May 1940. By and large, however, Germans were left alone to pursue their lives and occupations as best they could.[17]

In the years following the war, events such as the celebration of Saskatchewan's Golden Jubilee in 1955 and Canada's Centennial in 1967 helped to foster a greater appreciation of the city's ethnic diversity. A provincial Ukrainian cultural festival was held in Regina in 1955 as part of the province's Golden Jubilee celebrations, for instance. In that same year the German-Canadian Harmonie Club began to mark Oktoberfest. It became an annual event, as did a more ambitious undertaking launched by the Regina Folk Arts Council 1965. This annual Mosaic Festival presents the cuisine, song and dance of Regina's various ethnic groups in "pavilions" scattered across the ciy. The popularity of the festival also reflected a new interest on the part of the younger members of many of Regina's ethnic communities in the preservation of their cultural heritage. This was especially so in the case of the Ukrainians, by 1961 the second-largest non-British ethnic group in the city (Appendix, Table VIII). Ukrainian parents were quick to take advantage of a 1974 amendment to the provincial school law that again permitted instruction in languages other than English. A total of 161 pupils were receiving instruction in Ukrainian at three separate schools in Regina by 1978.[18]

A substantial influx of Native people also altered the character of Regina, but for them acceptance came more slowly. Long a marginal element in the city's population, their numbers suddenly began to increase rapidly during the 1950s and 1960s (Appendix, Table VIII). The migration was fuelled by a high Native birth rate and the limited economic opportunities available on the reserves and in rural Saskatchewan generally. Jobs, or at least the prospect of jobs, drew them to Regina. Many did find work, but others did not. An early survey (1958) put the Native unemployment rate in the city at 25 per cent. The founding of the Indian and Métis Friendship Centre in 1961 helped to ease the transition to a new and unfamiliar urban environment. Only the second of its kind to appear in Canada, the centre offered assistance in obtaining housing and employment, set up recreational programs for young people, helped those who ran afoul of the law and took some tentative steps to foster an interest in traditional Native culture.[19] The provincial government became active, too. In 1968 it established the Task Force on Indian and Métis Opportunity, which sought to encourage government departments, crown corporations and private firms to hire more Native people. But there have been no magic solutions, and poverty and unemployment remain the lot of many of the Native people who have come to live in the city.[20]

At first Reginans were largely oblivious to the growing Native presence, but in the 1970s a combination of circumstances brought it forcibly to their attention. One was the very size of what had become the city's most visible minority. The census found 2,860 Native people in Regina in 1971, but unofficial estimates put the total closer to 30,000 by mid-decade. If such estimates were accurate, some observers noted, then Regina had the highest per capita population of Native people of any Canadian city. Whatever the numbers, there were clearly more Native and Métis children in city schools. By the late 1970s Native children comprised a majority in some inner-city schools, such as Albert School north of the CPR tracks, and a sizeable minority in others.[21]

Further, a much-publicized increase in violent crime in the

High-rise office buildings and apartments in what had once been a single family residential area south of Victoria Park, 1974.

A Toronto developer, Principal Investments Limited, beat MacCallum Hill and Company in the race to build Regina's first suburban shopping centre. The Golden Mile Centre opened in 1960. Many low-rise apartments were built nearby in Parliament Place.

city was generally attributed to the growing Native presence. The police responded by stepping up its downtown patrols, indeed creating a special "task force" for the purpose in 1975. With only one Native constable on the Regina police force at the time, relations between the police and the Native community became very tense. There were repeated allegations of police brutality against Natives, and it was predicted in 1978 that "within the next few years Regina could be facing racial strife similar to that experienced during the late 1960s and early 1970s by the American cities of Detroit, New York, Chicago and Los Angeles."[22]

Although the Native population continued to grow,[23] tensions between Natives and whites in fact eased somewhat. In 1977 Native organizations joined with the city police to establish the Regina Native Race Relations Association (RNRRA). It was the first of its kind in North America, and its mandate was simple: to improve relations between Regina's Native population and the police. By providing an impartial method of investigating Native people's complaints against the force, it appeared to be acheiving its goal as the decade drew to a close. The RNRRA instituted a program of cross-cultural training for the city police that also had a beneficial effect.[24] To help Native and Métis children better adjust to an unfamiliar classroom setting, the public school board began to hire Native teacher's aides (the first were placed in Albert School in 1979) and then to recruit Native teachers. A more significant step forward in Native education was taken by Native people themselves: the founding of the Saskatchewan Indian Cultural College, which since 1976 has been affiliated with the University of Regina.[25]

The character and composition of Regina's trade union movement also began to change during and after the Second World War. Historically, the building and printing trades had formed the core of organized labour in the city. Craft union organizers had largely overlooked workers in the service sector, trade and commerce and manufacturing. Then in the late 1930s the concept of "industrial unionism" began to attract a following in Regina, as it did elsewhere across North America. Oil refinery workers were the first to be organized in Regina, in 1942. Others followed and the Regina Labour Council (RLC), comprised of all unions affiliated with the Canadian Congress of Labour, was established in 1943. The craft unions associated with the older Regina Trades and Labour Council responded to this challenge by launching an aggressive campaign of their own, organizing retail clerks, General Hospital employees and the city police force. The rivalry continued after the war, but when the Canadian Congress of Labour and the Trades and Labour Congress of Canada merged in 1956, the RTLC and the RLC followed suit.

Provincial civil servants were the most significant postwar additions to the ranks of organized labour. The Saskatchewan Civil Service Association (SCSA), founded in 1913, had at first been concerned chiefly with promoting social activities, but during the 1920s it had also begun to press for improvements in wages and fringe benefits, especially a superannuation scheme (granted in 1927). By the early 1940s the SCSA was beginning to explore the possibility of transforming itself from an association of employees into a real trade union. The change was facilitated by the new CCF government, which, after taking office in 1944, moved quickly to grant collective-bargaining rights to civil servants. With a little prodding from Premier T.C. Douglas (who did not want the SCSA to embarrass his government by not seizing the opportunity), the association was certified as the bargaining agent for most provincial government employees in 1945. The SCSA (later the Saskatchewan Government Employees' Association) in time became the largest single trade union in the city. Thus, the labour movement in Regina also came more and more to bear the imprint of the city's status as the provincial capital.[26]

THE URBAN LANDSCAPE

There was little building activity in Regina during the war years (Appendix, Table XI) and hence little change in its physical character and appearance. In 1945, as in 1939 or even 1929 for that matter, the built-up area of Regina was still easily accommodated within the city's 1911 boundaries. Indeed, large vacant tracts continued to separate the city proper from its outer limits. As it had for more than three decades, R. H. Williams's Glas-

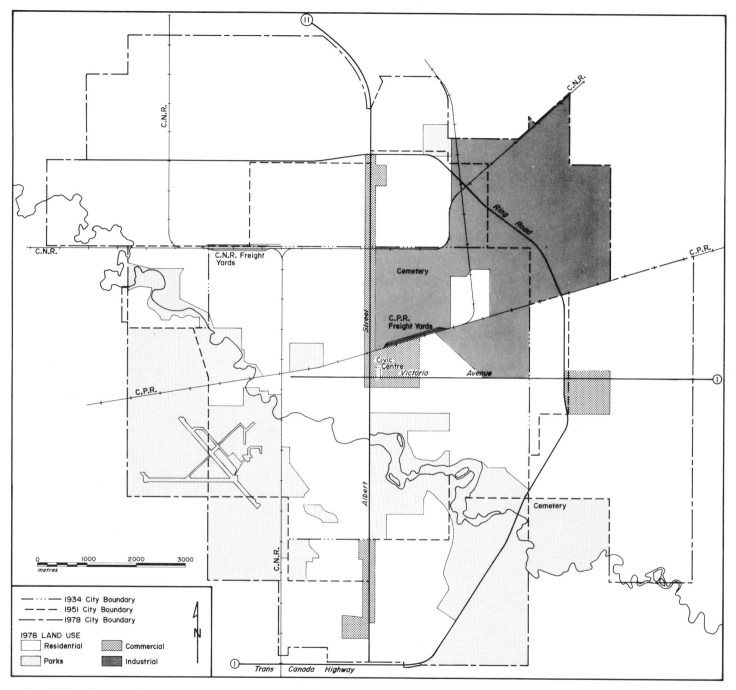

9 Land Use in Regina, 1978: Contemporary Regina is indeed a "man-made city." Successive city councils have directed industrial growth to the northeast. The city and provincial governments and the university have jointly created a 2,300-acre park centred on Wascana Lake. The Civic Centre is part of the legacy of Eugene Faludi's master plan. Postwar residential growth, too, has been influenced more by Regina's man-made features than by any natural-site factors.

gow House (soon to be acquired by the Robert Simpson Company) marked the economic centre of the city. Most of Regina's retail shops and stores were concentrated in the downtown core within easy walking distance for those who lived in nearby residential neighbourhoods, a short streetcar ride for those farther out. Regina was a small, physically compact city at war's end, solid and unpretentious.

Postwar prosperity, rapid population growth and the proliferation of automobile ownership made Regina a very different place by the 1970s. Private developers turned vacant land into low-density residential subdivisions and suburban shopping centres, and the city extended its boundaries to embrace other vacant tracts so that the process could be repeated. Private developers and the provincial government also reshaped the downtown core, adding new department stores and office towers that transformed Regina's skyline.

Although there was much that changed in Regina's urban landscape after the Second World War, there were also elements of continuity with earlier periods in its history. One was the city's determination to control the direction of industrial growth through its ownership of land suitable for this purpose. It was certainly in a position to do so. By 1946 city-owned land acquired through tax default and the balance of the 1904 grant from the federal government that had not yet been disposed of together amounted to 25 per cent of all property in Regina.[27] Tax-delinquent property in Tuxedo Park had in fact been set aside in the late 1920s for future industrial growth. But because the city made no accommodation for the existing residences, a conflict in land uses resulted when it began to offer sites for sale there after the war. The matter was not resolved until 1965, when under a joint federal-provincial-municipal agreement, the Tuxedo Park Urban Renewal Scheme, the city finally purchased the remaining houses. In 1953 the city also decided to develop another vacant parcel of land north of the original warehouse district for industrial purposes.

As late as 1955 almost all industrial activity in Regina was still concentrated in the warehouse district, but the city continued to acquire land to meet future needs. Its most important initiative came in 1959, when it purchased 830 acres of farm land immediately east of the warehouse district and north of Tuxedo Park. The tract was ideal: sewer and water lines and railway spurs could readily be extended to it, and apart from the Interprovincial Pipe Line right-of-way there were no physical barriers to future expansion. Development of Ross Industrial Park, as it became known, proceeded in an orderly fashion. During the 1970s the city purchased additional property to the east (where the Imperial Oil refinery had been located) and to the north. Thus, because Regina had the foresight to bank land in the late 1950s, when market prices were low, the price of serviced industrial land there remained significantly lower than in most other prairie cities.[28] Its virtual monopoly of suitable land also enabled Regina to ensure that industrial growth remained concentrated in the northeast sector of the city (see Map 9).

The city's ownership of large numbers of tax-delinquent lots also enabled it to exercise some influence over the pattern and pace of residential development, at least through the 1950s when overcrowding and a lack of housing were the most serious problems confronting Regina. The housing shortage was a legacy of the Depression years, and the war only made it worse. War plants such as Regina Industries Limited drew more workers to the city, and the establishment of three local training schools under the British Commonwealth Air Training Plan placed a greater strain on the available accommodation. Large houses were remodelled into apartments and even garages were converted into dwellings. Some newcomers moved north of the city limits to North Annex or Highland Park, and built or rented small houses on unserviced lots.[29]

Wartime Housing Limited, the federal crown corporation established to build temporary housing for war workers, initially looked with sympathy upon Regina's plight. It proposed in May 1942 to erect fifty houses near the city's largest war plant, but then withdrew the offer upon further investigation of housing conditions. By the end of the year city officials were insisting that the situation had reached crisis proportions, and even went so far as to publicly discourage farmers from moving to Regina for the winter. In August 1945 a city housing registry still had nearly 1,000 applications on file, and the medical health officer

In the 1950s and 1960s the Mother-well Building (left) and the Sas-katchewan Power Corporation head office (centre) joined the Hotel Sas-katchewan and the art deco Dominion Government Building along Victoria Avenue.

The Cornwall Centre nears comple-tion, 1980.

Downtown Regina looking west toward the Exhibition Grounds, 1976.

Premier Woodrow S. Lloyd (left), Minoru Yamasaki (center) and Thomas Church (right) examine a model of the proposed Wascana Centre, 1962.

Reginans use Wascana Lake exten-sively for canoeing and sailing. A marina at the eastern end of the lake is a legacy of the 1975 Western Canada Summer Games.

Reginans enjoy Wascana Centre on Canada Day, 1975.

estimated that when the situation returned to normal nearly as many houses ought to be condemned as unfit. Little wonder that a survey of postwar spending intentions showed that one of Reginans' top priorities would be to acquire a new or better home.[30]

Regina was included in the various postwar federal programs to provide homes for veterans. Wartime Housing and Housing Enterprises Limited (a joint venture of the federal government and the major Canadian insurance companies) built 1,147 houses in Regina between 1945 and 1952. The city cooperated by providing the land; it owned 2,854 vacant lots on sewer and water lines at the end of the war. Still determined to encourage compact residential development, the city wished to see these "wartime houses" erected near existing dwellings. In some cases they were, but most were clustered together in new residential districts south and west of the built-up area of the city. The three largest were Coventry Place, Normandy Heights and Arnheim Place. Private contractors were busy, too, building 1,383 single and duplex housing units in Regina between 1947 and 1952.[31]

The city's determination to influence patterns of residential growth also explains its renewed interest in town planning after 1945. Work on a master plan for Regina had begun in 1930, but was interrupted by the Depression and the war. In September 1945 the Town Planning Commission recommended that the city hire E. G. Faludi, a Toronto planning expert, to assist in completing it. He was given the job, and his thirty-year development plan was presented to the city in 1947. To create better residential neighbourhoods and improve housing conditions, Faludi proposed that in vacant city-owned subdivisions the rigid and monotonous gridiron street layout be replaced by more curvilinear designs. He also recommended that neighbourhood shopping centres be established within existing and new suburban residential areas. While Faludi was thus encouraging the creation of low-density residential neighbourhoods, he also concluded that the city possessed sufficient reserves of land to meet its housing and industrial needs for thirty years (by which time Faludi projected Regina would have a population of 90,000). Hence, no major annexations would be necessary for the foreseeable future. Faludi's report touched upon other issues as well. He urged the extension and beautification of the land adjacent to Wascana Lake and Creek, and the development of other parks in the city. His plan contained a proposal for a civic centre, comprising a new city hall and other municipal, provincial and federal buildings to be erected between Victoria Park and Albert Street in the downtown core. He made several recommendations to relieve congestion on Regina's main traffic arteries, the most ambitious of which was the eventual relocation of most railway branch lines outside the city limits.[32]

Taken together, Faludi's proposals were to have a far-reaching impact upon the urban landscape. His recommendations concerning future land use were almost immediately incorporated into a new zoning by-law. Crescents replaced the original rectangular grid street layout when a vacant tract south of Hill Avenue in Lakeview was replotted, and work began on a new North Side park. The city also began acquiring land for the civic centre and erected the first building there (a public health clinic) in 1951. That same year Regina hired a city planner, King Tegart, and in 1957 created a full-fledged planning department.[33]

Faludi's contention that vacant land within Regina's existing boundaries could accommodate projected future growth made the city cool to annexation proposals from North Regina and other lightly populated fringe areas. But North Regina, Highland Park and North Annex residents were insistent, and in April 1950 the provincial government gave notice of its intention to add these areas (as well as three others and a portion of the Imperial Oil refinery) to the city. Regina at first strongly protested, contending that any increased tax revenues it would derive from these outlying areas would not begin to offset the cost of extending municipal services to them. But recognizing that annexation was probably inevitable, the city soon changed its stand and insisted that all adjacent fringe areas and the entire Imperial Oil property be added at a single stroke in order to give it greater control over future growth. The province agreed, and the annexation became effective in 1951 (see Map 9). It added 5.5 square miles and some 5,000 people to the city.[34]

Other annexations soon followed. In 1953 the Consumers'

During the winter months the Wascana Centre Authority clears part of Wascana Lake for public skating and maintains cross-country ski trails along the shore line.

Regina's last streetcar run, September 11, 1950.

Co-operative Refinery was brought within the city limits, and land was acquired to permit future airport expansion and the extension of the park area along Wascana Creek. There was another modest annexation in 1955 and a much larger one in 1956, as the city began to annex extensive tracts of vacant land for residential development. This pattern continued through the 1960s and 1970s, as more and more farm land was detached from the Rural Municipality of Sherwood and brought under city control. By 1978 Regina embraced an area of 40.4 square miles, more than four times what it had been at the end of the Second World War.

Extensions of Regina's boundaries after 1951 were not marked by the same degree of acrimony as had characterized the earlier annexation. In every case it was the city that took the initiative in presenting annexation proposals to the provincial government, and, generally speaking, the province accepted them, although it did not always authorize as large an addition as the city had requested. The creation in 1951 of a District Planning Committee, comprised of representatives from both the rural municipality and the city, provided for a measure of joint control over development in the fringe areas surrounding Regina. Of course, it did not completely eliminate friction. When Regina first sought in 1968 to bring industries such as the IPSCO steel mill within its boundaries, the rural municipality objected on the ground that its tax base would be seriously eroded. In this case the province sided with the rural municipality, and Regina's repeated attempts to annex the industrial areas north of the city were not successful.[35]

The city sold most of its remaining tax-delinquent lots suitable for residential building purposes in the early 1950s. The largest tracts became new subdivisions: Assiniboia East and River Heights, both adjacent to Wascana Creek, and Rosemont, in northwest Regina. Another new subdivision, Regent Park, was laid out in 1959 on land the city had acquired as a result of its first postwar annexation. During the 1950s and 1960s it took no significant steps to replenish its supply of residential land (as Saskatoon did, for instance), leaving to the private sector the prime responsibility for meeting the housing needs of Reginans.[36]

One of the oldest land developers in Regina, McCallum Hill and Company, also proved to be one of the most active. Wholly controlled by the Hill family after 1939, the firm began to dispose of the last of its Lakeview lots in 1952. Two years later it acquired additional land south of Twenty-third Avenue on which to develop a new and equally prestigious subdivision, known as Hillsdale. This development was to consist only of "high-standard residential properties" with a minimum sixty-foot frontage. There were to be no back lanes (a first for Regina) and the street layout featured "short loops and cul-de-sacs minimizing traffic hazards to family living."[37] Farther south another consortium was quick to follow McCallum Hill's lead and proceeded to lay out Whitmore Park in 1956. A portion of the proposed Hillsdale subdivision, and all of Whitmore Park, lay outside Regina's existing boundaries, but the city obligingly extended them.[38] To accommodate McCallum Hill's extensive development plans, the city also agreed to relocate a portion of Broad Street and build a new bridge across Wascana Creek to replace the existing structure, which dated from 1908. Regina ratepayers, however, rejected the scheme in 1957. In the end McCallum Hill decided to proceed with construction of the bridge, on the understanding that the city would reimburse the firm once it had secured the ratepayers' approval. There was another vote in 1959, but the ratepayers rejected this arrangement as well. The controversial bridge was finally completed in 1960, and in 1978 McCallum Hill donated it to the city.[39]

Other developers were drawn to Regina from outside the province. They too laid out new subdivisions and built and sold houses. Some also accumulated substantial tracts of farm land on the outskirts of the city in anticipation of future growth, particularly during the 1970s. After 1973 the city itself became involved in the residential land-assembly process. In concert with the provincial government it began to purchase land on the northern and southeastern fringes of Regina; this partnership was accounting for 25 per cent of annual suburban lot sales in the city by the end of the decade.[40]

The direction of postwar residential growth in Regina was determined not so much by geography as by the city's man-made features (see Map 9). The presence of the airport and of

Constable William ("Whistling Willie") Greer. In the 1950s and early 1960s his downtown beat included one of Regina's busiest intersections, Hamilton Street and Eleventh Avenue. Greer's wrath was quick to fall on anyone who disobeyed the "Don't Walk" sign or tried to jaywalk.

CCF victory celebration, 1948. Charles Cromwell Williams (at the microphone) and Clarence Fines carried the two Regina seats in the provincial election.

Regina's sewage treatment facilities prevented much residential growth to the west. In 1973 the city did give its approval for a new subdivision immediately south and east of the airport. Indeed, it approved the subdivision plan for Westridge even before it had applied to the province to annex the land. The provincial government judged that this piece of land's proximity to the airport made it unsuitable for residential purposes, however, and refused to permit the city to proceed.[41] Similarly, the city's success in concentrating industrial development in the northeast also effectively prevented expansion in that direction. Thus, through these postwar decades residential expansion occurred chiefly to the east and southeast (Douglas Park, Glencairn, Glencairn Village and University Park), to the south (Hillsdale, Whitmore Park and Albert Park) and to the north and northwest (Regent Park, Normanview, Walsh Acres, Argyle Park and Uplands). Like their counterparts south of Wascana Creek, Regent Park and the other new northern suburbs featured the latest curvilinear street designs, neighbourhood shopping facilities, parks and spacious lots. This diminished the historic disparity between north and south as preferred places of residence in the city.

The detached single-family house predominated in these new suburban areas, but apartment living also became more popular. There was a resurgence of apartment construction during the late 1950s, and by 1965 there were more than 300 apartment blocks in the city. Most were two-and-a-half-storey walk-up structures erected by small builders for local owners, but larger firms built them as well. One built ninety, many of them clustered together in Parliament Place south of Twenty-fifth Avenue in what later came to be criticized as an "apartment jungle." The designs were monotonous and there were few amenities, but the rents were within the reach of most Reginans. More luxurious high-rise apartments also began to appear; Tower Gardens was the first, in 1955. Others followed in the 1960s and 1970s, with the area immediately south of the downtown core (and particularly Fifteenth and College Avenues) being the preferred location.[42]

Other postwar housing developments were designed to meet the needs of lower-income families. A Calgary firm was

Allan E. Blakeney represented Regina in the provincial legislature for twenty-nine years. He held several portfolios in the government of Premier Woodrow S. Lloyd and became premier in his own right in 1971. His New Democratic Party ruled the province until 1982; Blakeney continued to lead the party in opposition until 1988.

Gordon B. Grant was mayor of Regina, 1952-1953, and sat in the provincial legislature for three terms, 1964-1975. He served as minister of highways and later minister of industry in Ross Thatcher's Liberal government.

responsible for Gladmer Park, located in southeast Regina on twenty-three acres of land purchased from the provincial government. When it opened in 1955, Gladmer Park provided accommodation for 320 families. The city also became active in this field. Regina's first two public housing projects, Regent Court (1959) and Greer Court (1966), were also relatively large; each covered nine acres and provided housing for 115 and 141 families respectively. There were to be no other high-density projects of this kind, the city preferring thereafter to integrate the low-income housing units it built into neighbourhoods across Regina. The Saskatchewan Housing Corporation, a provincial crown corporation which after 1979 assumed the leading role in the provision of social housing in Regina, followed a similar approach.[43]

Suburban growth and the increasingly widespread use of the automobile encouraged the development of large retail shopping centres located on main thoroughfares on the periphery of the city. McCallum Hill was first in the field, proposing in 1955 to build a large shopping centre on Broad Street as part of its Hillsdale subdivision. Within a few months a Toronto developer, Principal Investments Limited, submitted a proposal for a similar facility to be located on Albert Street south of Twenty-fifth Avenue. Unable or unwilling to choose between them, the city gave both firms permission to proceed. Only one actually did so. Principal Investments' Golden Mile Centre opened in 1960. Construction of the Hillsdale shopping centre was said to be dependent on the completion of a new Broad Street bridge, but although the bridge was eventually built, the shopping centre never was.[44] Several other smaller neighbourhood shopping centres appeared in succeeding years, and another large one, the Northgate Shopping Centre (on Albert Street on the city's northern outskirts) in 1965. The Southland Mall, larger still, was built at the southern edge of the city (and again on Albert Street) a decade later.

While these suburban shopping centres proliferated, Regina's commercial core stagnated. The lack of convenient parking became a chronic source of complaint, persisting long after Simpson's opened the city's first parkade in 1959. In addition, there was little construction in the downtown area during the 1950s, private developers and the provincial and federal governments alike preferring to erect new office buildings elsewhere. Thus, the federal government's Motherwell Building was located on Victoria Avenue, the Financial Building (a private venture) south of Victoria Park and the province's new Administration and Health buildings south of Wascana Lake.

The steadily deteriorating condition of the city hall afforded an opportunity for the city to take the lead in revitalizing the downtown core. It put the site up for sale during the 1950s, but there were no takers. Finally compelled to abandon the fifty-four-year-old building and seek temporary quarters in 1962, the city again attempted to interest developers in the site. This time it was successful, selling the land in 1964. A nine-storey office tower, shopping mall and parkade, the Midtown Centre, was completed four years later. The city also disposed of a parcel of land on Broad Street (which had originally been set aside as a park) to another developer, who proceeded to build a hotel and another retail mall.[45] After much controversy, a new city hall was eventually included in the civic centre site that E. G. Faludi had first proposed after the war. Completed in 1978, it was the final link in the cluster of public buildings (the others were a federal office building, a provincial courthouse and a new home for the Regina Public Library) situated on the block bounded by Victoria and Twelfth avenues and McIntyre and Smith streets (see Map 9).

Although some lamented the loss of open space, the sale of the old city hall and Broad Street Park properties did contribute to the revitalization of Regina's downtown core. So did the Hudson's Bay Company's decision to build a department store on Twelfth Avenue in 1965, forty years after it had first acquired the site. There was also a flurry of office construction in the area during the 1960s and early 1970s. The Saskatchewan Power Corporation built a graceful new head office on Victoria Avenue in 1963, and three other high-rise office buildings went up along Hamilton Street over the next decade. A far more ambitious redevelopment scheme — the Cornwall Centre — was initiated by the city and the province in 1976.[46] It covers a three-block area north of Eleventh Avenue and includes the head offices of two other provincial crown corporations, Saskatchewan Govern-

In the postwar years the grounds surrounding the Legislative Building have become an increasingly common location for popular protest. This "Keep Our Doctors" rally took place during the 1962 doctors' strike over the introduction of Medicare. Premier Woodrow S. Lloyd is hanging in effigy.

Off-field fund-raising activities, such as the formation of a "booster club" and an annual $100-per-plate dinner, became necessary to keep professional football alive in Regina after the Second World War.

ment Insurance and Saskatchewan Telecommunications, Sears and Eaton's department stores and more than ninety other retail outlets.

The city and the province also cooperated to make Wascana Lake the focal point of a 2,300-acre inner-city park whose grounds provide a setting for the University of Regina, the Museum of Natural History, the Saskatchewan Centre of the Arts, the Legislative Building and government offices. Administered jointly by the city, the province and the university since 1962, the park also provides opportunities for a wide range of recreational activities. Reginans use the lake extensively for canoeing and sailing (a marina at the eastern end of Wascana Lake was a legacy of the Western Canada Summer Games that were held in the city in 1975), and its picnic areas are invariably crowded on warm summer evenings and weekends. During the winter months the Wascana Centre Authority clears areas of the lake for public skating and maintains ski trails along the shore line. The city has developed other parks itself: Douglas Park on the eastern edge of Regina, Mount Pleasant Park to the north (located on what had formerly been the city dump) and A. E. Wilson Park in the northwest.[47]

Suburban growth and the automobile altered the physical character and appearance of postwar Regina in other ways. With middle- and upper-income families abandoning the inner city for the suburbs, Regina's oldest residential areas began to decline. South of Victoria Park, homes were demolished to make way for office buildings and apartments, and the surviving housing stock in what had once been the city's most desirable residential neighbourhood increasingly fell into the hands of absentee landlords and speculators. The Cathedral Area (as the West End came to be known) and older neighbourhoods north of the CPR tracks were not subjected to the same redevelopment pressures, but they too became blighted. In the 1970s the city began to take steps to arrest their decline, through the federal Neighbourhood Improvement (NIP) and Residential Rehabilitation Assistance Programs, for instance. NIP projects were initiated in two older North Side neighbourhoods in 1974 and 1977. There was also a resurgence of local neighbourhood democracy — dormant since the 1930s — as residents of several inner city areas organized to demand more input into the planning process.[48]

In Regina's downtown core traffic congestion became a serious problem, one which was only partly alleviated by the introduction of one-way streets in 1955. The city's main north-south and east-west thoroughfares, such as Albert Street and Victoria Avenue, became clogged as well. To relieve the congestion the city built Ring Road, which encircles Regina (a recommendation first advanced in 1961 and incorporated into the "Community Planning Scheme" that superseded the Faludi Plan). The city also began to plan new arterial roads that would utilize land freed up by the relocation of some of the railway branch lines that had long impeded internal traffic flow. The removal of a CPR line permitted the widening of Arcola Avenue to provide better access to new subdivisions in the southeast. Similarly, a new north-south thoroughfare, Lewvan Drive, took the place of a line that the Grand Trunk Pacific had built on Regina's western outskirts in 1910. At the end of the 1970s the city was about to embark on a far more ambitious scheme: the relocation of the Canadian National marshalling yards to a new site north of Regina and the redevelopment of the old yards as a residential area. (The second phase of Regina's rail relocation plans would see the Canadian Pacific yards and main line moved as well).[49]

THE URBAN COMMUNITY: SOCIAL AND POLITICAL LIFE

Postwar prosperity and a healthy civic treasury enabled Regina to repair the ravages of the Depression on its streets, sidewalks and utilities, and to extend municipal services to outlying areas. Antiqated streetcars began to give way to electric trolley buses in 1948, and the last streetcar was retired two years later. In fact the changeover was hastened along by a fire that destroyed the car barns and most of the old streetcars in 1949. To keep pace with the growth of new suburbs, the Regina Transit System added more routes in the 1950s and 1960s and began to acquire diesel buses, abandoning the last of its electric trolleys in 1966. But neither could compete effectively with the private automobile; ridership declined sharply after the Second World War (until the mid-1960s at any rate) and the deficit soared. During the 1970s the city experimented with a Telebus service using small buses that came right to the door. Introduced in four south Regina suburbs in 1971, it was intended to complement the fixed-route service offered in the more densely populated core. In time it was extended to other suburban areas, but the Telebus service has since been discontinued.[50]

Obtaining a larger and more assured supply of water became another high priority of postwar city councils as Regina began to experience periodic shortages, during the summer months especially. With the city's existing underground sources of supply at Boggy Creek, Mallory Springs and Mound Springs apparently having reached their limit, the city began again in 1948 to give serious consideration to the feasibility of bringing water by pipeline from the South Saskatchewan River. Its initial preference was for the construction of a pipeline all the way from the river to Regina, but this scheme was soon abandoned in favour of a less costly alternative utilizing Buffalo Pound Lake, a shallow body of water situated northwest of the provincial capital (see Map 8).

It was easy to enlist Moose Jaw's support. That city also needed more water, although at the time it could promise no financial aid, since a default during the 1930s had made its debentures anathema to investors. Securing assistance from the senior governments proved difficult as well, but success finally came in 1950. The federal government agreed to augment the supply of water in Buffalo Pound Lake by pumping water from the South Saskatchewan River into the Qu'Appelle River. From there it would flow naturally into this lake, which would, in effect, become a storage reservoir for the city of Regina (and Moose Jaw too if it chose to participate in the scheme). The province agreed to bear the cost of constructing a filtration plant at Buffalo Pound Lake; the city was to be responsible for laying the thirty-six-mile pipeline that would bring the water to Regina.[51]

Regina proceeded at once, securing approval for its $4,500,000 share of the $7,000,000 project in a by-law vote that same year. By the time the project was completed in June 1955,

"Drawing to the button" in the Saskatchewan Civil Service Curling League, 1953.

Mayor Henry Baker reads an address of welcome to the Ernie Richardson rink at City Hall. In all, Richardson (standing to Baker's right) won four world curling championships, in 1959, 1960, 1962 and 1963.

Moose Jaw had also agreed to participate, sharing the water obtained from Buffalo Pound Lake and the cost of operating the filtration plant and associated facilities. The subsequent construction of the Gardiner Dam on the South Saskatchewan River at Outlook permitted the diversion of water into Buffalo Pound Lake by gravity flow. As the 1970s drew to a close this lake was supplying Regina with more than half of its water needs in the peak summertime period.

The city also augmented the capacity of its electrical generating plant on Wascana Lake, rejecting overtures from the province in the early 1950s to become part of the integrated provincial network that the Saskatchewan Power Corporation (SPC) was then beginning to construct. Regina's decision to go it alone was a product of several factors, but two were particularly important. One was civic pride in what had been for many years the province's largest electrical utility, and which at the beginning of the decade still produced the cheapest power. A second was the city's long-standing reliance on the surpluses generated by the plant to bolster civic revenues and stabilize the mill rate. Suspicion of SPC and antagonism between some civic officials and the provincial CCF government were probably less significant.

By the end of the 1950s, however, the merits of continued municipal operation of Regina's power plant were no longer so clear. A succession of dry years reduced water levels on Wascana Lake and the ability of the plant to meet the city's power needs in peak periods. Indeed, Regina was compelled to turn to the SPC for assistance in 1958 and 1959. Future expansion of the Regina plant was limited not only by the capacity of the lake, but also by provincial legislation in 1958 that restricted the area to be served by any municipal utility to that city's existing boundaries. Areas annexed after that date would be served by SPC. The completion of its Boundary Dam thermal generating station near Estevan finally gave the crown corporation an edge in electricity rates, and the extension of its high-capacity transmission line north to Weyburn and Moose Jaw (whose plants it acquired in 1959 and 1960 respectively) brought cheaper power to Regina's doostep. Some members of city council were quick to recognize the implications of all of this, but convincing a majority of their colleagues to sell Regina's aging plant proved

Students at Regina College, 1952.

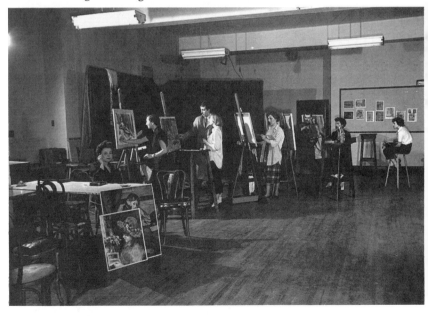

Kenneth Lochhead instructing an art class at Regina College, 1952. Lochhead would receive national acclaim as a member of the innovative "Regina Five" group of painters.

*Bill Dow (left), Michael Caruana (center) and Gordon Milroy
(right) in a scene from Black Powder: Estevan, 1931 at The
Globe Theatre.*

difficult. The debate was long and acrimonious, but finally in 1963 the SPC offer was put to the citizens in a special referendum. They endorsed the sale of the plant by a margin of 2 to 1. Further negotiations with SPC followed and two years later Regina's power plant, long the darling of civic officials, passed into provincial hands.[53]

Although the worst of the Depression was over by 1939, it left its imprint on municipal politics for another decade and a half. Political allegiances continued to be sharply drawn, as they had been during the 1930s. On one side was the business-dominated Civic Voters' Association (CVA), which had managed to wrest control of city hall away from Labour in 1939. On the other were a succession of civic political parties loosely allied with organized labour, the CCF and the Labour-Progressive Party (LPP), as the Communist Party became known in 1943. Labour did regain some lost ground in 1941 when C. C. Williams captured the mayoralty. He held it for three years, but Labour could not dislodge the CVA's firm hold on city council. In 1944 the CVA won back the mayoralty, and for the next decade it enjoyed complete mastery over Labour, sweeping every civic election from 1946 to 1953.

Civic Political Parties in Regina, 1939-1976

Name	Elections Contested
Civic Voters Association	1939-1969
Civic Labour Association	1939-1940
United Labour Association	1941-1945, 1947-1948
Civic Labour Committee	1946
Co-operative Labour League	1947-1948
Independent Labour	1950
Civic Reform Committee	1950
Civic Election Labour League	1951-1956, 1963-1965
Regina Civic Association	1953
Regina Citizens' Association	1954-1970
Regina Labour Election Committee	1958, 1961
Civic Action League	1964-1965
Regina Municipal New Democratic Party	1973-1976
Committee of Progressive Electors	1976

Voting patterns across the city followed a familiar pattern. CVA strength lay chiefly in the residential areas south and west of the downtown core, while Labour drew most of its support from neighbourhoods farther north and east. But on balance the CVA had the broader political base. Among the candidates whom it endorsed for civic office were men of moderate socialist views such as Garnet Menzies. A printer by trade and once a CCF candidate (in the 1934 provincial election), Menzies served four terms as a CVA alderman and three as mayor. Labour, on the other hand, was handicapped by the internecine warfare that periodically erupted in its ranks between moderate socialists aligned with the CCF and the more doctrinaire supporters of the LPP.[54]

Of course the CVA was not without its detractors. Some claimed that its absolute control of civic government had contributed to a growing apathy at election time. More than half of the city's eligible voters cast ballots in 1945, but only a third did so in 1947 and 1948 and scarcely a quarter in the early 1950s. Even an otherwise sympathetic *Leader-Post* was moved to observe in 1950 that "in virtually destroying radical opposition, CVA unfortunately has closed the door to desirable candidates who might offer alternatives to its slate." The low turnouts helped to revive interest in the ward system in 1953 and 1954, but the CVA showed no enthusiasm for a change, and neither did the Chamber of Commerce.[55] Others accused the CVA of becoming arrogant and high-handed, ignoring the objections of Victoria Avenue residents to the widening of their street when it was designated as part of the route of the Trans-Canada Highway through Regina in 1953, for instance. Out of that protest there emerged a new civic political party, the Regina Civic Association (RCA). (Its name was changed to the Regina Citizens' Association in 1954.) The RCA finally ended the CVA's long dominance in municipal politics, winning a majority of the council seats in 1955 and the mayoralty in 1956.

With the emergence of the RCA civic elections became more spirited affairs, and turnouts improved somewhat. Over the next fourteen years (the CVA finally disappeared following the 1969 contest) control of city hall see-sawed back and forth. The CVA regained its majority on city council in 1957, lost it two

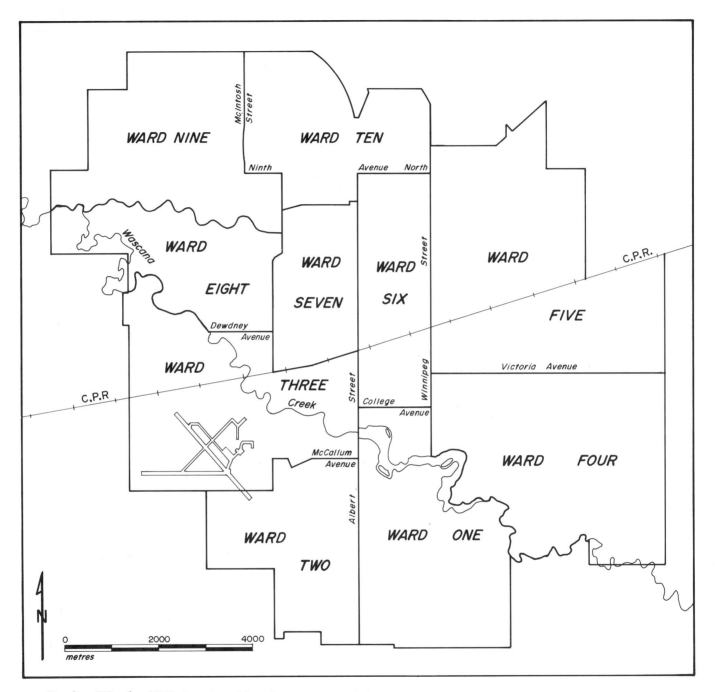

10 Regina Wards, 1979: Provincial legislation imposed the ward system on Regina in 1973. While the ward boundaries changed slightly through the 1970s as a result of successive annexations and population shifts, generally speaking they respected the city's neighbourhoods. This helped to facilitate the re-emergence of local neighbourhood democracy, dormant since the 1930s.

years later, and won it back in 1960. Not until 1968 did the RCA again manage to win a majority of the council seats. It would be wrong to make too much of this, for party lines in fact were never tightly drawn. The CVA made a point of giving the men and women whom it endorsed complete independence to vote in council as they saw fit. The RCA, while it had a platform to which its candidates were expected to adhere, was divided on controversial issues, such as the sale of the power plant.

Throughout the 1950s and 1960s the mayoralty remained securely in RCA hands, as first T. H. Cowburn (1957-58) and then Henry Baker (1959-70) occupied the city's highest elected office. Indeed, with his sixth triumph at the polls in 1968, Baker became Regina's longest-serving mayor. His relationship with city council was often stormy. In 1966, for instance, council abandoned the city-commissioner form of municipal administration in favour of a city manager largely to eliminate what was regarded as Baker's too-frequent meddling in the day-to-day operation of city departments.[57] (As mayor, Baker was *ex officio* a city commissioner.) Nevertheless, Henry Baker was a very successful politician. He acquired a well-merited reputation for being sensitive to the wishes of ordinary citizens, particularly those who lived in the city's older neighbourhoods, but his political appeal extended into the traditional CVA enclaves south of Wascana Lake as well. Defeated finally in 1970, he returned in triumph three years later and held the mayoralty until 1979. Thus, Baker outlasted even the RCA, which disappeared following the 1970 civic election. No party has since nominated a complete slate of civic candidates, not even the Regina Municipal New Democratic Party, which contested the 1973 and 1976 elections.

Aside from the virtual disappearance of civic slates, the other significant change that occurred in Regina during the 1970s was the reintroduction of the ward system, imposed by provincial legislation upon Saskatchewan's two largest cities in 1973. Reginans subsequently endorsed the change by a wide margin (more than 2 to 1) in 1977. The ward boundaries again respected the city's neighbourhoods (see Map 10), and thus helped to facilitate the re-emergence of local neighbourhood democracy. (But what the provincial government could give it could also take away — and did, in 1988, abolishing the ward system of election as it existed in Regina and Saskatoon).[58]

The CCF and its succesor the NDP have enjoyed considerable success in provincial and federal elections in Regina. The Second World War proved to be a turning point for the party there as it did across the province. Its program of postwar reforms — social security legislation, economic planning, labour legislation and guaranteed minimum prices for farm products — appealed to voters who still had memories of the Depression, and who feared a postwar slump such as had occurred following the First World War. Even Saskatchewan's capital city, long a bulwark of the Liberal party, fell to the CCF in 1944, and the party captured the Regina federal seat a year later. During the period 1944-78 the provincial CCF and NDP never failed to capture a majority of Regina's seats. (Regina still had only two seats in the legislature at the outset of this period, but it gained a third in 1952 and more as the population of the city increased in succeeding decades. By 1975 it had nine seats.) The city enjoyed strong representation in the CCF, Liberal and NDP governments which ruled the province during these years. C. M. Fines served for a decade and a half as CCF provincial treasurer, and C. C. Williams even longer as minister of labour. Gordon Grant was minister of highways and later minister of industry in the government of Premier Ross Thatcher. Allan E. Blakeney, who held senior portfolios in the last CCF government and became the province's first NDP premier in 1971, also represented Regina in the legislature. So did Henry Baker, the city's most successful mayor, who doubled as one of its MLAs after 1964.

In federal elections the CCF/NDP's hold was almost as strong. The CCF lost Regina to the Liberals in 1949, but regained it in 1953 only to be engulfed by the Diefenbaker landslide in 1958. The Progressive Conservatives held the riding for a decade, spoiling even T. C. Douglas's bid for a seat in the House of Commons in 1962 after he had left provincial politics to lead the federal NDP. In 1968 Regina gained a second federal seat, and that year the NDP took them both. The Progressive Conservatives gained one back in 1972 but lost it again to the NDP in 1979.[59]

Regina's social and cultural life flourished during these prosperous postwar decades. The city was subjected to the same homogenizing influences — Hollywood and television especially — which carried American habits, amusements and popular culture to the far corners of the globe. (Hence, a prediction in 1956 that Regina teenagers would not warm to rock'n'roll, the latest American music craze, proved to be far wide of the mark.) But local artists and playwrights also found a receptive audience for their work, and that work increasingly sought to articulate the experience of the province and the region, thereby contributing to the development of distinctive expressions of prairie culture.

Its size and isolation have enabled Regina to maintain a strong sense of community. Regina prides itself on being able to support a professional football team, though in fact the Saskatchewan Roughriders (as they have been known since 1948) draw fans from across the province to Taylor Field, built after the war where Park Hughes and Park de Young once stood. Ticket revenues alone would never have ensured the surival of the team, and it has had to resort to a variety of fundraising schemes (an annual $100-per-plate dinner began in 1953) to remain competitive. And competitive it has been, particularly in the 1960s and 1970s. Led by diminutive quarterback Ron Lancaster and fullback George Reed, the Roughriders played in eleven consecutive Western Conference finals and three national championship games, winning the Grey Cup for the first and as yet only time in 1966. No other team was able to achieve the same following in postwar Regina; not the junior Regina Rams (though they won several national championships), not the junior Regina Pats (who won the Memorial Cup again in 1974) and most certainly not the city's short-lived (1945-1951) entry in the professional Western Canada Hockey League.

If Reginans only watched football and hockey, they still participated in other sports in large numbers. Golf and curling continued to have the greatest mass appeal. In the latter sport Reginans enjoyed considerable success in national and international competition during these years.[60]

A long-standing urge for an institution of higher learning in the city was finally realized in 1959, when Regina College was raised to full degree-granting status as the University of Saskatchewan, Regina Campus. It became a fully autonomous institution, the University of Regina, in 1974 and its presence continued to enrich the city's cultural life. Norman Mackenzie's bequest formed the nucleus of the city's first art gallery, opened in 1953 as part of Regina College. Its School of Art, revitalized under Kenneth Lochhead, who became director in 1950, acquired a national reputation for the innovative work of the "Regina Five" group of painters: Lochhead, Art McKay, Ron Bloore, Doug Morton and Ted Godwin.[61]

There have been important developments in other fields of artistic endeavor as well. In 1966 Ken and Sue Kramer came to the city from Edmonton to found a touring company, the Globe Theatre, that would bring drama to Regina's and Saskatchewan's schools. Four years later the Kramers established a resident company in Regina. Some of its most successful plays, such as *Medicare!* and *Black Powder: Estevan, 1931,* both the work of its writer-in-residence, Rex Deverell, drew upon the Saskatchewan experience and thereby helped to foster a stronger sense of local and provincial identity. The Globe Theatre commissioned plays from a variety of other new Canadian writers, and toured them across southern Saskatchewan. On another front, television brought the city to the country. The new medium reached Regina in 1954.[62] Like radio a generation earlier, it extended Regina's cultural influence even as Saskatchewan and indeed the nation as a whole were becoming part of the "global village."

If Regina enjoyed a wider range of cultural facilities than ever before in its history, this was due in part to its status as the capital of Saskatchewan. It was the province which built the Museum of Natural History in Wascana Park in 1955 and the Saskatchewan Centre of the Arts a decade and a half later. Another museum bears testimony to the city's long association with the RCMP. The collection of artifacts relating to the history of the force had begun in the 1930s, and in 1973 a new facility was opened at the RCMP barracks to display them.[63] These museums, no less than Rex Deverell's plays or the annual Mosaic Festival, reflected a determination to preserve and celebrate the distinctive character of Saskatchewan and of its capital city.

CONCLUSION

Regina's history largely mirrors the experience of other Canadian cities, but in some respects it is unique. Regina was part of the new urban landscape created by the Canadian Pacific Railway when it extended its prairie line from Winnipeg to the Rockies. It was the CPR that determined the actual location of the town; the CPR also profoundly influenced Regina's street layout and general land-use patterns. Equally important in shaping the character of Regina was the federal government's decision to locate the capital of the North-West Territories there. Throughout its history Regina has always been a government centre. That status has brought handsome public buildings, a spacious park and substantial civil-service payrolls, along with the incalculable prestige that attaches to a capital city.

Regina possessed few natural advantages, situated as it was on a treeless plain with the meandering Pile of Bones Creek its only nearby source of water. The site had never possessed any commercial importance before the coming of the railway, yet from such meagre resources was fashioned a city that early became the largest in Saskatchewan and one of the largest in the prairie region. Regina was the author of its own success. In this respect it was, and is, very much a "man-made" city, the creation of a business elite whose aims and aspirations have dominated civic government and politics for most of its history.

Still, Regina's success was less than complete. It was compelled to share the province with rivals such as Moose Jaw and more especially Saskatoon, and of course with Winnipeg. While Regina's economy prospered in the twentieth century with the expansion of cereal agriculture (and faltered when prices fell or harvests were poor or both), the city was and to a considerable extent still remains part of Winnipeg's hinterland. Extensive oil and potash discoveries in the 1950s and 1960s helped to diversify the Saskatchewan economy and made Regina less susceptible to the whims of "King Wheat," but again it was compelled to share those benefits with others. Calgary and Edmonton were arguably the principal beneficiaries of Saskatchewan's postwar oil boom; potash conferred far greater benefits upon Saskatoon than upon any other Saskatchewan city.

The pattern of ethnic and class relationships in Regina has also been to some degree different from that of other cities. To be sure, Regina's "British" character was modified by the arrival of large numbers of Europeans during the early decades of this century, class distinctions became more observable, and neighbourhoods increasingly came to be identified with different social strata. But Regina did not experience the same degree of polarization as Winnipeg, for instance. There has been no event in Regina's history to match the 1919 general strike in the Manitoba capital. The closest parallel — the 1935 On-to-Ottawa Trek and the riot at Market Square on July 1 — was the product of forces that to a large extent originated outside the city. And neither the trek nor the riot left any permanent mark on civic politics or labour-management relations. Ethnic divisions quickly softened too, as succeeding generations born in Regina were absorbed into its broader Anglo-Saxon culture and no fresh influx of newcomers arrived from overseas to renew Regina's ethnic communities. Thus, while Vancouver and especially Toronto have become more cosmopolitan since the Second World War, Regina has become much less so.

Regina will never rival Winnipeg, or Calgary or Edmonton, but neither is it simply a scaled-down version of one of those larger prairie cities. It is unique in its own right. Although the circumstances of its founding in 1882 were inauspicious and the site unattractive, Reginans have managed to transform cheerless prairie into a city of shaded parks and streets, and have fashioned an urban community possessing many of the amenities of cities more favourably endowed.

Appendix
Statistical Tables

TABLE I
THE GROWTH OF MANUFACTURING IN REGINA, 1891-1981

YEAR	POPULATION	NUMBER OF FIRMS*	NUMBER OF EMPLOYEES	PAYROLL $ (000)	VALUE OF PR $ (000)
1891	-	28	88	35	113
1901	2,249	-	-	-	-
1911	30,213	23	561	358	1,313
1921	34,432	43	1,211	1,910	13,022
1931	53,209	89	2,218	3,037	17,537
1941	58,245	106	2,269	3,272	25,938
1951	71,319	137	2,968	7,879	61,896
1961	112,141	124	3,521	15,116	100,632
1971	139,469	146	3,131	23,047	198,239
1981	164,313**	150	6,192	130,100	929,300

*The discrepancy between 1891 and 1901 is accounted for by the fact that the 1891 figure includes *all* establishments, regardless of size, while the figures for 1901-81 are based on firms with *five or more* employees.

**The 1981 figure is for the Census Metropolitan Area.

Sources: *Censuses of Canada, 1891-1911; Manufacturing Industries of the Prairie Provinces, 1931; Canada Year Books, 1924, 1943-44, 1955, 1965, 1974, 1985.*

TABLE II
NUMBER OF MALES PER 1,000 FEMALES IN REGINA, 1901-81*

YEAR	NUMBER OF MALES	NUMBER OF FEMALES	RATIO
1901	1,208	1,041	1,160.4
1911	19,767	10,446	1,892.3
1916	13,655	12,472	1,094.8
1921	17,801	16,631	1,070.3
1926	18,460	18,869	978.3
1931	26,682	26,527	1,005.8
1936	25,820	27,534	937.7
1941	28,432	29,813	953.6
1946	28,801	31,445	915.9
1951	34,147	37,172	918.6
1956	43,977	45,778	960.6
1961	55,471	56,670	978.8
1966	64,291	66,836	961.9
1971	68,259	71,210	958.5
1976	73,010	76,585	953.3
1981	80,095	84,220	951.0

*Figures are not available for 1906. The 1981 figures are for the Census Metropolitan Area.

Sources: *Censuses of Canada, 1901-1981; Censuses of Prairie Provinces, 1916-1946.*

TABLE III
URBAN POPULATION GROWTH AND DISTRIBUTION
IN SASKATCHEWAN, 1906-81

YEAR	POPULATION OF REGINA*	POPULATION OF SASKATCHEWAN	REGINA'S POPULATION AS % OF TOTAL POP.	URBAN POP. OF SASK.**	REGINA'S POPULATION AS % OF TOTAL URBAN POP.
1906	6,169	257,763	2.4	22,494	27.4
1911	30,213	492,432	6.1	79,502	38.0
1916	26,127	647,835	4.0	97,435	26.8
1921	34,432	757,510	4.5	127,622	26.9
1926	37,329	820,738	4.5	141,238	26.4
1931	53,209	921,785	5.8	186,144	28.6
1936	53,354	931,547	5.7	177,621	30.0
1941	58,245	895,992	6.5	190,738	30.5
1946	60,246	832,688	7.2	208,872	28.8
1951	71,319	831,728	8.6	251,018	28.4
1956	89,755	880,665	10.2	318,013	28.2
1961	112,141	925,181	12.1	395,868	28.3
1966	131,127	955,344	13.7	464,979	28.2
1971	139,469	926,242	15.0	485,159	28.7
1976	149,593	921,323	16.2	510,048	29.3
1981	164,313	968,310	16.9	563,170	29.2

*The 1981 figure is for the Census Metropolitan Area.
**Includes all incporporated cities and towns of 1,000 and over only.

TABLE IV
POPULATION GROWTH IN SASKATCHEWAN
AND PRAIRIE CITIES, 1901-81

YEAR	REGINA	SASKATOON	MOOSE JAW	WINNIPEG	EDMONTON	CALGARY
1901	2,249	113	1,558	42,340	2,626	4,392
1906	6,169	3,011	6,249	90,153	11,167	11,967
1911	30,213	12,004	13,823	136,035	24,900	43,704
1916	26,127	21,048	16,934	163,000	53,846	56,514
1921	34,432	25,739	19,285	179,087	58,821	63,305
1931	53,209	43,291	21,299	218,785	79,197	83,761
1936	53,354	41,934	19,805	215,814	85,774	83,407
1941	58,245	43,027	20,753	221,960	92,817	88,904
1951	71,319	53,268	24,355	235,710	159,631	129,060
1961	112,141	95,526	33,206	265,429	281,027	249,641
1971	139,469	126,449	31,854	246,246	438,152	403,319
1981	164,313*	154,210*	36,057	584,842*	657,057*	592,743*

*The 1981 figure is for the Census Metropolitan Area.
Sources: *Censuses of Canda, 1901-1981; Census of Population and Agriculture of the Northwest Provinces, 1906; Census of Prairie Provinces, 1916, 1936.*

TABLE V
POPULATION GROWTH IN REGINA, 1901-81*

YEAR	POPULATION	NUMERICAL CHANGE	PERCENT CHANGE
1901	2,249	-	-
1906	6,169	3,920	174.3
1911	30,213	24,044	389.7
1916	26,127	-4,086	-13.5
1921	34,432	8,305	31.8
1926	37,329	2,897	8.4
1931	53,209	15,880	42.5
1936	53,354	145	0.3
1941	58,245	4,891	9.2
1946	60,246	2,001	3.4
1951	71,319	11,073	18.4
1956	89,755	18,436	25.8
1961	112,141	22,384	24.9
1966	131,127	18,986	16.9
1971	139,469	8,342	6.4
1976	149,593	10,124	7.2
1981	164,313	14,720	9.8

*The 1981 figures are for the Census Metropolitan Area.

Sources: *Censuses of Canada, 1901-81; Census of Population and Agriculture of the Northwest Provinces, 1906; Census of Prairie Provinces, 1916-46.*

TABLE VI
BIRTHPLACE OF REGINA'S CANADIAN-BORN POPULATION, 1911-81*

BIRTHPLACE	1911 NUMBER	%	1921 NUMBER	%	1931 NUMBER	%	1941 NUMBER	%	1951 NUMBER	%	1961 NUMBER	%	1971 NUMBER	%	1981 NUMBER	%
Maritimes**	883	3.0	824	2.4	949	1.8	871	1.5	906	1.3	1,097	1.0	-	-	1,690	1.0
Quebec	543	1.8	570	1.6	615	1.1	615	1.0	739	1.0	840	0.7	-	-	1,360	0.9
Ontario	8,373	27.7	6,637	19.3	6,772	12.7	5,605	9.6	5,262	7.4	5,382	4.8	-	-	6,450	4.0
Manitoba	801	2.6	1,322	3.8	2,648	4.9	3,071	5.3	3,527	5.0	5,334	4.8			8,215	8.0
Saskatchewan	3,875	12.8	9,591	28.0	21,432	40.3	31,018	53.2	43,775	61.4	76,005	67.8	102,990	73.8	120,365	74.0
Alberta	80	0.3	192	0.5	483	1.0	713	1.2	1,082	1.5	2,541	2.3	-	-	4,415	2.7
British Columbia	63	0.2	134	0.4	239	0.5	298	0.5	595	0.8	1,314	1.2	-	-	2,330	1.5
Yukon and Territories	50	0.1	1		3		11		9		66	0.1	-	-	145	0.1
Not Given	268	0.9	141	0.4	36	-	1	-	-	-	-	-	-	-	-	-
Total Canadian-Born	14,936	49.4	19,412	56.4	33,177	72.3	42,203	72.3	55,895	78.4	92,579	82.7	121,075	86.8	144,975	89.2
Total Population	30,213	100.0	34,432	100.0	53,209	100.0	58,245	100.0	71,319	100.0	112,141	100.0	139,430	100.0	164,313	100.0

*The 1981 figures are for the Census Metropolitan Area.
**Includes Newfoundland in 1951, 1961, 1971, 1981.
Source: *Censuses of Canada, 1911-1981.*

TABLE VII
BIRTHPLACE OF REGINA'S FOREIGN-BORN POPULATION, 1911-81*

BIRTHPLACE	1911 NUMBER	%	1921 NUMBER	%	1931 NUMBER	%	1941 NUMBER	%	1951 NUMBER	%	1961 NUMBER	%	1971 NUMBER	%	1981 NUMBER	%
Great Britain	8,447	28.0	9,038	26.3	10,390	19.5	8,224	14.1	6,856	9.6	6,339	5.6	5,125	3.7	3,995	2.4
United States	1,451	4.8	1,860	5.4	2,442	4.6	2,229	3.8	2,136	3.0	2,310	2.0	2,470	1.8	2,270	1.4
Scandinavia	130	0.4	151	0.4	323	0.6	248	0.4	271	0.4	374	0.3				
Germany	475	1.6	211	0.6	462	0.9	272	0.5	475	0.7	1,889	1.7	1,800	1.3	1,360	0.9
Russia**	4,395	14.5	3,208	9.3	4,943	9.3	3,964	6.8	1,426	2.0	1,605	1.4	1,505	1.0	905	0.6
Poland			70	0.2	810	1.5	551	1.0	871	1.2	1,065	1.0	1,075	0.8	835	0.5
Italy	22	0.1	9		8		15	0.1	15		322	0.3	490	0.4	610	0.4
Asia	144	0.5	270	0.8	329	0.6	263	0.5	207	0.3	465	0.4	1,150	0.8	2,580	1.6
Other	213	0.7	203	0.6	325	0.6	276	0.5	3,167	4.4	5,193	4.6	4,740	3.4	4,870	3.0
Total Foreign-Born	15,277	50.6	15,020	43.6	20,032	37.6	16,042	27.7	15,424	21.6	19,562	17.3	18,355	13.2	17,410	10.8
Total Population	30,213	100.0	34,432	100.0	53,209	100.0	58,245	100.0	71,319	100.0	112,141	100.0	139,430	100.0	164,313	100.0

*The 1981 figures are for the Census Metropolitan Area.
**Russia includes the following: 1901 — Romania; 1911 — Austria, Bohemia, Bukovina, Bulgaria, Galicia, Hungary and Romania; 1921 — Austria, Bulgaria, Czechoslovakia, Galicia, Hungary, Romania, Ukraine and Yugoslavia; 1931 — Austria, Czechoslovakia, Hungary, Romania, Ukraine and Yugoslavia; 1941 — Austria, Bulgaria, Czechoslovakia, Hungary, Romania and Yugoslavia; 1951, 1961, 1971, 1981 — U.S.S.R
Source: *Censuses of Canada, 1911-1981.*

TABLE VIII
ETHNIC ORIGINS OF REGINA'S POPULATION, 1901-81*

ETHNIC GROUP	1901 NUMBER	%	1911 NUMBER	%	1921 NUMBER	%	1931 NUMBER	%	1941 NUMBER	%	1951 NUMBER	%	1961 NUMBER	%	1971 NUMBER	%	1981 NUMBER	%
Asian	6	.2	89	.3	273	.8	403	.7	400	.7	367	.5	890	.8	1,350	1.0	3,495	2.2
British	1,891	71.5	20,960	69.4	25,515	74.1	35,823	67.3	37,501	64.4	40,191	56.4	52,539	46.8	64,650	46.4	77,650	47.8
French	31	1.2	520	1.7	700	2.0	1,086	2.0	1,855	3.2	2,565	3.6	4,714	4.2	6,145	4.4	7,315	4.5
German	478	18.1	2,758	9.1	2,902	8.4	7,160	13.5	7,428	12.8	11,944	16.7	22,370	20.0	30,375	21.8	29,345	18.1
Italian	1		25	.1	18	.1	46	.1	65	.1	104	.1	638	.5	990	.7	1,200	.8
Dutch	13	.5	63	.2	242	.7	490	1.0	904	1.5	1,056	1.5	2,138	2.0	2,155	1.5	2,125	1.0
Scandinavian	7	.2	238	.8	448	1.3	1,081	2.0	1,522	2.6	2,418	3.4	4,532	4.0	5,260	3.8	4,325	2.7
Russian**	174	6.6	3,352	11.1	2,410	7.0	3,476	6.5	4,286	7.4	3,643	5.1	1,679	1.5	900	.6	575	.4
Ukrainian	-	-	299	1.0	162	.5	1,074	2.0	1,831	2.6	2,702	3.8	5,741	5.1	8,720	6.3	9,820	6.1
Polish	-	-	118	.4	156	.5	719	1.4	1,024	1.7	1,584	2.2	3,032	2.7	3,730	2.7	2,990	1.8
Jewish	-	-	130	.4	860	2.5	1,010	1.9	944	1.6	660	1.0	653	.6	865	.6	720	.5
Native Peoples	39	1.5	6		16		8		39	.1	160	.2	539	.5	2,860	2.0	6,405	4.0
Others and Unspecified	5	.2	1,655	5.5	730	2.1	833	1.6	746	1.3	3,925	5.5	12,674	11.3	11,435	8.2	16,420	10.1
Total	2,645	100.0	30,213	100.0	34,432	100.0	53,209	100.0	58,245	100.0	71,319	100.0	112,141	100.0	139,435	100.0	162,385	100.0

*The 1981 figures are for the Census Metropolitan Area.

**Russian includes the following: 1901 — Austro-Hungarian; 1911 — Austrian, Bulgarian, Hungarian and Romanian; 1921, 1931, 1941 — Austrian, Czech, Hungarian, Romanian and Slovak; 1951 — Austrian, Czech, Hungarian and Slovak; 1961, 1971, 1981 — U.S.S.R.

Source: *Censuses of Canada, 1901-81.*

TABLE IX
MAJOR RELIGIOUS AFFILIATIONS OF REGINA'S POPULATION, 1901-81*

RELIGION	1901 NUMBER	%	1911 NUMBER	%	1921 NUMBER	%	1931 NUMBER	%	1941 NUMBER	%	1951 NUMBER	%	1961 NUMBER	%	1971 NUMBER	%	1981 NUMBER	%
Anglican	520	19.7	7,372	24.4	9,174	26.6	11,236	21.1	11,228	19.3	10,829	15.2	12,478	11.1	13,025	9.3	12,480	7.7
Baptist	112	4.2	1,416	4.7	1,301	3.8	1,975	3.7	2,020	3.5	2,056	2.9	2,586	2.3	2,560	1.8	3,030	1.9
Greek Orthodox	9	0.4	2,312	7.7	1,083	3.1	1,720	3.2	1,931	3.3	2,505	3.5	3,709	3.3	3,840	2.7	3,690	2.3
Jewish	129	0.4	860	2.5	1,007	1.9	932	1.6	740	1.0	817	0.7	795	0.6	710	0.6	710	.4
Lutheran	103	3.9	1,255	4.1	1,069	3.1	2,914	5.5	3,470	6.0	6,507	9.1	13,341	11.9	16,445	11.8	18,195	11.2
Presbyterian	797	30.1	6,875	22.8	9,243	26.9	6,758	12.7	5,581	9.6	4,034	5.6	3,754	3.3	3,835	2.7	2,815	1.7
Roman Catholic	617	23.3	4,750	15.7	5,573	16.2	10,540	19.8	11,785	20.2	16,305	22.9	31,147	27.8	42,945	30.8	52,430	32.3
Ukrainian Catholic							604	1.0	798	1.1	1,667	1.5	2,920	2.1	3,465	2.1	3,465	2.1
United Church**	429	16.2	4,969	16.4	4,391	12.8	14,324	27.0	17,304	2937.0	24,199	34.0	36,741	32.8	38,910	28.0	40,965	25.2
Other and No Religion	58	2.2	1,135	3.8	1,738	5.0	2,735	5.1	3,390	5.8	3,346	4.7	5,901	5.3	14,165	10.2	24,605	15.2
Total	2645	100.0	30,213	100.0	34,432	100.0	53,209	100.0	58,245	100.0	71,319	100.0	112,141	100.0	139,440	100.0	162,385	100.0

*The 1981 figures are for the Census Metropolitan Area.
**Includes Congregationalists and Methodists until 1931.

Sources: *Censuses of Canada, 1901-81.*

TABLE X
AGE COMPOSITION OF REGINA'S POPULATION, 1921-81*

YEAR	0-14 NUMBER	%	15-44 NUMBER	%	45-64 NUMBER	%	65+ NUMBER	%	Age Not Given NUMBER	%	Total Population
1921	10,639	30.9	19,321	56.1	3,798	11.0	614	1.8	60	0.2	34,432
1931	15,148	28.5	28,377	53.3	8,278	15.6	1,398	2.6	8	-	53,209
1941	13,363	23.0	30,640	52.5	11,605	20.0	2,637	4.5	-	-	58,245
1951	17,859	25.0	34,786	48.8	13,199	18.5	5,475	7.7	-	-	71,319
1961	35,332	31.5	50,385	45.0	18,069	16.1	8,355	7.4	-	-	112,141
1971	41,060	29.4	61,980	44.4	25,040	18.0	11,385	8.2	-	-	139,465
1981	38,770	23.6	81,590	49.6	28,875	17.6	15,095	9.2	-	-	164,330

*The 1981 figures are for the Census Metropolitan Area.

Source: Censuses of Canada, 1921-81.

TABLE XI
VALUE OF BUILDING PERMITS ISSUED IN REGINA 1904-79

YEAR	VALUE ($)	YEAR	VALUE ($)	YEAR	VALUE ($)
1904	210,000	1930	2,971,543	1956	18,369,087
1905	750,000	1931	1,598,440	1957	20,624,300
1906	2,000,000	1932	277,069	1959	29,150,656
1907	1,177,840	1933	376,392	1959	35,125,341
1908	516,656	1934	291,696	1960	24,432,124
1909	749,479	1935	632,944	1961	32,573,315
1910	2,351,288	1936	358,865	1962	29,798,338
1911	5,099,340	1937	463,941	1963	36,020,471
1912	8,047,309	1938	477,780	1964	38,554,915
1913	4,018,350	1939	587,615	1965	50,857,990
1914	1,765,875	1940	1,052,919	1966	39,358,983
1915	464,065	1941	1,149,791	1967	38,330,827
1916	222,075	1942	755,349	1968	38,824,533
1917	416,460	1943	455,855	1969	30,364,703
1918	1,006,000	1944	1,166,623	1970	25,325,228
1919	1,699,020	1945	2,803,279	1971	51,888,743
1920	2,597,920	1946	6,024,876	1972	38,891,636
1921	2,160,030	1947	3,900,532	1973	69,499,884
1922	1,784,124	1948	5,070,785	1974	92,364,048
1923	1,264,030	1949	6,124,849	1975	152,106,979
1924	939,785	1950	6,475,623	1976	177,670,675
1925	1,208,403	1951	6,068,657	1977	183,918,786
1926	4,242,402	1952	12,736,939	1978	163,499,481
1927	3,482,090	1953	27,124,358	1979	180,018,487
1928	6,619,200	1954	19,284,639		
1929	10,022,631	1955	24,358,332		

Source: City of Regina, Municipal Manual, 1930; City of Regina Community Profile, 1981-82.

TABLE XII
THE LABOUR FORCE OF REGINA BY INDUSTRY, 1911-81*

INDUSTRY	1911 NUMBER	%	1921 NUMBER	%	1931 NUMBER	%	1941 NUMBER	%	1951 NUMBER	%	1961 NUMBER	%	1971 NUMBER	%	1981 NUMBER	%
Primary: Agriculture, Forestry, Fishing, Trapping and Mining	346	2.1	530	3.6	512	2.3	494	2.2	602	2.0	816	1.7	765	1.3	1,860	2.1
Manufacturing	1,414	8.6	1,578	10.8	2,721	12.2	3,282	14.5	3,662	11.5	4,681	10.0	5,880	10.2	7,675	9.0
Construction	4,712	28.8	1,211	8.3	2,172	9.8	1,306	5.8	2,145	6.7	3,682	8.0	3,475	6.0	6,180	7.2
Transportation	1,799	11.0	1,514	10.3	2,097	9.4	2,032	9.0	3,102	9.7	5,805	12.4	6,670	11.6	8,925	10.3
Trade and Commerce	3,446	21.0	3,840	26.2	5,717	25.7	6,719	29.7	10,007	31.4	13,319	28.5	15,520	27.0	24,130	28.0
Government Employees (all levels)	2,049	12.5	1,804	12.3	2,392	10.7	2,932	13.0	5,096	16.0	6,245	13.4	8,290	14.4	11,085	12.9
Services	2,615	16.0	3,414	23.3	5,486	24.7	5,239	23.2	6,968	21.9	10,989	23.6	16,515	28.6	26,340	30.5
Other or Unspecified	-	-	758	5.2	1,158	5.2	586	2.6	242	.8	1,135	2.4	505	.9	-	-
Total	16,381	100.0	14,649	100.0	22,255	100.0	22,590	100.0	31,824	100.0	46,672	100.0	57,620	100.0	86,195	100.0

*The 1981 figures are for the Census Metropolitan Area.
**Total including Active Service is 25,805.

Source: *Censuses of Canada, 1911-81.*

TABLE XIII
WHEAT ACREAGE, PRODUCTION AND VALUE
IN SASKATCHEWAN, 1905-76

Year	Acreage (millions of acres)	Yield (bushels/ acre)	Production (millions of bushels)	Value (millions of dollars)*	Year	Acreage (millions of acres)	Yield (bushels/ acre)	Production (millions of bushels)	Value (millions of dollars)*
1905	1.1	23.0	26.1	-	1948	14.3	13.3	191.0	311.3
1906	1.7	21.4	37.0	-	1949	15.7	11.8	186.0	299.4
1907	2.0	13.5	27.6	-	1950	16.5	16.5	272.0	405.2
1908	3.7	13.6	50.6	-	1951	15.6	20.8	325.0	494.0
1909	4.0	22.1	90.2	-	1952	16.6	27.0	449.0	713.9
1910	4.6	15.5	72.6	-	1953	16.8	23.3	391.0	520.0
1911	5.2	18.5	97.2	-	1954	16.6	10.2	169.3	204.4
1912	5.3	19.9	107.1	-	1955	14.1	22.7	320.0	441.6
1913	5.7	19.5	112.3	-	1956	14.5	24.4	355.0	440.2
1914	6.0	12.4	74.6	-	1957	13.8	16.6	229.0	295.4
1915	8.5	25.2	214.7	-	1958	14.2	15.0	213.0	281.1
1916	9.0	16.3	147.5	188.9	1959	15.8	16.0	253.0	333.9
1917	8.2	14.3	117.9	229.9	1960	15.8	20.7	327.0	516.6
1918	9.2	10.0	92.4	184.0	1961	16.0	8.5	137.0	239.7
1919	10.5	8.5	89.9	208.7	1962	17.3	20.4	354.0	591.1
1920	10.0	11.2	113.1	175.3	1963	17.9	27.5	493.0	862.7
1921	13.5	13.9	188.0	142.8	1964	19.2	18.1	348.0	556.8
1922	12.3	20.3	250.1	212.6	1965	18.5	21.6	400.0	680.0
1923	12.7	21.2	271.6	176.5	1966	19.4	27.7	537.0	950.4
1924	13.0	10.2	132.9	160.8	1967	19.6	17.2	339.0	549.1
1925	12.5	18.8	235.4	294.2	1968	19.0	19.6	372.0	499.9
1926	13.5	16.2	219.6	237.2	1969	16.6	27.0	448.0	577.9
1927	12.9	19.5	252.5	244.9	1970	8.0	26.2	210.0	304.5
1928	13.7	23.3	321.2	247.3	1971	12.9	26.7	345.0	465.7
1929	14.4	11.1	160.5	165.3	1972	13.9	23.5	326.0	612.8
1930	14.3	14.4	206.7	97.1	1973	15.4	24.0	370.0	1,702.0
1931	15.0	8.8	132.4	50.3	1974	14.5	21.0	304.0	1,316.0
1932	15.5	13.6	211.5	74.0	1975	15.2	25.5	387.0	1,412.5
1933	14.7	8.7	128.0	60.1	1976	17.4	31.5	548.0	1,625.4
1934	13.2	8.6	114.2	69.6					
1935	13.2	10.8	142.1	85.3					
1936	14.7	7.5	110.0	101.2					
1937	13.8	2.6	36.0	37.8					
1938	13.7	10.0	137.8	79.9					
1939	14.2	19.1	271.3	146.5					
1940	15.5	17.1	266.7	154.6					
1941	12.1	12.1	147.0	86.7					
1942	12.3	24.7	305.0	234.8					
1943	9.6	15.2	146.0	166.4					
1944	13.2	18.3	242.1	302.6					
1945	13.6	12.4	168.1	275.6					
1946	14.2	14.6	208.0	336.9					
1947	14.2	12.2	173.0	281.9					

*Comparable figures are not available for the period 1905-15.
Source: Saskatchewan, Department of Agriculture, Annual Reports, 1905-15;

Endnotes

Abbreviations
SAB   Saskatchewan Archives board
CRA   City of Regina Archives
CSP   Canada Sessional Papers
GAI   Glenbow-Alberta Institute
PAC   Public Archives of Canada

Introduction

[1] J. H. Archer, *Saskatchewan: A History* (Saskatoon, 1980), pp. 52-67; G. W. D. Abrams, *Prince Albert: The First Century, 1866-1966* (Saskatoon, 1966), pp. 18-34. The construction of Canada's first transcontinental railway and its impact on prairie settlement and townsite location have been examined in considerable detail. H. A. Innis, *History of the Canadian Pacific Railway* 2nd ed.(Toronto, 1971) and W. K. Lamb, *History of the Canadian Pacific Railway* (New York, 1977) both advance the traditional view concerning the CPR's abandonment of the original northern route. So does W. A. Waiser, "A Willing Scapegoat: John Macoun and the Route of the CPR," *Prairie Forum*, Vol. 10, No. 1 (Spring, 1985), pp. 65-81. P. Berton, *The Last Spike: The Great Railway, 1881-1885* (Toronto, 1971) argues that the company wished to avoid competition with established real estate interests. The role of the CPR as a townsite promoter, and its relationship with the Canada North-West Land Company, are explored briefly in J. B. Hedges, *Building the Canadian West: The Land and Colonization Policies of the Canadian Pacific Railway* (New York, 1939). A fuller account, with particular emphasis on Regina, can be found in J. W. Brennan, "Business-Government Co-operation in Townsite Promotion in Regina and Moose Jaw, 1882-1903," in A. F. J. Artibise, ed., *Town and City: Aspects of Western Canadian Urban Development* (Regina, 1981), pp. 95-100.

[2] *CSP, 1884*, No. 12, p. 3; *Saskatchewan Herald*, 30 September 1882.

[3] Brennan, pp. 100-101; J. B. D. Larmour, "Edgar Dewdney, Commissioner of Indian Affairs and Lieutenant Governor of the North-West Territories, 1879-1888," unpublished M.A. thesis, University of Saskatchewan, Regina, 1969, pp. 105-16.

[4] *Manitoba Free Press*, 26 September 1882, 4 October 1882.

[5] Ibid., 28 October 1882; W. B. Scarth to J. A. Macdonald, 10 November 1882, J. A. Macdonald Papers, PAC, pp. 142881-83.

[6] *Manitoba Free Press*, 28 October 1882; G. Stephen to J. A. Macdonald, 28 October 1882, J. A. Macdonald Papers, PAC, pp. 121556-57, emphasis in original; J. A. Macdonald to D. McIntyre, 12 December 1882, ibid., letterbooks, vol. 22; Brennan, p. 100.

[7] *Manitoba Free Press*, 10 October 1882, 2 December 1882, 11 December 1882, 9 February 1883.

[8] Ibid., 13 November 1882, 2 December 1882, 8 December 1882; J. Murray to J. M. Egan, 14 March 1883, Department of the Interior Records, Dominion Lands Branch, PAC, file 70199; W. B. Scarth to J. A. Macdonald, 2 January 1883, E. Dewdney Papers, GAI; same to same, 17 January 1883, J. A. Macdonald Papers, PAC, p. 142885.

[9] E. Dewdney to Minister of the Interior, 29 December 1882, Department of the Interior Records, Dominion Lands Branch, PAC, File 54657; W. H. Gibbs and D. L. Scott to W. B. Scarth, 15 February 1883, J. A. Macdonald Papers, PAC, pp. 46059-61; *Manitoba Free Press*, 15 February 1883; *CSP, 1884*, No. 12, p. 3; *Regina Leader*, 28 June 1883, 19 July 1883, 2 August 1883.

[10] *Manitoba Free Press*, 16 February 1883; *Order-In-Council No. 2778, of Dec. 29th 1900 Approving Report, Evidence and Cash Statements Submitted by the Townsite Commissioners Appointed by Order-In-Council No. 1527 of June 19th, 1900*, SAB (hereafter cited as *Townsite Report*), pp. 11, 109; C. B. Koester, *Mr. Davin, M.P.: A Biography of Nicholas Flood Davin* (Saskatoon, 1980), pp. 1-58.

[11]*Regina Leader*, 19 July 1883, 9 August 1883, 11 October 1883; *North-West Territories Gazette*, 8 December 1883; A. N. Reid, "Informal Town Government in Regina, 1882-3," *Saskatchewan History*, Vol. VI, No. 3 (Autumn, 1953), pp. 81-88.

[12]*Regina Leader*, 10 January 1884, 17 January 1884.

[13]*The Assiniboia Club, Regina*, (Regina, 1945), p. 3; *Manitoba Free Press*, 19 December 1882; *Regina Leader*, 22 November 1883, 13 January 1885.

[14]*Manitoba Free Press*, 21 March 1883; *Regina Leader*, 17 May 1883, 6 December 1883; *CSP, 1883*, No. 23, pp. 142-43, *1884*, No. 12, pp. 18-19, *1885*, No. 13, pp. 10-11.

[15]*Moose Jaw News*, 18 January 1884; *Regina Leader*, 28 February 1884; N. F. Davin to J. A. Macdonald, 13 June 1884, J. A. Macdonald Papers, PAC, p. 195468.

Chapter One

[1]Canada, *Statutes*, 46 Vict., Chapter 72; *Regina Leader*, 21 April 1885, 26 May 1885; C. Martin, *"Dominion Lands" Policy* 2nd ed. (Toronto, 1973), pp. 51-72.

[2]*Regina Leader*, 8 June 1886, 20 August 1889, 1 July 1890; Lamb, p. 177.

[3]*Regina Leader*, 4 April 1892, 25 April 1892, 23 May 1892, 30 May 1892, 14 July 1892, 15 August 1892, 25 August 1892.

[4]Innis, pp. 176-78; *Regina Leader*, 24 February 1885, 9 March 1886, 16 March 1886, 30 March 1886; Regina Town Council, Minute Book, 25 March 1886.

[5]A. F. J. Artibise, *Winnipeg: An Illustrated History* (Toronto 1977), p. 32; D. Kerr, "Wholesale Trade on the Canadian Plains in the Late Nineteenth Century: Winnipeg and Its Competition," in H. Palmer, ed., *The Settlement of the West* (Calgary, 1977), pp. 130-52; *The New West* (Winnipeg, 1888), p. 115.

[6]*Regina Leader*, 29 June 1886, 9 November 1886, 28 February 1888, 31 July 1888, 4 September 1888, 8 April 1890, 25 August 1891, 15 September 1891, 23 March 1893.

[7]Canada, Dominion Bureau of Statistics, *Census of the Three Provisional Districts of the North-West Territories, 1884-5 (Ottawa, 1886)*, p. 3; *Fourth Census of Canada, 1901* (Ottawa, 1902), vol. 1, p. 5; *CSP, 1886-1898*, Reports of the Land Board, Department of the Interior; A. N. Lalonde, "The North-West Rebellion and Its Effects on Settlers and Settlement in the Canadian West," *Saskatchewan History*, vol. 27, no. 3 (Autumn, 1974), 95-102.

[8]Regina Town Council, By-Law no. 18, 19 October 1885; idem. no. 109, 5 October 1891; idem. no. 116, 15 February 1892; *Regina Leader*, 4 August 1891.

[9]F. H. Auld, "The Territorial Exhibition, 1895," *Saskatchewan History*, vol. 15, no. 1 (Winter 1962), pp. 19-29; Regina Town Council, Minute Book, 19 May 1896.

[10]*Regina Leader*, 31 May 1887, 6 September 1887; J. W. Powers, *The History of Regina, Its Foundation and Growth* (Regina, 1887), p. 67; J. Hawkes, *The Story of Saskatchewan and Its People* (Chicago, 1924), vol. 2, pp. 1288-93, vol. 3, pp. 1686-88.

[11]*Regina Leader*, 1 May 1888, 26 March 1896, 1 December 1898. The role of the southern Alberta ranching community in providing capital for early manufacturing ventures in Calgary is discussed in M. Foran, *Calgary: An Illustrated History* (Toronto, 1978), p. 30.

[12]*Regina Leader*, 24 March 1885, 15 September 1898; L. H. Thomas, "The Saskatchewan Legislative Building and Its Predecessors," Royal Architectural Institute of Canada, *Journal*, vol. 32, no. 7 (July 1955): 250.

[13]*Regina Leader*, 6 April 1886, 19 June 1888, 6 May 1897.

[14]*CSP, 1880-81*, no. 3, pp. 8-9; *CSP, 1884*, no. 125, p. 32; R. B. Deane, *Mounted Police Life in Canada: A Record of Thirty-one Years' Service* (London, 1916), p. 22.

[15]*Regina Leader*, 24 March 1885; *CSP, 1886*, no. 50, pp. 1-60.

[16]*CSP, 1886-1906*, North-West Mounted Police Annual Reports; *Regina Leader*, 20 September 1887.

[17]*Regina Leader*, 14 September 1886; *CSP, 1887*, no. 7, p. 13; *CSP, 1888*, no. 28, pp. 12-13; *CSP, 1890*, no. 13, p. 8; *CSP, 1906*, no. 28, p. 14.

[18]*Regina Leader*, 27 July 1886, 26 June 1888, 4 December 1888, 25 December 1888. On the Davin-Herchmer feud see R. C. Macleod, *The North-West Mounted Police and Law Enforcement, 1873-1905* (Toronto, 1976), pp. 53-55.

[19]L. W. Herchmer to F. White, 26 November 1888, NWMP Records, Comptroller's Office, PAC, File 79-1888; memoran-

dum prepared by F. White, 27 June 1889, idem., file 79-1889; *Manitoba Free Press*, 10 April 1890.

[20]*Regina Leader*, 27 March 1902, 24 April 1902, 12 June 1902, 25 December 1902.

[21]Ibid., 23 January 1902, 20 April 1904.

[22]*The New West*, p. 115; *Homes for Millions* (Ottawa, 1892), p. 43.

[23]Macleod, pp. 74-82.

[24]*Regina Leader*, 19 July 1900, 22 October 1903; H. Lehmann, *The German Canadians, 1750-1937: Immigration, Settlement and Culture*, trans. and edited by G. P. Bassler (St. John's, 1986), pp. 113, 116, 213-37 passim.

[25]B. Z. Kazymyra, *Early Ukrainian Settlement in Regina, 1890-1920* (Regina, 1977), pp. 32-38.

[26]*Regina Leader*, 27 August 1885. Anti-Oriental sentiment seems to have been far stronger in Calgary, for example; see Foran, pp. 40-44, and J. B. Dawson, "The Chinese Experience in Frontier Calgary: 1885-1910," in A. W. Rasporich and H. Klassen, eds., *Frontier Calgary: Town, City and Region, 1875-1914* (Calgary, 1975), pp. 124-40.

[27]*Regina Leader*, 31 March 1885, 7 April 1885; *CSP, 1886*, no. 43, p. 237.

[28]J. Wilson and C. Gass to W. Laurier, 1 March 1905, W. Laurier Papers, PAC, p. 208845; T. M. Marshall to W. Laurier, 2 March 1905, idem., p. 208894.

[29]J. F. Fraser, *Canada As It Is* (London, 1905), p. 153; *Regina Leader*, 29 October 1885.

[30]*Regina Leader*, 18 March 1890, 25 March 1890, 23 September 1890.

[31]Regina Town Council, By-law no. 103, 27 April 1891; *Regina Leader*, 13 March 1902.

[32]*Regina Leader*, 21 May 1903, 5 October 1904, 11 October 1905.

[33]Regina Town Council, By-law no. 131, 19 December 1892; *Regina Leader*, 24 August 1893, 24 July 1902.

[34]Regina Town Council, Minute Book, 3 October 1887, 15 February 1892; *Regina Leader*, 7 February 1888.

[35]Regina Town Council, Minute Book, 23 September 1889; *Regina Leader*, 12 September 1901.

[36]*Regina Standard*, 1 December 1898; *Regina Leader*, 12 December 1901.

[37]*Townsite Report*, pp. 68, 130. For a fuller discussion of this controversy see Brennan, pp. 106-12.

[38]*Regina Leader*, 4 July 1892; J. Feather, "Hospitals in Saskatchewan in Territorial Days," *Saskatchewan History*, vol. 40, no. 2 (Spring, 1987), pp. 62-71; E. Saddlemeyer, "Regina Victoria Hospital," unpublished student essay, SAB.

[39]Regina Town Council, Minute Book, 16 March 1885, 19 April 1886; F. White to N. F. Davin, 3 August 1891, NWMP Records, Comptroller's Office, PAC, file 361-91.

[40]Regina Town Council, Minute Book, 4 February 1889; *Regina Leader*, 12 March 1889, 21 October 1890, 11 August 1891, 18 August 1891; Regina Town Council, By-law no. 123, 23 July 1892. Regina's experience with prostitution was hardly unique, as S. W. Horrall has demonstrated in "The (Royal) North-West Mounted Police and Prostitution on the Canadian Prairies," *Prairie Forum*, vol. 10, no. 1 (Spring, 1985), pp. 105-27.

[41]Regina Town Council, Minute Book, 5 May 1890; *Regina Leader*, 6 May 1890, 23 November 1893, 18 December 1902, 26 March 1903.

[42]*Regina Standard*, 22 December 1898.

[43]*Regina Leader*, 30 August 1887, 1 October 1903; Regina City Council, Minute Book, 31 December 1904.

[44]*Regina Leader*, 26 August 1890, 16 December 1890, 8 June 1893, 4 December 1902; Regina City Council, Minute Book, 19 January 1903.

[45]Regina City Council, Minute Book, 5 January 1903, 19 January 1903; *Regina Leader*, 22 January 1903; North-West Territories, *Ordinances*, 1903, chapt. 28.

[46]Regina City Council, By-Law No. 305, 25 April 1904; *Regina Leader*, 9 July 1903, 1 June 1904, 4 January 1905.

[47]Memorandum of agreement signed by J. G. Turriff and F. T. Griffin, 27 March 1902, Department of the Interior Records, Dominion Lands Branch, PAC, file 69563; F. T. Griffin to Tupper, Phippen and Tupper, 30 June 1902, Canada North-West Land Company Records, GAI, file 59; Regina City Council, By-Law no. 306, 2 May 1904.

[48]Koester, pp. 71-174, 191-210; D. H. Bocking, "Premier Walter Scott: His Early Career," *Saskatchewan History*, vol. 13, no. 3 (Autumn, 1960), pp. 81-99.

[49]*Daily Standard*, 13 March 1905; J. Balfour and J. F. Bole to W. Scott, 10 June 1905, W. Scott Papers, SAB, pp. 5085-90; W. Scott to J. Balfour, 17 June 1905, idem., pp. 5091-92; W. Scott to J. M. Young, 14 July 1905, idem., pp. 7079-82.

[50]W. Scott to L. B. Cochrane, 20 December 1905, W. Scott Papers, SAB, p. 37981; Regina City Council, Minute Book, 2 January 1906. A more detailed account of the provincial capital question can be found in J. E. Murray, "The Provincial Capital Controversy in Saskatchewan," *Saskatchewan History,*vol. 5, no. 3 (Autumn, 1952), pp. 81-106 and D. Kerr and S. Hanson, *Saskatoon: The First Half-Century* (Edmonton, 1982), pp. 37-39.

[51]*Leader-Post*, 16 May 1955, 18 June 1963; P. D. Routledge, "The North-West Mounted Police and Their Influence on the Sporting and Social Life of the North-West Territories, 1870-1904" unpublished M.A. thesis, University of Alberta, 1978; R. B. Shepard, "Symbol of Empire: Government House, Regina," *Saskatchewan History*, vol. 36, no. 1 (Winter, 1983), 20-30; H. Kallmann, G. Potvin and K. Winters, eds., *Encyclopedia of Music in Canada* (Toronto, 1981), p. 802; E. G. Drake, *Regina: The Queen City* (Toronto, 1955), chapt. 3-9 *passim*; Koester, pp. 175-90.

[52]*Regina Leader*, 6 April 1886, 3 February 1891, 19 April 1894, 13 January 1904; J. Archer, *Honoured With the Burden: A History of the Regina Board of Education* (Regina, 1987), pp. 15-35.

[53]*Regina Leader*, 6 September 1905.

Chapter 2

[1]S. B. Steele, *Forty Years in Canada* (London, 1915), p. 412.

[2]*Morning Leader*, 23 February 1907.

[3]T. D. Regehr, *The Canadian Northern Railway: Pioneer Road of the Northern Prairies, 1895-1918* (Toronto, 1976), pp. 172, 177-79, 198-209; D. S. Richan, "Boosterism and Urban Rivalry in Regina and Moose Jaw, 1902-1913," unpublished M.A. thesis, University of Regina, 1981, pp. 56-63; M. L. Bladen, "Construction of Railways in Canada, Part II: From 1885 to 1931," *Contributions to Canadian Economics,*vol. 7 (1934), 83, 93-100; Regina City Council, Minute Book, 19 June 1911, 3 July 1911.

[4]J. L. Moser, "The Impact of City Council's Decisions Between 1903 and 1930 on the Morphological Development of Regina" (unpublished M.A. thesis, University of Regina, 1978), pp. 3-10; Richan, pp. 63-78; W. T. Jackman, *Economic Principles of Transportation* (Toronto, 1935), pp. 248, 376-78; H. Darling, *The Politics of Freight Rates: The Railway Freight Rate Issue in Canada* (Toronto, 1980), pp. 33-43.

[5]*Morning Leader*, 8 May 1913; *Greater Regina* (Regina, 1910); Hawkes, vol. 3, pp. 1984-87.

[6]*Henderson's Directory of Regina*, 1908, 1912; Thomas, "Saskatchewan Legislative Building," p. 252; *CSP, 1909*, no. 28, p. 16; *CSP, 1912, No. 28, pp. 133-34*; *CSP, 1913, No. 28, pp. 138-39*; *CSP, 1914*, No. 28, pp. 154-55.

[7]*Regina Leader*, 5 February 1903; *Morning Leader*, 31 July 1912; *Leader-Post*, 3 February 1938; Hawkes, vol. 3, p. 1968.

[8]*Morning Leader*, 8 May 1913.

[9]*Regina. The Queen City of the Middle West. The Undisputed Business Centre of the Wheat Fields of Canada* (Regina, 1911); Greater Regina Club, *Regina: The Capital of Saskatchewan, Canada. Its Commercial and Industrial Opportunities* (Regina, 1910); *Regina Standard*, 1 February 1905; *Morning Leader*, 27 April 1907; *Daily Province*, 17 May 1912.

[10]Regina City Council, Minute Book, 20 March 1905; Richan, pp. 146-47; H. E. Bronson, "The Developing Structure of the Saskatchewan Meat Packing Industry: A Study of Economic Welfare,"(unpublished Ph.D. dissertation, University of Saskatchewan, 1965), pp. 16-23.

[11]Richan, pp. 147-50, 157; Kerr and Hanson, pp. 131-32, 137-38; R. C. Brown and R. Cook, Canada, 1896-1921: A Nation Transformed (Toronto, 1974), p. 195.

[12]*Morning Leader*, 29 November 1910, 8 December 1910.

[13]Saskatchewan, *Report on Coal and Power Investigation* (Regina, 1913), pp. 130-31.

[14]*Morning Leader*, 29 November 1912, 1 November 1913; C. O. White, *Power for a Province: A History of Saskatchewan Power* (Regina, 1976), pp. 6-20.

[15]Canada, Dominion Bureau of Statistics, *Fifth Census of Canada, 1911* (Ottawa, 1912), Vol. III, pp. 354, 364; *Morning Leader*, 8 May 1913.

[16] J. K. Hunter to J. A. Calder, 10 November 1908, J. A. Calder Papers, SAB, pp. 7197-98; *Daily Standard*, 16 May 1912; *Daily Province*, 18 May 1912; *Morning Leader*, 18 May 1912, 15 November 1913; Saskatchewan, *Statutes*, 3 Geo. V, Chapter 27, 4 Geo V, chapt. 42.

[17] *Morning Leader*, 23 November 1912, 30 November 1912, 21 July 1913; Saskatchewan, Department of Agriculture, *Annual Report, 1913* (Regina, 1914), pp. 95-99, 108-9.

[18] J. S. Woodsworth, *Report of a Preliminary and General Social Survey of Regina* (1913), pp. 19-20.

[19] *Morning Leader*, 16 November 1912, 19 November 1912. Since 1892 the law had required that all schools be taught in the English language, though French could also be used as a language of instruction in the first two grades. In 1901 the scope of the legislation was widened, permitting instruction in "any language other than English" during the last hour of the school day as well. One or more "competent persons" could be employed to provide such instruction, and the regulations stipulated that the cost of employing a "competent person" who was not the teacher normally in charge of the school would be borne by a special levy on the parents of the pupils. (North-West Territories, *Ordinances*, 1892, no. 22, 1901, chapt. 29.)

[20] Woodsworth, p.9; *Leader Post*, 4 June 1966; F. Gerein, *Outline of History of the Archdiochese of Regina* (Regina 1961). p. 112; K Tischler, "The German Canadians in Saskatchewan with Particular Refernce to the Language Problem, 1900-1930"(unpublished M.A. thesis, University of Saskatchewan, 1978), pp. 2-17, 39-50.

[21] K. H. Burmeister, ed., *Western Canada 1909: Travel Letters by Wilhelm Cohnstaedt* (Regina, 1976), p. 10; Woodsworth, pp. 36-39.

[22] Kazymyra, pp. 38-42; M. P. Toombs, "A Saskatchewan Experiment in Teacher Education, 1907-1917," *Saskatchewan History*, vol. 17, No. 1 (Winter, 1964), pp. 1-11; R. Radecki and B. Heydenkorn, *A Member of a Distinguished Family: The Polish Group in Canada* (Toronto, 1976), pp. 63-65; H. L. Kutarna, "Polish People in Regina, A Case History: St. Anthony's Roman Catholic Parish," (unpublished student essay, SAB).

[23] *Morning Leader*, 28 October 1907, 5 April 1913; *Daily Standard*, 15 December 1910.

[24] *Morning Leader*, 24 November 1913, 26 March 1914, 15 June 1914; R. Huel, "Pastor vs. Politician: The Reverend Murdoch MacKinnon and Premier Walter Scott's Amendment to the School Act," *Saskatchewan History*, vol. 32, no. 2 (Spring, 1979), 61-73. A fuller account of the prewar prohibition movement can be found in E. Pinno, "Temperance and Prohibition in Saskatchewan,"(unpublished M.A. thesis, University of Saskatchewan, Regina, 1971), pp. 1-48.

[25] *Morning Leader*, 30 July 1912; Woodsworth, pp. 26, 46-48.

[26] *Morning Leader*, 7 January 1914, 12 January 1914, 19 January 1914, 2 February 1914.

[27] *Regina: The Capital of Saskatchewan*, p. 39; *Daily Standard*, 9 August 1907; *Morning Leader*, 10 August 1907, 12 August 1907, 29 November 1907.

[28] W. J. C. Cherwinski, "Organized Labour in Saskatchewan: The T.L.C. Years, 1905-1945," unpublished Ph.D. dissertation, University of Alberta, 1971, p. 327; Saskatchewan, *Statutes*, 2 Geo. V, chapt. 17; Saskatchewan, Bureau of Labour, *Annual Report, 1912* (Regina, 1913), pp. 34-37, 41-42 idem., *1913* (Regina, 1914), p. 46; *Morning Leader*, 20 August 1913.

[29] Saskatchewan, Bureau of Labour, *Annual Report, 1911* (Regina, 1912), pp. 39-45, *1913*, p. 35-43; Regina City Council, Minute Book, 7 June 1909, 18 March 1912, 1 April 1912; Cherwinski, pp. 7-34, 276-77; G. Makahonuk, "Painters, Decorators and Paperhangers: A Case Study in Saskatchewan Labourism, 1906-1919," *Prairie Forum*, Vol. 10, No. 1 (Spring, 1985), pp. 189-99.

[30] *Regina Leader*, 13 January 1904; Moser, pp. 10-14, 27-30.

[31] *Morning Leader*, 2 December 1910.

[32] Regina City Council, By-Law no. 355, 17 April 1906; idem. Minute Book, 7 May 1906.

[33] J. A. Calder to W. Scott, 14 June 1906, Department of Public Works Records, SAB, file 119G; W. Scott to Calder, 19 June 1906, idem.; *Morning Leader*, 23 June 1906.

[34] Regina City Council, Minute Book, 4 July 1906, 1 October 1906; W. Scott to J. K. Hunter, 9 August 1906, W. Scott Papers, SAB,

pp. 52158-59; Hunter to Scott, 28 September 1906, Department of Public Works Records, SAB, File 119G.

[35]F. G. Todd to F. J. Robinson, 30 January 1907, Department of Public Works Records, SAB, file 119G; *Morning Leader*, 3 March 1908, 17 March 1908; R. E. Laporte, "The Development of Parks in Regina, 1882-1930: Private Initiative and Public Policy,"(unpublished M.A. thesis, University of Regina, 1984), pp. 82-85.

[36]*Morning Leader*, 27 April 1907; J. K. Hunter to D. D. Mann, 2 August 1909, City Clerk's Records, CRA, file 1028; Regina City Council, Minute Book, 29 April 1912.

[37]*Morning Leader*, 19 July 1910; *Daily Standard*, 25 July 1910.

[38]Regina City Council, Minute Book, 23 November 1910; Saskatchewan, *Statutes*, 3 Geo. V, Chapter 65; Board of Trade, *Annual Report, 1910* (Regina, 1910), p. 28.

[39]*Morning Leader*, 31 July 1912; Saskatchewan, Department of Municipal Affairs, *Annual Report*, 1913-1914 (Regina, 1914), p. 98.

[40]Regina City Council, Minute Book, 7 November 1910; *Morning Leader*, 27 March 1911; "Map of the City of Regina," 1913, SAB, A 20/87. On the relationship between boosterism and the expansion of civic boundaries see A. F. J. Artibise, "Boosterism and the Development of Prairie Cities, 1871-1913," in *Town and City*, pp. 209-35.

[41]Moser, pp. 36-44; C. Hatcher, *Saskatchewan's Pioneer Streetcars: The Story of the Regina Municipal Railway* (Montreal, 1971), pp. 8-27; Regina City Council, Minute Book, 3 July 1911; Macintosh and Hyde, *City of Regina Report and Financial Statement as at 31st of December, 1914* (Calgary, 1915), p. 27, CRA.

[42]B. Pullen-Burry, *From Halifax to Vancouver* (London, 1912), p. 239.

[43]F. G. Todd to J. K. Hunter, 6 March 1907, City Clerk's Records, CRA, File 762; *Morning Leader*, 27 April 1907.

[44]Woodsworth, p. 9; W. G. Van Egmond, "Public Buildings at Regina," *Construction*, vol. 8, no. 1 (January 1915), pp. 13-21; F. C. Pickwell, "Residential Work of Regina," idem., pp. 23-26; Hawkes, vol. 3, pp. 1795-96.

[45]*Morning Leader*, 26 February 1910, 6 September 1912.

[46]Ibid., 3 July 1912, 30 June 1913; P. H. Brennan, "It's An Ill Wind That Blows Nobody Good: Regina Faces Catastrophe, 1912 and 1918," (unpublished student essay, SAB).

[47]*Morning Leader*, 11 May 1911, 31 October 1912, 6 January 1913.

[48]*Daily Standard*, 11-13 September 1912; *Daily Province*, 12 September 1912, 14 September 1912; *Morning Leader*, 17 September 1912, 19 October 1912; Regina City Council, Minute Book, 18 October 1912.

[49]*Daily Province*, 13 September 1912; *Morning Leader*, 10 December 1912. A fuller account of the controversy surrounding the location of the GTP hotel in Wascana Park can be found in Laporte, pp. 134-40.

[50]*Morning Leader*, 15 March 1913.

[51]Regina City Council, Minute Book, 17 June 1913; *Morning Leader*, 1 July 1913; Laporte, pp. 87-89, 115-27.

[52]Richan, pp. 36-41.

[53]Saskatchewan, *Statutes*, 6 Edw. VIII, chapt. 46. The original draft of Regina's charter also contained a provision for cumulative voting, permitting ratepayers additional votes on money by-laws according to the value of their property up to a maximum of four votes for an assessment of $8,000. This proved to be too much for the farmer-dominated legislature, and it threw the clause out (*Morning Leader*, 15-16 May 1906, 18 May 1906).

[54]*Morning Leader*, 18 September 1906, 8 October 1909; Regina City Council, By-Law no. 544, 6 June 1910.

[55]City of Regina, Financial Statement, 1915, CRA; J. H. Perry, *Taxes, Tariffs, and Subsidies: A History of Canadian Fiscal Development* (Toronto, 1955), vol. 1, pp. 120, 124-33.

[56]*Morning Leader*, 7 December 1905, 9 December 1905, 13 December 1905; Regina City Council, By-law no. 368, 5 November 1906.

[57]*Morning Leader*, 11 February 1913, 8 October 1913. Similar ratepayers' associations were established in Wards One and Four as well during 1913 (Idem., 25 April 1913, 14 October 1913).

[58]Drake, pp. 190-91; *Morning Leader*, 15 November 1913, 29 November 1913.

[59]*Morning Leader*, 30 April 1912, 11 May 1912, 21 May 1912.

[60]Hatcher, pp. 21-22; *Morning Leader*, 25 November 1912; Regina City Council, Minute Book, 29 November 1912.

[61]Saskatchewan, *Statutes*, 3 Geo V, Chapter 27; *Morning Leader*, 9 December 1913, 9 July 1914, 10-11 August 1914.

[62]*Morning Leader*, 6 March 1908, 28 November 1911, 27 November 1912; J. R. Bothwell, *The First 50: 1909-1959* (Regina, 1959).

[63]*Morning Leader*, 29 November 1910, 28 November 1911, 27 November 1912.

[64]Regina City Council, By-Law no. 394, 5 June 1907, no. 657, 8 May 1912; *Morning Leader*, 28 November 1911, 26 November 1912; Gerein, pp. 229-30.

[65]Richan, pp. 97-128; R. M. Haig, *The Exemption of Improvements From Taxation in Canada and the United States* (New York, 1915), pp. 40-41; City of Regina, Financial Statement, 1913, CRA.

[66]Saskatchewan, *Statutes*, 8 Edw. VII, chapt. 15-16, 4 Geo. V, Chapter 41; *Morning Leader*, 9 October 1913.

[67]*Morning Leader*, 15 May 1908; Regina Board of Trade to W. Laurier, 8 April 1911, W. Laurier Papers, PAC, p. 184511; *CSP, 1909*, no. 18, pp. 444-47, *1911-1912*, no. 18, pp. 448-52.

[68]*Daily Province*, 14 March 1912; *Morning Leader*, 13 March 1912, 15 March 1912.

[69]M. Hayden, *Seeking a Balance: The University of Saskatchewan, 1907-1982* (Vancouver, 1983), pp. 5-45; J. E. Murray, "The Contest for the University of Saskatchewan," *Saskatchewan History*, vol. 12, no. 1 (Winter 1959): 1-22.

[70]*Morning Leader*, 15 February 1910; 4 June 1910; J. M. Pitsula, *An Act of Faith: The Early Years of Regina College* (Regina, 1988), pp. 1-35; T. J. D. Powell, "The Church of England in the Dioceses of Qu'Appelle and Saskatchewan: Their Establishment, Expansion and Response to Immigration, 1874-1914," (unpublished M.A. thesis, University of Regina, 1980), pp. 158-61.

[71]*Morning Leader*, 26 November 1909, 6 June 1914; Archer, *Honoured With the Burden*, pp. 37-46, 53-55, 172; Gerein, p. 50.

[72]R. N. Reid, "A History of the Wascana Country Club, Regina, Saskatchewan," (unpublished manuscript), SAB; *Morning Leader*, 13 October 1917; P. B. O'Neill, "Regina's Golden Age of Theatre: Her Playhouses and Players," *Saskatchewan History*,

vol. 28, no. 1 (Winter, 1975), pp. 29-37; Kallmann, Potvin and Winters, pp. 802-3.

[73]B. Zeman, *Hockey Heritage: 88 Years of Puck Chasing in Saskatchewan* (Regina, 1983), pp. 15-35; B. Calder and G. Andrews, *Rider Pride: The Story of Canada's Best-Loved Football Team* (Saskatoon, 1984), pp. 3-18; Drake, pp. 126-27, 141; Laporte, pp. 32, 93-95.

[74]Quoted in D. Taylor, *For Dignity, Equality and Justice: A History of the Saskatchewan Government Employees' Union* (Regina, 1984), p. 1.

[75]Woodsworth, pp. 26, 47.

[76]*Morning Leader*, 1 February 1910.

[77]Ibid., 7 January 1908, 21 January 1913, 24 January 1913; J. M. Pitsula, *Let the Family Flourish: A History of the Family Service Bureau of Regina, 1913-1982* (Regina, 1982), pp. 8-19.

Chapter 3

[1]Saskatchewan, Department of Agriculture, *Annual Report, 1914* (Regina, 1915), pp. 107-9, 175-77; *Evening Province and Standard*, 1 June 1914; *Morning Leader*, 25 June 1914, 15 July 1914, 4-5 August 1914; Regina City Council, Minute Book, 15 September 1914.

[2]*Morning Leader*, 19 July 1915, 11 December 1915, 29 September 1917, 13 September 1919.

[3]G. T. Bloomfield, "'I Can See a Car in That Crop: Motorization in Saskatchewan, 1906-1934," *Saskatchewan History*, vol. 37, no. 1 (Winter 1984), pp. 3-18; J. H. Thompson, *The Harvests of War: The Prairie West, 1914-1918* (Toronto, 1978), p. 65; *Morning Leader*, 17 January 1918.

[4]Saskatchewan, *A Submission by the Government of Saskatchewan to the Royal Commission on Dominion-Provincial Relations* (Regina, 1937), pp. 136-38; G. L. Fairbairn, *From Prairie Roots: The Remarkable Story of Saskatchewan Wheat Pool* (Saskatoon, 1984), pp. 17-73.

[5]*Morning Leader*, 12 September 1925, 27 November 1926, 21 September 1929.

[6]Canada, Dominion Bureau of Statistics, *Seventh Census of Canada*, 1931 (Ottawa, 1936), vol. 8, p. 589; Saskatchewan, *Sub-*

mission, pp. 138-41; R. B. Shepard, "Tractors and Combines in the Second Stage of Agricultural Mechanization on the Canadian Plains," *Prairie Forum*, vol. 11, no. 2 (Fall, 1986), pp. 253-71; R. Bellan, *Winnipeg First Century: An Economic History (Winnipeg, 1978), pp. 155, 174.*

[7]Saskatchewan, *Submission*, pp. 175, 179; *Report of the Royal Commission on Agriculture and Rural Life* (Regina, 1955), no. 2, pp. 27, 42.

[8]Fairbairn, pp. 87-114; G. E. Britnell, *The Wheat Economy* (Toronto, 1939), pp. 34-99, 197-201; *Leader-Post*, 7 April 1931.

[9]*Leader-Post*, 22 March 1932, 30 December 1938; Regina City Council, Minute Book, 29 December 1936, 1 November 1938, 20 June 1939.

[10]Saskatchewan, Department of Agriculture, *Annual Report*, 1929 (Regina, 1929), p. 363; Department of Railways, Labour and Industries, *Annual Report*, 1930 (Regina, 1930), p. 10.

[11]*Morning Leader*, 22 September 1917; *Leader-Post*, 16 November 1937; J. F. C. Wright, *Prairie Progress: Consumer Co-operation in Saskatchewan* (Saskatoon, 1956), pp. 122-49; T. Phalen, *Co-operative Leadership: Harry L. Fowler* (Saskatoon, 1977), pp. 89-106.

[12]Regina Board of Trade, *Annual Report*, 1928 (Regina, 1928), pp. 4-5; *Morning Leader*, 1 June 1928; *Regina Daily Star*, 15 August 1930; *Leader-Post*, 6 March 1931, 3 September 1937, 3 January 1938, 24 October 1939.

[13]Bronson, pp. 20-31.

[14]Unpublished history of Houston Willoughby, pp.1-31, Pemberton Houston Willoughby, Regina.

[15]*Regina. Center of the World's Hard Wheat Area* (Regina, 1926), p. 24.

[16]L. A. Thornton to J. D. Reid, 6 September 1919, Department of Railways and Canals Records, PAC, file 20469; S. C. Burton to H. W. Thornton, 3 January 1922, Canadian National Railways Records, PAC, file 450-6; Thornton to Burton, 13 October 1923, 22 April 1924, idem.; *Morning Leader*, 3 October 1924.

[17]Regina City Council, Minute Book, 1 April 1919; *Morning Leader*, 23 May 1927; Regina Board of Trade, *Annual Report, 1928*, pp. 6-7; E. J. Hart, *The Selling of Canada: The CPR and the Beginnings of Canadian Tourism* (Banff, 1983), pp. 107-109; Kallmann, Potvin and Winters, pp. 240-41.

[18]*Regina. Canada* (Regina, 1928), p. 28.

[19]*Regina. Center of the World's Hard Wheat Area*, p. 24; Bloomfield, pp. 11, 18-21.

[20]*Morning Leader*, 21 April 1920; R. H. Crone, "Aviation Pioneers in Saskatchewan," *Saskatchewan History*, vol. 28, no. 1·(Winter 1975), 9-28.

[21]*Morning Leader*, 10 July 1928, 18 July 1928; Regina City Council, Minute Book, 21 August 1928, 20 June 1938; K. M. Molson, *Pioneering in Canadian Air Transport* (Altona, 1974), pp. 37-44.

[22]Britnell, p. 23.

[23]*Morning Leader*, 21 September 1929; *Leader-Post*, 19 June 1930, 7 April 1931, 5 November 1936, 13 November 1936; Wright, p. 206; *CSP, 1921*, No. 28, p. 5.

[24]*Regina Daily Star*, 24 November 1933; *Leader-Post*, 12 November 1934, 17 September 1937; Canada, Dominion Bureau of Statistics, *Census of Canada, 1941* (Ottawa, 1944), vol. 2, p. 128.

[25]Saskatchewan, *Journals of the Legislative Assembly, 1932* (Regina, 1932), pp. 198-201; Sessional Paper no. 42, Session 1939, Saskatchewan Legislative Assembly Records, SAB.

[26]Saskatchewan, Department of Public Health, *Annual Report on Saskatchewan Vital Statistics, 1960* (Regina, 1960), p. 10; Regina, Development and Public Relations Department, *City of Regina Community Profile, 1981-1982* (Regina, 1982), p. VIII-19.

[27]German Canadian Provincial Alliance of Saskatchewan to R. L. Borden, 21 September 1914, R. L. Borden Papers, PAC, pp. 106108-112; *Morning Leader*, 17 August 1914; Cherwinski, p. 43.

[28]A. B. Perry to Comptroller, RNWMP, 31 August 1914, R. L. Borden Papers, PAC, pp. 105963-66; memorandum from Comptroller, RNWMP, 4 September 1914, idem., p. 105993; E. J. Chambers to E. N. H. Mercer, 10 March 1916, Chief Press Censor Records, PAC, file 119-C-1; E. J. Chambers to Secretary of State, 11 January 1918, ibid.; W. Entz, "The Suppression of the German Language Press in September 1918 (With Special Reference to the Secular German Language Papers in Western Canada)," *Canadian Ethnic Studies*, vol. 8, no. 2 (1976), pp. 56-70.

[29]*Daily Province*, 4 December 1914; *Morning Leader*, 5 December 1914, 5 January 1915; W. F. A. Turgeon to J. A. Calder, 27 July 1918, W. F. A. Turgeon Papers, SAB, General files 1918 C; R.

Huel, "The French Canadians and the Language Question, 1918," *Saskatchewan History*, vol. 23, no. 1 (Winter 1970), pp. 1-15.

[30]*Morning Leader*, 9 November 1914; Toombs, p. 8; Kazymyra, pp. 40-44; Ukrainian Senior Citizens of Regina, *From Dreams to Reality: A History of the Ukrainian Senior Citizens of Regina and District, 1896-1976* (Winnipeg, 1977), pp. 152, 155; D. Hayden, *Let the Bells Ring: Knox-Metropolitan United Church, Regina, 1882-1982: An Illustrated History* (Regina, 1981), pp. 43-46.

[31]Pinno, pp. 48-289.

[32]*Morning Leader*, 30-31 July 1918, 1 August 1918; *Regina Daily Post*, 23 October 1918.

[33]*Regina Daily Post*, 8 May 1919; Cherwinski, pp. 63-67, 85-87.

[34]*Morning Leader*, 27 May 1919; Cherwinski, pp. 67-75, 88-95. For Saskatchewan farm opinion on the Winnipeg General Strike see *Grain Growers' Guide*, 25 June 1919.

[35]Saskatchewan, Department of Labour, *Annual Report, 1961* (Regina, 1961), p. 42.

[36]*Morning Leader*, 20 August 1924, 8 October 1924, 17 November 1925; Regina City Council, Minute Book, 1 June 1926; Saskatchewan, *Statutes*, 17-18 Eliz. II, Chapter 24.

[37]Lehmann, pp. 238-39, 276-78, 288-89; Tischler, pp. 132-33; K. Mitchell, *Luther: The History of a College* (Regina, 1981).

[38]*Morning Leader*, 3 October 1927; Cherwinski, p. 141; N. F. Dreisziger et al., *Struggle and Hope: The Hungarian-Canadian Experience* (Toronto, 1982), pp. 105-6; Gerein, pp. 118-20; Kazymyra, pp. 44-45; Ukrainian Senior Citizens, pp. 102-14, 126-36.

[39]*Morning Leader*, 4 July 1927; J. H. Hawkins to J. E. Huckins, 17 October 1927, J. G. Gardiner Papers, SAB, p. 12677; W. Calderwood, "The Rise and Fall of the Ku Klux Klan in Saskatchewan," (unpublished M.A. thesis, University of Saskatchewan, Regina, 1968).

[40]Saskatchewan, *Statutes*, 6 Geo. V, chapt. 21; Regina City Council, Minute Book, 5 August 1924; Moser, pp. 59-64.

[41]Regina City Council, Minute Book, 5 August 1924; Moser, pp. 88-89.

[42]Regina City Council, Minute Book, 17 May 1927, 22 January 1931, 3 February 1931, 29 December 1931, 6 February 1934.

[43]Moser, pp. 64-67.

[44]Ibid., pp. 57-58, 67-68; Laporte, pp. 156-62.

[45]Saskatchewan, *Statutes*, 8 Geo. V, chapt. 70; T. H. Mawson, *Regina: A Preliminary Report on the Development of the City* (London, 1921); *Morning Leader*, 24 November 1922, 1 December 1922, 11 January 1923; M. E. Robinson, *Pile O' Bones: History of Wascana Creek* (Regina, 1975), p. 42.

[46]Regina City Council, By-Law no. 1378, 20 September 1927; *Leader-Post*, 12 February 1931; Moser, pp. 81-87; Laporte, pp. 179-84.

[47]Morning Leader, 1 June 1927.

[48]Hatcher, pp. 29-45; M Hughes, "The Functional Hierarchy of Business Centres in Regina" (unpublished M.A. thesis, University of Saskatchewan, Regina, 1971), pp. 82-83.

[49]*Morning Leader*, 14 March 1919, 25 November 1922, 3 April 1926; *CSP, 1923*, no. 19; history of Houston, Willoughby, p. 12.

[50]*Leader-Post*, 5 August 1935, 17 October 1936, 25 February 1938, 9 September 1938; J. Bowker, "The Canadian Federal Government's Entry into Housing: The Origins and Implementation of the Dominion Housing Act of 1935," (unpublished paper presented to the Canadian Historical Association, 1982).

[51]Pitsula, *Let the Family Flourish*, pp. 14-23.

[52]City of Regina, Financial Statements, 1913-18, CRA; D. B. Climenhaga, "Public Finance in Saskatchewan During the Settlement Process, 1905-1929," (unpublished M.A. thesis, University of Saskatchewan, 1949), pp. 72-73.

[53]*Morning Leader*, 9 December 1914, 22 November 1918, 4 December 1918; *Daily Province*, 15 December 1914; *Evening Province and Standard*, 14 December 1915.

[54]The widening of the municipal franchise had actually begun during the war years. In 1915 the vote was extended to all men and women who either met the minimum property qualification (still fixed at $200) or paid at least $100 annually in rent. The qualifications were further relaxed in 1917; henceforth any resident who paid at least $10 in licence fees could vote. Finally in 1920 the $200 minimum for property owners was dropped altogether. (Saskatchewan, *Statutes*, 6 Geo. V, chapt. 16; 7 Geo. V, chapt. 11; 10 Geo. V, chapt. 23.)

[55]W. D. Young, "M. J. Coldwell, the Making of a Social Democrat," *Journal of Canadian Studies*, vol. 9, no. 3 (August, 1974): 50-55. For a brief biographical sketch of James McAra see *Morning Leader*, 25 November 1926.

[56]City of Regina, Financial Statements, 1919-1929, CRA; Climenhaga, p. 74; J. H. Perry, *Taxes, Tariffs, and Subsidies: A History of Canadian Fiscal Development* (Toronto, 1955), vol. 1, p. 168; *Morning Leader*, 14 March 1923.

[57]*Morning Leader*, 21 November 1919, 22 November 1924, 27 November 1926; Hatcher, pp. 29-45.

[58]*Morning Leader*, 17 May 1928; White, pp. 22-51.

[59]White, pp. 55-76, 119-23; *Leader-Post*, 22 November 1941.

[60]*Morning Leader*, 9 August 1919, 1 November 1919, 28 July 1921; "Report of Conference Between Delegates on Water Supply for Southern Saskatchewan and Members of the Saskatchewan Government, 12 November 1919," W. M. Martin Papers, SAB, pp. 42652-95; Synopsis of Report of the Saskatchewan Water Supply Commission on the Feasibility of Diverting a Supply of Water from the South Saskatchewan River for Domestic and Industrial Purposes in the Moose Jaw-Regina District (Regina, 1920); Sessional Paper no. 7, Session 1921-22, Saskatchewan Legislative Assembly Records, SAB.

[61]*Morning Leader*, 21 December 1928; *Leader-Post*, 23 June 1931, 26 October 1943; *Regina Daily Star*, 30 September 1931; N. S. Hill, R. O. Wynne-Roberts and H. E. Simpson, *Reports on Regina Water Supply* (Regina, 1930); Regina City Council, Minute Book, 16 October 1930, 16 June 1931, 7 July 1931.

[62]Canada, Dominion Bureau of Statistics, *Seventh Census of Canada, 1931* (Ottawa, 1934), Vol. VI, p. 1268; *Census of the Prairie Provinces, 1936* (Ottawa, 1938), Vol. II, p. 606; City of Regina, Financial Statements, 1929-37, CRA.

[63]Regina City Council, Minute Book, 27 October 1931, 1 December 1931; P. H. Brennan, "Public Works Relief in Saskatchewan Cities, 1929-1940," (unpublished M.A. thesis, University of Regina, 1981), pp. 91, 123. This thesis provides the fullest account of these various public works relief projects in Regina.

[64]P. Brennan, "Public Works Relief," pp. 134-35; *Leader-Post*, 23 October 1932.

[65]Regina City Council, Minute Book, 6 October 1931, 16 February 1932; Pitsula, *Let the Family Flourish*, pp. 27-53.

[66]*Leader-Post*, 11 November 1939; P. Brennan, "Public Works Relief," p. 134.

[67]Regina City Council, Minute Book, 19 May 1932; *Leader-Post*, 7 November 1933.

[68]*Leader-Post*, 22 November 1930, 27 November 1930, 2 May 1931, 26-29 October 1932. The role of the Communist Party in organizing the unemployed in Regina and other Canadian cities during the 1930s is discussed in more detail in I. Avakumovic, *The Communist Party in Canada: A History* (Toronto, 1975), pp. 54-95.

[69]*Regina Daily Star*, 1 November 1932; *Leader-Post*, 19 November 1932.

[70]*Leader-Post*, 25-27 August 1932, 24 November 1932; Regina City Council, Minute Book, 22 February 1933, Appendix A; *Regina Daily Star*, 3 March 1933.

[71]*Regina Daily Star*, 25 November 1930.

[72]*Leader-Post*, 5 November 1931, 23-24 November 1932. Cornelius Rink was one of a number of populist figures who rose to prominence and power in civic politics during this turbulent decade. For other examples see J. H. Taylor, "Urban Social Organization and Urban Discontent: The 1930s," in D. J. Bercuson, ed., *Western Perspectives 1* (Toronto, 1974), pp. 33-44; and "Mayors a la Mancha: An Aspect of Depression Leadership in Canadian Cities," *Urban History Review* vol. 9, no. 3 (February, 1981), pp. 3-14.

[73]*Leader-Post*, 24-27 October 1933, 5 November 1933, 18 November 1933.

[74]*Regina Daily Star*, 18 May 1934, 5 July 1934.

[75]Regina City Council, Minute Book, 15 February 1934, 3 July 1934, 7 August 1934, 25 October 1934; Pitsula, *Let the Family Flourish*, pp. 54-55.

[76]*Leader-Post*, 15 November 1934; C. M. Fines, "The Impossible Dream: An Account of People and Events Leading to the First CCF Government, Saskatchewan, 1944," (unpublished memoirs, 198)2, SAB.

[77]*Leader-Post*, 18 October 1933, 31 March 1934; *Regina Daily Star*, 27 November 1934; Regina City Council, By-Law no. 1799, 18 December 1934.

[78]*Leader-Post*, 6 March 1935, 20 March 1935, 22 March 1935, 3 October 1935, 5 October 1935, 7-8 October 1935.

[79]Ibid., 4 June 1935.

[80]Ibid., 15 June 1935, 17 June 1935. For a fuller account of the events leading up to the Regina Riot see V. Howard, *"We Were the Salt of the Earth!" A Narrative of the On-to-Ottawa Trek and the Regina Riot* (Regina, 1985) and L. Brown *When Freedom Was Lost: The Unemployed, the Agitator, and the State* (Montreal, 1987).

[81]*Leader-Post*, 11 September 1935, 19 October 1935.

[82]Ibid., 21 November 1935.

[83]Ibid., 26 November 1935.

[84]Ibid., 16 January 1936, 18 March 1936; Regina City Council, Minute Book, 22 January 1936, 7 April 1936; Howard, pp. 130-31.

[85]*Leader-Post*, 31 January 1936, 1 February 1936, 5 February 1936.

[86]Ibid., 7 January 1936; Pitsula, *Let the Family Flourish*, pp. 55-61.

[87]*Leader-Post*, 8 July 1936; City of Regina Financial Statements, 1929-1936, CRA; P. Brennan, "Public Works Relief," p. 177.

[88]*Leader-Post*, 12 November 1936, 14 November 1936, 17 November 1936.

[89]Regina City Council, Minute Book, 19 December 1935; *Leader-Post*, 19 February 1936, 30 October 1936, 24 November 1936. The ward system was defeated by a margin of 6,681 to 6,499.

[90]*Leader-Post*, 4 October 1938.

[91]City of Regina, Financial Statements, 1929-39, CRA; *Leader-Post*, 10 November 1936, 11 November 1939, 14 November 1939.

[92]*Leader-Post*, 13 January 1939, 31 January 1939, 2 February 1939; P. Brennan, "Public Works Relief," pp. 179-84, 205-25.

[93]*Leader-Post*, 1 November 1939, 13 November 1939, 15 November 1939, 17 November 1939.

[94]A great deal of attention has been devoted to Saskatchewan's political history during the First World War and the two postwar decades, but to date little has been written about urban voting patterns in either provincial or federal elections. The best published accounts are S. M. Lipset, *Agrarian Socialism: The Co-operative Commonwealth Federation in Saskatchewan* (Berkeley, 1950) and D. E. Smith, *Prairie Liberalism: The Liberal Party in Saskatchewan, 1905-71* (Toronto, 1975). Also of value are J. W. Brennan, "A Political History of Saskatchewan, 1905-1929," (unpublished Ph.D. dissertation, University of Alberta, 1976), R. J. A. Huel, "*La Survivance* in Saskatchewan: Schools, Politics and the Nativist Crusade for Cultural Conformity," unpublished Ph.D. dissertation, University of Alberta, 1975, and J. W. Warren, "From Pluralism to Pluralism: The Political Experience of Organized Labour in Saskatchewan from 1900 to 1938," (unpublished M.A. thesis, University of Regina, 1985). On the 1930 federal contest in Regina see J. W. Brennan, "C. A. Dunning, 1916-30: The Rise and Fall of a Western Agrarian Liberal," in J. E. Foster, ed., *The Developing West: Essays on Canadian History in Honour of Lewis H. Thomas* (Edmonton, 1983), pp. 263-65.

[95]*Leader-Post*, 28 February 1938, 21 March 1938, 7 April 1938, 16 April 1938, 19 April 1938. For a fuller account of this "unity" campaign see Lipset, pp. 110-14; F. Steininger, "George H. Williams: Agrarian Socialist" (unpublished M.A. Thesis, University of Regina, 1976), pp. 230-79; and K. Andrews, "'Progressive' Counterparts of the C.C.F.: Social Credit and the Conservative Party in Saskatchewan, 1935-1938," *Journal of Canadian Studies*, vol. 17, no. 3 (Fall, 1982), pp. 58-74.

[96]*Grain Growers' Guide*, 15 March 1927; *Leader-Post*, 27 July 1942; Zeman, pp. 369-71. For a fuller discussion of the impact of American popular culture in Canada during the interwar period, see J. H. Thompson and A. Seager, *Canada, 1922-1939: Decades of Discord* (Toronto, 1985), pp. 158-92.

[97]*Morning Leader*, 15 July 1926; *Leader-Post*, 16 May 1955; Zeman, pp. 40-42, 51-59, 151-63, 210-11; D. Shury, "The Chicago Black Sox and Their Saskatchewan Connection," *Saskatchewan Historical Baseball Review*, 1987, pp. 60-61; Calder and Andrews, pp. 19-63.

[98]Kallman, Potvin and Winters, pp. 135, 241, 370-71, 802-803, 1004; M. Hayden, pp. 120-23, 134-35, 166-69; Pitsula, *An Act of Faith*, pp. 36-163; S. Bland, "The Development of the Visual

Arts in Regina and Saskatoon, 1920-1950," (unpublished student essay).

Chapter 4

[1] *Leader-Post*, 5 May 1942; Regina City Council, Minute Book, 15 May 1941; Archer, *Honoured With the Burden*, pp. 64-65; City of Regina, Financial Statements, 1939-46, CRA.

[2] V. Fowke, "Economic Effects of the War on the Prairie Economy," *Canadian Journal of Economics and Political Science*, vol. 12, No. 3 (August, 1945), pp. 373-87.

[3] Regina City Council, Minute Book, 4 March 1941; *Leader-Post*, 1 February 1940, 28 February 1941, 24 March 1941, 11 June 1941, 9 May 1942, 7 June 1944, 4 July 1945; Canada, Department of Munitions and Supply, Economics and Statistics Branch, *War Employment in Canada Geographical Report* 5th ed. (Ottawa, 1944,), p. 135.

[4] *Leader-Post*, 9 November 1973, 24 November 1976; Bronson, pp. 50-85.

[5] For an early discussion of this phenomenon in postwar Saskatchewan agriculture, see C. Schwartz, *The Search for Stability* (Toronto, 1959).

[6] Saskatchewan, Department of Agriculture, *Annual Report, 1972* (Regina, 1972), p. 74; Canada, Dominion Bureau of Statistics, *Eighth Census of Canada, 1941* (Ottawa, 1950), vol. 1, p. 36; *Ninth Census of Canada, 1951* (Ottawa, 1953), vol. 1, p. 15-9; *1976 Census of Canada* (Ottawa, 1978), Catalogue 92-807, Table 7.

[7] City of Regina, Planning Department, *An Analysis of the Structural Components and Role of the Regina Economy* (Regina, 1971), pp. 3-17; *City of Regina Community Profile, 1981-1982*, p. III-1.

[8] C. Purden, *Agents for Change: Credit Unions in Saskatchewan* (Regina, 1980); J. Richards and L. Pratt, *Prairie Capitalism: Power and Influence in the New West* (Toronto, 1979), p. 112; I. MacPherson, *The Story of CIS Ltd.: Co-operative Insurance Services* (Regina, 1974); *Leader-Post*, 4 June 1969, 8 February 1985; unpublished history of Houston Willoughby, pp. 36-54.

[9] B. Banks, "The Political Economy of Petroleum Development in Saskatchewan, 1940-1960," unpublished M.A. thesis, University of Regina, 1986, pp. 11-72; *Western Business and Industry*, March 1948, February 1952.

[10] *Western Business and Industry*, September 1956, September 1957, June 1958; Saskatchewan, Department of Mineral Resources, *Mineral Statistical Year Book*, 1966 (Regina, 1966), p. 3; White, pp. 295-303; Richards and Pratt, pp. 178, 202.

[11] *Leader-Post*, 18 August 1954, 23 September 1958, 4 September 1976, 21 June 1978, 29 September 1978; *Western Business and Industry*, March 1957; Banks, pp. 103-104, 130-37; Richards and Pratt, pp. 258-59.

[12] *Leader-Post*, 23 August 1956, 9 August 1957, 19 September 1958, 13 May 1959, 7 September 1963, 25 April 1967; *Western Business and Industry*, March 1962, February 1963; *Report on Business Magazine*, March 1986.

[13] *Leader-Post*, 22 May 1975, 26 May 1975; C. Caviedes, "The Functional Structure of Regina," in E. H. Dale, ed., *Regina: Regional Isolation and Innovative Development* (Victoria, 1980), pp. 67-69. By 1981 Saskatoon had surpassed Regina in terms of the number of firms and employees in the manufacturing sector, but Regina continued to hold its lead in salaries and value of production. (Statistics Canada, *Canada Year Book, 1985* [Ottawa, 1985], p. 526.)

[14] *Leader-Post*, 26 April 1963; Richards and Pratt, pp. 137-39, 187-96, 259-75.

[15] E. A. Tollefson, *Bitter Medicine: The Saskatchewan Medicare Feud* (Saskatoon, 1963); J. Pitsula, "The CCF Government in Saskatchewan and Social Aid, 1944-1964," in J. W. Brennan, ed., *"Building the Co-operative Commonwealth": Essays on the Democratic Socialist Tradition in Canada* (Regina, 1985), pp. 205-25; Caviedes, pp. 63-66; *An Analysis of the Structural Components and Role of the Regina Economy*, pp. 24-27.

[16] F. I. Hill, ed., *Canadian Urban Trends* (Ottawa, 1976), vol. 2, Table 5.1; Saskatchewan, Department of Health, *Annual Report on Saskatchewan Vital Statistics, 1960*, p. 10; *1965*, p. 10; *1971*, p. 10; *1977*, p. 15; *1981*, p. 13; *City of Regina Community Profile, 1981-1982*, pp. viii 19-VIII 20; D. G. Ross, "Population Growth, the Catalyst of Spatial Changes in Regina, 1945 to 1975, with a Projection to the Future," unpublished M.A. thesis, Univer-

sity of Regina, 1979, pp. 21-40; Archer, *Honoured With the Burden*, pp. 91-123, 172-73.

[17]*Leader-Post*, 29 October 1938, 17-18 May 1940; J. Wagner, "The *Deutscher Bund Canada* in Saskatchewan," *Saskatchewan History*, vol. 31, no. 2 (Spring, 1978), pp. 41-50. The federal government's treatment of Germans in Canada during the Second World War is discussed more fully in R. H. Keyserlingk, "'Agents Within the Gates': The Search for Nazi Subversives in Canada during World War II," *Canadian Historical Review*, vol. 66, no. 2 (June, 1985), pp. 211-39.

[18]*Leader-Post*, 18 June 1965, 23 October 1973, 20 December 1978; *From Dreams to Reality*, pp. 157-58; "Final Report of 75th Anniversary Committee, 1978," Regina Multicultural Council Records, SAB, File 7; M. R. Lupul, "Ukrainian-language Education in Canada's Public Schools," in M. R. Lupul, ed., *A Heritage in Transition: Essays in the History of Ukrainians in Canada* (Toronto, 1982), pp. 227-28.

[19]*Leader-Post*, 1 November 1957, 31 October 1958, 6 July 1961, 28 December 1963, 9 February 1965; A. B. Robe, *Tour of Canadian Friendship Centres* (Ottawa, 1971), reel 7, side 1, Interviews 2-3.

[20]*Leader-Post*, 13 September 1968, 14 November 1968; D. Eisler, *Rumours of Glory: Saskatchewan and the Thatcher Years* (Edmonton, 1987), pp. 253-56; S. J. Clatworthy and J. Hull, *Native Economic Conditions in Regina and Saskatoon* (Winnipeg, 1983).

[21]Ibid., 31 October 1974, 11 September 1975, 23 September 1975; L. Krotz, *Urban Indians: The Strangers in Canada's Cities* (Edmonton, 1980) pp. 41, 88.

[22]*Leader-Post*, 14 May 1975, 4 September 1975, 8 September 1975, 11 March 1978; Krotz, pp. 40, 130.

[23]The 1981 census appears to significantly underestimate the size of the native population in Regina, as it does in other cities. This has been attributed to the fact that Native people are highly transient. For a more detailed discussion of the impact of Native transiency on the census returns see J. S. Frideres, *Native People in Canada: Contemporary Conflicts* (Scarborough, 1983, 2nd ed.), pp. 187-98.

[24]*Leader-Post*, 26 September 1978, 16 February 1979.

[25]Krotz, pp. 89-91; Archer, *Honoured With the Burden*, pp. 137-40; *Leader-Post*, 28 May 1976.

[26]Cherwinski, pp. 211-28, 294-98; Taylor, pp. 1-70; G. Makahonuk, "Masters and Servants: Labour Relations in the Saskatchewan Civil Service, 1905-1945," *Prairie Forum*, vol. 12, no. 2 (Fall, 1987), pp. 257-76; T. H. McLeod and I. McLeod, *Tommy Douglas: The Road to Jerusalem (Edmonton, 1987), pp. 156-63.*

[27]J. L. Moser, "Regina: Development by Controls — Prelude to Town Planning, 1903-1946," in Dale, p. 196.

[28]Regina City Council, Minute Book, 1 December 1953, 6 January 1955; *Leader-Post*, 11 September 1959; G. M. Lipinski, "A Review and Post-Planning Evaluation of the Development of the Ross Industrial Park, Regina, Saskatchewan"(unpublished M.A. thesis, University of Regina, 1984).

[29]*Leader-Post*, 20 September 1940, 3 November 1941, 4 November 1948.

[30]Regina City Council, Minute Book, 14 May 1942, 16 June 1942, 7 August 1945; *Leader-Post*, 25 November 1942, 25 May 1944. There is a good discussion of the operations of Wartime Housing Limited in J. Wade, "Wartime Housing Limited, 1941-1947: Canadian Housing Policy at the Crossroads," *Urban History Review*, vol. 15, No. 1 (June, 1986): 41-59.

[31]Regina City Council, Minute Book, 17 April 1945, 21 May 1946, 16 December 1947, 3 January 1952, Appendix A; *Leader-Post*, 7 October 1952.

[32]Regina City Council, Minute Book, 18 September 1945, 6 November 1945; E. G. Faludi, *A Thirty Year Program for Development: Regina 1946-1976* (Toronto, 1947).

[33]Regina City Council, By-Law no. 2356, 8 June 1949; idem.Minute Book, 5 February 1957, Appendix F; *Leader-Post*, 4 April 1951, 28 November 1951, 11 April 1953.

[34]Regina City Council, Minute Book, 19 October 1948, Appendix D; 16 May 1950, Appendix B; 10 August 1950, Appendix B; *Leader-Post*, 23 November 1950; City of Regina, Planning Department, *Housing Survey Report* (Regina, 1961), p. 20.

[35]*Leader-Post*, 17 August 1951, 10 June 1955, 1 August 1968, 17 July 1969, 19 December 1974, 6 January 1977, 23 June 1978; Ross, pp. 43-50.

[36]*Leader-Post*, 2 October 1954, 10 February 1955, 16 January 1960; City of Regina, Planning Department, *Land Acquisition for*

Residential Development (Regina, 1971). Saskatoon's more ambitious efforts are discussed in D. P. Ravis, *Advance Land Acquisition by Local Government: The Saskatoon Experience* (Ottawa, 1973).

[37]*Leader-Post*, 23 September 1952, 29 October 1954, 26 March 1955.

[38]Ibid., 8 February 1956, 13 February 1957; Ross, p. 46.

[39]*Leader-Post*, 29 April 1955, 7 November 1957, 20 December 1957, 19 June 1959, 3 July 1959, 5 November 1959, 30 May 1978.

[40]A. E. O. Troyer, "Causes of Regina's Rental Housing Shortage and its Effects on Residential Satisfaction, 1972-1978," (unpublished M.A. thesis, University of Regina, 1980), pp. 36-38; City of Regina, Planning Department, *Housing Study 1985, Part V, Government Housing Programs* (Regina, 1985), pp. 20-22.

[41]Ross, pp. 49-50.

[42]*Leader-Post*, 25 April 1955, 28-29 April 1965, 1 May 1965; Troyer, pp. 27-30.

[43]City of Regina, Planning Department, *Public and Low Cost Housing in Regina* (Regina, 1970); *Housing Study 1985, Part V, Government Housing Programs*, pp. 1-7, Part VI, Groups Experiencing Special Problems; T. D. Gross, "Infill Housing in Regina: The Roles of the Actors in the Implementation Process," (unpublished M.A. thesis, University of Regina, 1984).

[44]Regina City Council, Minute Book, 17 April 1956, Appendix A; *Leader-Post*, 20 January 1956, 27 March 1956, 26 April 1960.

[45]*Leader-Post*, 9 October 1959, 22 November 1962, 11 September 1963, 2 September 1964, 29 September 1964.

[46]Ibid., 2 February 1965, 8 December 1976.

[47]E. H. Dale, "The Wascana Centre, Regina: Innovation in the Provision and Development of Open Space," in Dale, pp. 97-133.

[48]*Leader-Post*, 27-28 September 1976, 14 December 1976, 4 June 1977; City of Regina, Planning Department, *Regina RSVP: A Planning Strategy for Regina* (Regina, 1977), pp. 99-113.

[49]*Leader-Post*, 19 April 1955, 27 January 1961, 20 September 1966, 30 September 1969; City of Regina, Planning Department, *Regina Community Planning Scheme 1961* (Regina, 1961), pp. 54-56, idem. *Regina RSVP*, pp. 67-81.

[50]Hatcher, pp. 51-54; Ross, pp. 50-61; L. D. Tangjerd, "Innovation in Transportation: The Regina Telebus System," in Dale, pp. 163-85.

[51]Regina City Council, Minute Book, 24 November 1949, Appendix A; *Leader-Post*, 11 June 1948, 25 January 1949, 19 June 1950.

[52]*Leader-Post*, 29 September 1950, 4 June 1955, 12 October 1978; Regina City Council, Minute Book, 18 March 1952; D. R. Cullimore, "The Water Problems of a Growing City in a Semi-Arid Area," in Dale, pp. 135-61.

[53]*Leader-Post*, 7 November 1963, 17 January 1964; White, Chapters 7-10 passim.

[54]*Leader-Post*, 22 November 1941, 18 November 1948, 25 September 1951.

[55]Ibid., 3 November 1950, 7 November 1953, 3 April 1954, 9 April 1954, 29 April 1954.

[56]Ibid., 3 October 1953, 3 November 1955.

[57]Ibid., 13 July 1966, 27 July 1966, 20 October 1966.

[58]Saskatchewan, *Statutes*, 21-22 Eliz. II, Chapter 118, 38 Eliz. II, Chapter 61; *Leader-Post*, 8 December 1977.

[59]R. M. Sherdahl, "The Saskatchewan General Election of 1944," (unpublished M.A. thesis, University of Saskatchewan, Saskatoon, 1966); L. H. Thomas, "The CCF Victory in Saskatchewan, 1944," *Saskatchewan History*, vol. 34, no. 1 (Winter 1981), pp. 1-16. Postwar Saskatchewan politics has only begun to receive serious scholarly attention, and no published work has devoted much attention to urban voting patterns in either provincial or federal elections. On the decline of the Liberal party's fortunes in Saskatchewan see Smith, chapt. 7-8, and his more recent *The Regional Decline of a National Party: Liberals on the Prairies* (Toronto, 1981) as well as D. Eisler, *Rumours of Glory:* T. C. Douglas's unsuccessful bid for a Regina seat in 1962 is discussed in the context of the "Medicare Crisis" in J. L. Granatstein, *Canada, 1957-1967: The Years of Uncertainty and Innovation* (Toronto, 1986), pp. 169-97, and in McLeod and McLeod, pp. 225-29.

[60]*Leader-Post*, 17 November 1956; Calder and Andrews, pp. 64-199; Zeman, pp. 84-88, 170-87; S. F. Wise and D. Fisher, *Canada's Sporting Heroes: Their Lives and Times* (Don Mills, 1974), pp. 210-12.

[61]M. Hayden, pp. 232-38, 244-88; W. A. Riddell, *The First Decade: A History of the University of Saskatchewan, Regina Campus, 1960-1970* (Regina, 1974); *Leader-Post*, 24 September 1953, 26 September 1953, 1 December 1961.

[62]*Leader-Post*, 8 September 1954, 8 October 1968, 7 November 1970, 28 September 1973; D. Bessai, "The Prairie Theatre and the Playwright," in A. W. Rasporich, ed., *The Making of the Modern West: Western Canada Since 1945* (Calgary, 1984), pp. 211-13.

[63]*Leader-Post*, 21 November 1951, 4 December 1952, 18 July 1953, 12 May 1967, 24 August 1970.

Suggestions for Further Reading and Research

The published literature on Regina is not extensive and is of uneven quality. Much good work is beginning to appear in the form of unpublished M.A. theses. An extensive listing of articles, books and theses relating to Regina may be found in Alan F. J. Artibise, *Western Canada Since 1870: A Select Bibliography and Guide* (Vancouver, 1978), and Alan F. J. Artibise and Gilbert A. Stelter, *Canada's Urban Past: A Bibliography to 1980 and Guide to Canadian Urban Studies* (Vancouver, 1981). The purpose of this review essay is to highlight the best and most useful sources available, and to direct the reader's attention to recently completed work that does not appear in either of these bibliographies.

This book has drawn heavily upon such secondary sources as do exist, but it is also based upon extensive primary research. Those interested in exploring Regina's history will find its newspapers to be particularly valuable. Complete runs of the *Regina Leader* and of its rivals and successors are to be found in the Regina office of the Saskatchewan Archives Board. The holdings of the Saskatchewan Archives Board are described more fully in Christine MacDonald, *Historical Directory of Saskatchewan Newspapers, 1878-1983* (Regina, 1984). The provincial archives holds many other collections of private papers, territorial and provincial government records and publications, maps, and unpublished memoirs that also reveal a good deal about Regina's history. The City of Regina Archives, only recently established, has acquired the minutes (1884-1983) and bylaws (1884-1985) of the town and city councils. The more recent council minutes and bylaws can be consulted in the City Clerk's Office at city hall. The records of various city departments (in many cases up to the late 1970s) are also being transferred to the City of Regina Archives. As this material is inventoried and made more accessible, it will doubtless prove to be a valuable source for future research on Regina. There is also a wealth of material on Regina's physical growth in the library of the Urban Planning Department at city hall. As well, the Public Archives of Canada and the Glenbow-Alberta Institute have collections that should be consulted for information on Regina's early history. The former contains the records of the North-West Land Company.

Several institutions in Regina have extensive photograph collections that are an invaluable source for anyone interested in Regina's past. The Saskatchewan Archives Board has by far the largest and most accessible collection. The holdings of the Royal Canadian Mounted Police Museum, the Saskatchewan Sports Hall of Fame, the City of Regina Archives, the University of Regina Archives and the Regina Public Library's Prairie History Room are smaller but should certainly not be overlooked.

General Works

Several popular histories of Regina have appeared, but only Earl Drake, *Regina: The Queen City* (Toronto, 1955), provides anything like a detailed and critical narrative (and it does not extend far beyond the end of the Second World War). There is also a brief historical overview in Edmund H. Dale, ed., *Regina: Regional Isolation and Innovative Development* (Victoria, 1980). However, most of the essays in this eighteenth volume of the Western Geographical Series address contemporary themes such as planning, the development of Wascana Centre, Regina's Telebus experiment and changes in the city's economic functions. Similarly, the short "biography" of Regina in George A. Nader, *Cities of Canada*, Vol. 2, *Profiles of Fifteen Metropolitan Centres* (Toronto,

1976), is mainly concerned with the contemporary city and not its historical roots.

A careful reading of John Archer, *Saskatchewan: A History* (Saskatoon, 1980), will help to set Regina's development in a wider provincial context. Archer's discussion of the emergence of "King Wheat" and its implications for the province's economy, society and politics is particularly good. But urban themes *per se* are not treated extensively in this history of what has been until recently a predominantly rural province. J. Howard Richards and K. I. Fung, *Atlas of Saskatchewan* (Saskatoon, 1969), is also useful. The best history of the prairie region is Gerald Friesen's widely acclaimed *The Canadian Prairies: A History* (Toronto, 1984).

Specific Themes

The Origins and Incorporation of Regina

The role of the Canadian Pacific Railway as a townsite promoter and its relationship with the Canada North-West Land Company are explored briefly in James B. Hedges, *Building the Canadian West: The Land and Colonization Policies of the Canadian Pacific Railway* (New York, 1939), and Max Foran, "The CPR and the Urban West, 1881-1930," in Hugh A. Dempsey, ed., *The CPR West: The Iron Road and the Making of a Nation* (Vancouver, 1984), pp. 89-105. A fuller account, with particular emphasis on Regina, can be found in J. William Brennan, "Business-Government Co-operation in Townsite Promotion in Regina and Moose Jaw, 1882-1903," in Alan F. J. Artibise, ed., *Town and City: Aspects of Western Canadian Urban Development* (Regina, 1981), pp. 95-120. The controversy surrounding the selection of Regina as the capital of the North-West Territories in 1882, and Edgar Dewdney's subsequent efforts to influence the direction of the town's growth are discussed at length in Jean Larmour, "Edgar Dewdney, Commissioner of Indian Affairs and Lieutenant Governor of the North-West Territories, 1879-1888" (unpublished M.A. thesis, University of Saskatchewan, Regina, 1969). A. N. Reid has examined Regina's first tentative efforts at self-government in "Informal Town Government in Regina, 1882-3," *Saskatchewan History*, 6, no. 3 (Autumn 1953): 81-88.

Economic Growth and Metropolitan Development

Alan Artibise has done more than any other scholar in Canada to emphasize the role of boosterism in the city-building process. Most of his work has focused on Winnipeg, but his "Boosterism and the Development of Prairie Cities, 1871-1913," in Alan F. J. Artibise, ed., *Town and City*, pp. 209-35, and "Continuity and Change: Elites and Prairie Urban Development, 1914-1950," in Alan F. J. Artibise and Gilbert A. Stelter, eds., *The Usable Urban Past: Planning and Politics in the Modern Canadian City* (Toronto, 1979), pp. 130-54, deal with the wider prairie experience. Donald Richan has explored the same theme in a Regina context in "Boosterism and Urban Rivalry in Regina and Moose Jaw, 1902-1913" (unpublished M.A. thesis, University of Regina, 1981). Cesar Caviedes, "The Functional Structure of Regina," in Edmund H. Dale, ed., *Regina*, pp. 53-95, offers some useful insights into the changing structure of Regina's economy during the 1960s and 1970s. Paul Phillips takes a longer view and a wider regional focus in "The Prairie Urban System, 1911-1961: Specialization and Change," in Alan F. J. Artibise, ed., *Town and City*, pp. 7-30.

Much of the literature on prairie agriculture and related themes indirectly casts light on Regina's growth as a retail and wholesale distribution centre serving the farm community. Of particular value because of their focus on Saskatchewan are G. E. Britnell, *The Wheat Economy* (Toronto, 1939), and Charles Schwartz, *The Search for Stability* (Toronto, 1959). Garry Fairbairn's recent *From Prairie Roots: The Remarkable Story of Saskatchewan Wheat Pool* (Saskatoon, 1984) chronicles the rise of Canada's largest grain-handling concern, one of the few firms of any size to locate its head office in Regina. Of course, there was more to agriculture than wheat, even in its heyday, and scholars have begun to examine other lines of agricultural endeavour in the province. Some of this work contributes to a better understanding of the development of manufacturing in Regina (or the lack of such development). Gordon Church, *An*

Unfailing Faith: A History of the Saskatchewan Dairy Industry (Regina, 1985), is especially useful in this regard. There is as yet no comparable study of ranching in the province, but Harold Bronson, "The Developing Structure of the Saskatchewan Meat Packing Industry: A Study of Economic Welfare" (unpublished Ph.D. dissertation, University of Saskatchewan, 1965), provides a good analysis of the industry it serves.

A strong cooperative tradition took root early in rural Saskatchewan and in its towns and cities as well. The Saskatchewan experience is discussed briefly in Ian MacPherson's recent *Each for All: A History of the Co-operative Movement in English Canada, 1900-1945* (Toronto, 1979) and more fully in J. F. C. Wright, *Prairie Progress: Consumer Co-operation in Saskatchewan* (Saskatoon, 1956). Two books trace the rise of the credit union movement and the related financial institutions it spawned: Muriel Clements, *By Their Bootstraps: A History of the Credit Union Movement in Saskatchewan* (Toronto, 1965), and Christine Purden, *Agents for Change: Credit Unions in Saskatchewan* (Regina, 1980). Ian MacPherson has examined another manifestation of that cooperative tradition in *The Story of CIS Ltd.: Co-operative Insurance Services* (Regina, 1974).

Extensive oil and potash discoveries since the Second World War have helped to diversify Saskatchewan's economy. John Richards and Larry Pratt discuss this transformation in considerable detail in *Prairie Capitalism: Power and Influence in the New West* (Toronto, 1979). Brian Banks, "The Political Economy of Petroleum Development in Saskatchewan, 1940-1960" (unpublished M.A. thesis, University of Regina, 1986), is a valuable supplement; it examines the urban impact of the oil and gas boom in the province more fully.

Other themes in the economic history of Regina and other Saskatchewan cities have only begun to be examined in G. T. Bloomfield, "'I Can See a Car in That Crop': Motorization in Saskatchewan, 1906-1934," *Saskatchewan History* 37, no. 1 (Winter 1984): 3-24, and Ray H. Crone, "Aviation Pioneers in Saskatchewan," *Saskatchewan History* 28, no. 1 (Winter 1975): 9-28, for instance.

Population Growth and Ethnic Relationships

Regina's ethnic communities are only beginning to attract serious scholarly attention, and much remains to be done. There is as yet no full-scale study of any ethnic group in the city. The Germans are treated briefly in Heinz Lehmann, *Das Deutschtum in Westkanada* (Berlin, 1939). The book has recently been translated into English by Gerhard Bassler and republished (along with some of Lehmann's other work from the 1930s) as *The German Canadians, 1750-1937: Immigration, Settlement and Culture* (St. John's, 1986). Kurt Tischler, "The German-Canadians in Saskatchewan with Particular Reference to the Language Problem, 1900-1930" (unpublished M.A. thesis, University of Saskatchewan, 1978), is also of value, though of course his focus is not exclusively or even predominantly on Regina. The problems *Der Courier* encountered during the Second World War are discussed in W. Entz, "The Suppression of the German Language Press in September 1918 (with special reference to the secular German Language papers in Western Canada)," *Canadian Ethnic Studies* 8, no. 2 (1976): 56-70. The extent of Reginans' participation in the Deutscher Bund is explored in Jonathan Wagner, "The *Deutscher Bund Canada* in Saskatchewan," *Saskatchewan History* 31, no. 2 (Spring 1978), 41-50.

The experience of Regina's Ukrainians has been examined somewhat more fully. Bohdan Kazymyra, *Early Ukrainian Settlement in Regina, 1890-1920* (Winnipeg, 1977), is the best local ethnic history to appear to date. A useful supplement is the Ukrainian Senior Citizens of Regina, *From Dreams to Reality: A History of the Ukrainian Senior Citizens of Regina and District, 1896-1976* (Winnipeg, 1977). Other books that take a wider national focus, such as Manoly R. Lupul, ed., *A Heritage in Transition: Essays in the History of Ukrainians in Canada* (Toronto, 1982), also contain references to Regina's Ukrainian community or help to set the local experience in a larger context. Histories of other ethnic groups often do, too. Three particularly good recent works are H. Radecki and B. Heydenkorn, *A Member of a Distinguished Family: The Polish Group in Canada* (Toronto, 1976); N. F. Dreisziger *et al.*, *Struggle and Hope: The Hungarian-Canadian Experience* (Toronto, 1982); and E. Wickberg *et al.*, *From China to*

Canada: A History of the Chinese Communities in Canada (Toronto, 1982).

With the host society determined to enforce assimilation and many of Saskatchewan's ethnic groups seeking to preserve their distinctive language, culture and traditions, it should not have been surprising that schools and schooling long remained controversial issues. There is an extensive literature on the "school question." Of particular value are M. P. Toombs, "A Saskatchewan Experiment in Teacher Education, 1907-1917," *Saskatchewan History* 17, no. 1 (Winter 1964): 1-11; Ray Huel, "The French Canadians and the Language Question, 1918," *Saskatchewan History* 23, no. 1 (Winter 1970): 1-15; and Ray Huel, "Pastor vs. Politician: The Reverend Murdoch MacKinnon and Premier Walter Scott's Amendment to the School Act," *Saskatchewan History* 32, no. 2 (Spring 1979): 61-73. The Ku Klux Klan, which made considerable inroads in Regina and across Saskatchewan in the 1920s, has also been examined in detail. The best studies are William Calderwood, "The Rise and Fall of the Ku Klux Klan in Saskatchewan" (unpublished M.A. thesis, University of Saskatchewan, Regina, 1968 — from which he has spun off several articles), and Ray Huel, "*La Survivance* in Saskatchewan: Schools, Politics and the Nativist Crusade for Cultural Conformity" (unpublished Ph.D. dissertation, University of Alberta, 1975).

Large numbers of Native people began moving to Regina in the 1950s and 1960s, introducing a highly visible element into the city's population. This phenomenon has attracted a good deal of attention, and a substantial literature has begun to accumulate. Of particular value are Andrew Bear Robe, *Tour of Canadian Friendship Centres* (Ottawa, 1971); Larry Krotz, *Urban Indians: The Strangers in Canada's Cities* (Edmonton, 1980): Stewart J. Clatworthy and Jonathan P. Gunn, *Economic Circumstances of Native People in Selected Metropolitan Centres in Western Canada* (Winnipeg, 1981); and Stewart J. Clatworthy and Jeremy Hull, *Native Economic Conditions in Regina and Saskatoon* (Winnipeg, 1983).

The emergence of trade unions in Regina and Saskatchewan has also begun to be examined in some detail. W. J. C. Cherwinski, "Organized Labour in Saskatchewan: The T.L.C. Years, 1905-1945" (unpublished Ph.D. dissertation, University of Alberta, 1971), provides a good overview of the Saskatchewan experience, with numerous references to the situation in the provincial capital. Insofar as Regina is concerned, Cherwinski's pioneering efforts have been supplemented by Glen Makahonuk. His "The Regina Painters' Strike of 1912," *Saskatchewan History* 35, no. 3 (Autumn 1982): 108-15, "Painters, Decorators and Paperhangers: A Case Study in Saskatchewan Labourism, 1906-1919," *Prairie Forum* 10, no. 1 (Spring 1985): 189-204, and "Masters and Servants: Labour Relations in the Saskatchewan Civil Service, 1905-1945," *Prairie Forum* 12, no. 2 (Fall 1987): 257-76, are all useful. A fuller account of union activity among the province's civil servants can be found in Doug Taylor, *For Dignity, Equality and Justice: A History of the Saskatchewan Government Employees' Union* (Regina, 1984).

There are three good accounts of the On-to-Ottawa Trek and the Regina Riot. Two are recent works: Victor Howard, "*We Were the Salt of the Earth!" A Narrative of the On-to-Ottawa Trek and the Regina Riot* (Regina, 1985), and Lorne Brown, *When Freedom Was Lost: The Unemployed, the Agitator, and the State* (Montreal, 1987). The older Gladys Stone, "The Regina Riot, 1935" (unpublished M.A. thesis, University of Saskatchewan, Saskatoon, 1967), is still of value.

The Urban Landscape

Graduate students in history, and more especially in geography, have made the most important contributions in this field. The theses the author found most useful were: Timothy Gross, "Infill Housing in Regina: The Roles of the Actors in the Implementation Process" (unpublished M.A. thesis, University of Regina, 1984); Rodney Laporte, "The Development of Parks in Regina, 1882-1930: Private Initiative and Public Policy" (unpublished M.A. thesis, University of Regina, 1984); Gordon Lipinski, "A Review and Post-Planning Evaluation of the Development of the Ross Industrial Park, Regina, Saskatchewan" (unpublished M.A. thesis, University of Regina, 1984); John Moser, "The Impact of City Council's Decisions Between 1903 and 1930 on the Morphological Development of Regina" (unpublished M.A.

thesis, University of Regina, 1978); Donald Ross, "Population Growth, the Catalyst of Spatial Changes in Regina, 1945 to 1975, With a Projection to the Future" (unpublished M.A. thesis, University of Regina, 1979); and Elizabeth Troyer, "Causes of Regina's Rental Housing Shortage and Its Effects on Residential Satisfaction, 1972-1978" (unpublished M.A. thesis, University of Regina, 1980). There is as yet little published work of value apart from the essays in Edmund H. Dale, ed., *Regina*. The Saskatchewan Association of Architects, *Historic Architecture of Saskatchewan* (Regina, 1986), also contains some fine Regina examples of the architect's craft.

Civic Politics, Government and Services

The literature here is thin. There is almost nothing that focuses specifically on Regina, save for W. D. Young, "M. J. Coldwell, the Making of a Social Democrat," *Journal of Canadian Studies* 9, no. 3 (August 1974): 50-60, and Colin Hatcher, *Saskatchewan's Pioneer Streetcars: The Story of the Regina Municipal Railway* (Montreal, 1971). Other books and articles dealing with larger provincial, regional or national themes do include some comment (in some cases quite extensive comment) on Regina. Thus J. Harvey Perry, *Taxes, Tariffs, and Subsidies: A History of Canadian Fiscal Development*, 2 vols. (Toronto, 1955), discusses Regina's experiment with the single tax, and C. O. White, *Power for a Province: A History of Saskatchewan Power* (Regina, 1976), the acrimonious debate over the sale of Regina's electrical utility to the Saskatchewan Power Corporation. John Taylor devotes some attention to Regina in "Urban Social Organization and Urban Discontent: The 1930s," in D. J. Bercuson, ed., *Western Perspectives 1* (Toronto, 1974), pp. 33-44, and in "Mayors à la Mancha: An Aspect of Depression Leadership in Canadian Cities," *Urban History Review* 9, no. 3 (February 1981): 3-14, as does James D. Anderson in "The Municipal Government Reform Movement in Western Canada, 1880-1920," in Alan F. J. Artibise and Gilbert A. Stelter, eds., *The Usable Urban Past*, pp. 73-111. John Taylor, "Urban Autonomy in Canada: Its Evolution and Decline," in Gilbert A. Stelter and Alan F. J. Artibise, eds., *The Canadian Cities: Essays in Urban and Social History*, rev. ed.

(Ottawa, 1984), pp. 478-500, is also highly recommended; it too places the Saskatchewan experience in a wider context.

Index

Adams, Thomas, 125
Aerial Service Company, 110
Albert Park, 177
Albert School, 53, 140, 165, 167
Albert Street Bridge, 136
Alberta Stock Exchanges, 153
Alexandra School, 53
All Peoples' Mission, 67
Allan Cup, 147
Allen theatres, 95
Anderson, J. T. M., 146
Angus, R. B., 11
Armour, Hugh, 61, 62, 106
Arnheim Place, 173
Asiatic Exclusion League, 71
Assiniboia, 23, 37, 47
Assiniboia Agricultural Society of Regina, 25
Assiniboia Club, 95
Assiniboia East, 175
Assiniboia Provincial Rifle Association, 52
Assiniboia West, 47, 49
Association of Ukrainian-English Teachers, 66
Athabasca provincial district, 49

Baker, Henry, 187
Balfour Apartments, 126
Balfour, James, 128, 139
Balgonie, 35
Bank of Montreal, 37
baseball, 52, 95, 97
Beaver Lumber, 106
Bell Telephone Company, 44
Belle Plaine, 159
Bennett, R. B., 140, 146
Bijou Family Theatre, 95
Black, Henry, 116, 131, 145
Black, N. F., 84
Blakeney, Allan E., 187
Bloore, Ron, 188

Board of Railway Commissioners, 57
Boggy Creek, 43, 47, 89, 135, 181
Bole, J. F., 29, 84, 92
Bolshevik, 116
Boundary Dam, 183
Bow, Dr. Malcolm, 68
Brandon and McFee, 14
Bredt, Paul, 35, 65
British City Planning Association, 84
British Commonwealth Air Training Plan, 169
Broder Building, 119
Broder's Annex, 83
Brown, George, 23
Buchanan, W. F., 31, 33
Buffalo Pound Lake; reservoir, 181, 183
Bureau of Labour, 71
Bureau of Public Welfare, 128, 136
P. Burns and Company, 106, 151

Cameron, Dan, 148
Canada Life Building, 79
Canada North-West Land Company (CNWLC), 11, 41
Canadian Congress of Labour, 167
Canadian Hungarian Cultural Club, 119
Canadian Labour Defence League, 140
Canadian National Railway, 101, 110, 181
Canadian Northern Railway (CN), 33, 55, 57, 74
Canadian Pacific Railway (CPR), 47, 51, 73, 74, 87, 101, 110; branch lines, 33, 57; construction, 38; construction — "Soo Line," 21, 23; and establishment of Regina, 11-2, 14, 17, 37, 189; exemption from municipal taxation, 41, 43; festivals, 148; financial difficulties, 18; as future of Regina, 19; impact of tornado, 83; introduction of competition to, 55; presence in Moose Jaw, 61; townsite lots, 58; underpass, 136
CPR Park, 95
Canadian Patriotic Fund, 113
Canadian Unemployed Workers' Association, 137
Capitol Theatre, 119, 147
Carlyle, 33, 135

Carnegie Corporation, 149
Carnegie Foundation, 88
Case, J. I., 39
Catholic Mutual Benefit Association, 95
Celebrity Concert Series, 148
Champ, Wesley, 147
Chateau Qu'Appelle, 84, 110, 125
Children's Aid Society, 97
China, immigrants from, 35, 68, 117
Chinese Benevolent Society, 119
CHWC radio, 147
Citizens' Committee, 18, 128, 131
Citizens' Emergency Commitee, 140
City Act, 143
Civic Government Association (CGA), 139, 140, 143, 145
Civic Labour League (CLL), 143
Civic Relief Board, 137, 140, 143
Civic Voters' Association (CVA), 145, 185
CKCK radio, 147
Clark, Ed, 110
Clemesha and Portnall, 79
Co-operative Commonwealth Federation (CCF), 99, 140, 146, 147, 159, 183, 185, 187
Co-operative Fire and Casualty, 153
Co-operative Labour Party, 139
Co-operative Life, 153
Coldwell, M. J., 131, 146
Commission of Conservation, 125
Communist Party, 185
Communists, 137-9; May Day rally, 137; mayoralty candidate, 139
Community Chest, 143
Community Clothing Depot, 136, 139, 140
Community Planning Scheme, 181
Conservatory of Music, 92, 149
Consumers' Co-operative Refineries Limited, 104, 175
Cornwall Centre, 179
Cottage Hospital Fund, 43
Coventry Place, 173
Cowan, W. D., 91, 146
Cowburn, T. H., 187

Daily Province, 84
Daily Standard, 68, 84
Darke Block, 79

Darke, Frank, 58, 92, 149
Davin, Nicholas Flood, 17, 33, 47, 49, 52
Degelman Industries, 159
Department of Municipal Affairs, province of Saskatchewan, 91
Der Courier, 113, 119
Deutsch-Kanadisches Zentralkomitee, 119
Deutschcanadischer Provinzialverband von Saskatchewan, 65
Deutscher Bund Canada, 165
Deutscher Tage, 119
Deverell, Rex, 188
Dewdney Avenue, 31
Dewdney, Edgar, 12, 17, 21, 31, 37
Dewdney Place, 123
Diefenbaker, John, 187
District Planning Committee, 175
Dixon, Charles, 143
Doerr, J. E., 84
Dominion Government Building, 119
Dominion Housing Act, 128
Dominion Lands Office, 18, 23
Dominion Park, 95, 125, 148
Dominion Park School, 131
Dominion Securities, 106
Douglas Park, 123, 177, 180
Douglas, T. C., 155, 167, 187
Duncan, William H., 106
Dunning, Charles, 116, 146

Earl Grey, 95
East, Samuel B., 143, 146
T. Eaton Company, 101, 125, 126, 180
Elite Theatre, 95
Ellison, Alban C., 140, 143, 145, 147
Epworth League, 95
Estevan, 61
ethnic tensions, 113, 115
Europe; immigrants from, 35, 36
Exchequer Court, 125
Exhibition Grounds, 140, 148

Faludi, E. G., 173, 179
Faludi Plan, 181
Famous Players, 147
Felsch, Hap, 147
Financial Building, 179

Fines, Clarence M., 140, 187
First World War, 55, 58, 65, 97, 99, 111, 115, 187
football, 147-8
Forget, Lieutenant-Governor A. E., 51
Forman, Nellie, 115
Fort Carlton, 11
Fort Ellice, 11
Fort Pitt, 11
Fort Qu'Appelle, 11, 29; see also Qu'Appelle
Fort Walsh, 12
Fosterton, 155
Franco-Prussian War, 17
French language, use in Regina, 115

Gaiety Theatre, 95
Galt, John, 47
Gee, Fred M., 148
General Motors, 106, 123, 151
George, Henry, 84
German Baptist church, 119
German Mutual Improvement Society, 35
German language, use in Regina, 115
German-Canadian Harmonie Club, 165; Oktoberfest, 165
Germantown, 39, 65, 67, 76, 83
Germany, 61; immigrants from, 35, 67, 113, 117, 162; pro-Nazi sympathizers, 165
Gibbon, John Murray, 110
Gladmer Park, 178
Glasgow House, 29, 57
Glencairn Village, 177
Globe and Mail (Toronto), 14
Globe Theatre, 188
Godwin, Ted, 188
Golden Mile Centre, 178
Gordon, Ironside and Fares, 61
Government House, 51, 95
Grand Trunk Pacific Railway (GTP), 55, 57, 74, 83, 84, 87, 110
Grant, Gordon, 187
Grassick, James, 145, 146
Gratton Separate School, 53
Great Britain; demand for goods during WW1, 99; immigrants from, 35, 113, 162; influence on Regina, 51, 63, 65, 189; influence on Regina — evolution, 55

Great Depression, 102, 104, 106, 110-1, 113, 123, 126, 133, 135, 139, 143, 145, 147, 149, 151, 169, 173, 181, 185, 187
Great Peace River District, 14
Great War Veterans' Association, 131
Great West Canadian Folksong, Folkdance and Handicrafts Festival, 110, 148
Greater Regina Club, 58, 68, 97
Greer Court, 178
Grey Cup, 148, 188
Groome, Roland J., 110
Groves, Barney, 95
Gyro Club, 147

Hartney, 33
Haultain, F. W. G., 49, 68
Herbert Court, 139
Herchmer, L. W., 31, 33
Heseltine, Ralph, 139
Hewitt, Foster, 147
Highland Park, 123, 169, 173
Hill, W. H. A., 58, 79, 126
Hillsdale subdivision, 175, 177
Hitler, Adolph, 165
hockey, 52; development of local leagues, 52; rivalry with Moose Jaw, 52
Holy Rosary Cathedral, 83
Homeowners' Association, 145
Horticultural Society, 83
Hotel Saskatchewan, 110, 119, 147
Houston, William H., 106
Houston Willoughby and Company, 106, 153
Hudson's Bay, 23
Hudson's Bay Company (HBC), 11, 101, 104, 179
Hungarian Catholic parish, 119

immigrants; Anglo-Saxon influence on, 187; assistance for, 115; British, 162; Chinese, 35, 68, 117; Chinese — discrimination against, 68,70; European, 15, 35; German, 35, 61, 67, 110, 113, 117, 162; German — pro-Nazi sympathizers, 165; Russian, 35; Ukrainian, 35, 119, 162
immigration, 63, 65-67; influence of European immigrants on Regina, 189;
Imperial Oil Limited, 104, 110, 155, 157, 169, 173
Independent Labour Party (ILP), 137, 139, 146
Innismore, 123
Intercontinental Packers, 151

International Brotherhood of Maintenance of Way Employees, 71
International Typographical Union, 71
Interprovincial Pipe Line, 155
Interprovincial Steel and Pipe Corporation Limited (IPSCO), 157, 175
Irish Times (Dublin), 17

Kalium Chemicals, 159
Kamsack, 155
Katepwa Beach, 97
Kenderdine, Gus, 149
Kicking Horse Pass, 11
King Tegart, 173
King, William Lyon Mackenzie, 146
King's Hotel, 79, 97
Kinsmen Club, 147
Kiwanis Club, 147
Knox Presbyterian Church, 67, 79, 149
Kramer, Ken, 188
Kramer, L. L., 35, 87
Kramer, Sue, 188
Krauss, Andrew, 84
S. S. Kresge Company, 111
Kronau, 35
Ku Klux Klan, 119, 146

Labour-Progressive Party (LPP), 185
LaColle Falls, 61
lacrosse, 52, 95, 97
Laird, H. W., 73
Lakeview, 58, 79, 125, 126, 139, 173, 175
Lalonde, "Newsy", 97
Lancaster, Ron, 188
Land Titles Building, 58
Langley, George, 63
Last Mountain, 97, 135
Laubach, Frank L., 52, 95, 148
Laurier, Sir Wilfrid, 37, 62
Lawn Tennis Club, 52
Leader, 17, 33, 37, 47, 49
Leader-Post, 136, 145, 149, 185
Leduc, 155
Legislative Building, Saskatchewan, 58, 180
Lions Club, 147
Literary Society, 52
Lloydminster, 155

P. Lyall and Sons, 73
Local Government Board, 91
Lochhead, Kenneth, 188
Luther College, 119
Lutheran parish, 119
Lux Theatre, 95
P. Lyall and Sons, 71

Macdonald, Sir John A., 12, 14, 37
Mackenzie, Norman, 149
MacKinnon, Murdoch, 67
Mackintosh, Charles H., 25
MacPherson, M. A., 146
Majestic Theatre, 95
Mallory Springs, 135, 181
Market Square, 139, 140
Markwell, Mary, 52
Martin, Robert, 63, 84
Martin, W. M., 91
Masons, 51
Massey family, 92
Massey-Harris, 39
Mathieu, O. E. (Bishop), 67
Mawson, Thomas, 84, 125
Maxwell, Edward, 74
Maxwell, W. S., 74
McAra, James, 131, 139
McCallum, E. A., 58, 65
McCallum, E. D., 58, 65, 83, 126
McCallum Hill and Company, 73, 79, 175
McCallum Hill Building, 58, 119
McKay, Art, 188
McManus, T. G., 140, 143, 146
Mechanics and Literary Institute, 52
Melville, 57, 76
Memorial Cup, 148, 188
Menzies, Garnet, 146, 185
Métis, 23, 37
Métis Friendship Centre, 165
Metropolitan Methodist Church, 79
Metropolitan Opera, 52
Metropolitan Stores, 111
Midtown Centre, 179
Mikkelson, Peter, 140, 143

Mile Belt, 18
Military Hospitals Commission, 131
Ministerial Association, 140
Mirror subdivision, 73, 123
Moderation League, 115
Molloy, Thomas M., 71
Moose Jaw, 11, 21, 23, 35, 57, 61, 133, 135; economic benefits from North-West rebellion, 31; population growth, 55; sports teams' rivalries with Regina, 52; value of goods produced in, 62; water sharing with Regina, 183
Morning Leader, 68, 116, 147
Morton, Doug, 188
Mosaic Festival, 165, 188
Motherwell Building, 179
Motherwell, W. R., 146
Mound Springs, 135, 181
Mount Pleasant Park, 180
Mowat, Daniel, 29, 31
Murray, Walter, 92
Museum of Natural History, 180, 188
Music and Art Building, 149
Musical and Dramatic Society, 52

National Hockey League, 147
Natives in Regina, 35, 37, 165, 167; population, 167; social position, 35, 37
Neigborhood Improvement Projects (NIP), 180
New Democratic Party, 187
Normandy Heights, 173
Normanview, 177
North Annex, 123, 169, 173
North Regina, 61, 123, 173 *see also* Regina
North Saskatchewan River, 11, 21; river valley, 11
North Side Ratepayers' Association, 131
North-West Commercial Travellers' Association, 58
North-West Council, 18
North-West Mounted Police (NWMP),11, 17, 18, 31, 35, 37; barracks, 21; barracks — construction, 12, 58; economic impact on Regina, 31; local law enforcement, 43; popularity of sports with, 52
North-West Rebellion, 23, 31; economic benefits for Regina from, 31
North-West Territories, 21, 23, 25, 33, 35, 37, 189
Northern Crown Bank, 79
Northgate Shopping Centre, 178

Odd Fellows, 51

On-To-Ottawa-Trek, 140, 189
One Big Union (OBU), 116
Operatic Society, 95
Orange Lodge, 51, 67
Osler, E. B., 11

Park de Young, 148, 188
Park Hughes, 148, 188
Parker, L. D. "Pete," 147
Parks Hockey League, 147
Parliament Place, 177
Pasqua, 21, 23
Patriotic Revenue Tax, 128
Patrons of Industry, 49
Peat, Hugh, 71
Pemberton Securities, 153
Perley, Senator William D., 25
Perry, Harry, 128
Peverett, J. R., 91
Pile of Bones Creek (Wascana Creek), 11, 189 *see also* Wascana Creek
Pioneer Life, 153
Polish parishes, 66, 119
polo, 52, 95
Portal, 21
Potash Corporation of Saskatchewan, 159
Power Resources Commission, 133
Powers, J. W., 52
Prairie Pipe Manufacturing Company, 157
Princess Patricia's Canadian Light Infantry, 147
Princess Theatre, 95
Principal Investments Limited, 178
Progressive Conservative Party, 187
Progressive Party, 146
Prosvita Society, 119

Qu'Appelle, 17, 21, 31, 39, 97, 110
Qu'Appelle, Long Lake and Saskatchewan Railway, 17, 21, 39
Qu'Appelle River, 181
Quaker Oats Company, 61

Reed, George, 188
Regent Court, 175, 178
Regent Park, 177
Regina; East End, 128, 165; North Side, 53, 95, 131; North Side — grievances of residents, 87; North Side — impact of tornado on, 83; North Side — Neighbourhood Improvements projects, 180; North

Side — park construction, 173; North Side — support for Ward system, 140; North Side — as working class area, 74, 76; role as administrative centre, 31; West End, 139, 180
Regina Balmorals, 147
Regina Beach, 97
Regina Board of Trade, 33, 58, 83, 87, 91, 110, 151
Regina Boat Club, 97
Regina Brass Band, 52
Regina Brokerage and Investment Company, 106
Regina Bureau of Public Welfare, 97
Regina Capitals, 147
Regina Chamber of Commerce, 185;
Regina City Planning Association, 84
Regina Civic Association (RCA), later Regina Citizens' Association, 185
Regina College, 92, 148, 188
Regina College School of Art, 149, 188
Regina Collegiate Institute, 95
Regina Creamery Company, 31
Regina Curling Club, 52
Regina Daily Star, 146
Regina Electric Light and Power Company, 44, 61
Regina Five group of painters, 188
Regina Folk Arts Coucil, 165
Regina General Hospital, 89, 135, 139, 167
Regina Golf Club, 52
Regina Home Owners' and Taxpayers' Association, 143
Regina Industries Limited, 151, 169
Regina Little Theatre, 148
Regina Local Council of Women, 43, 140, 149; arts and letters committee, 149
Regina Male Voice Choir, 149
Regina Manifesto, 146
Regina Milling Company, 29
Regina Monarchs, 147
Regina Municipal New Democratic Party, 187
Regina Municipal Railway, 76, 79, 89, 91, 126, 131
Regina Nationals, 147
Regina Native Race Relations Association (RNRRA), 167
Regina Orchestral Society, 95
Regina Pats, 147, 188
Regina People's Forum, 131, 140
Regina Philharmonic Society, 52, 95
Regina Public Library, 179;
Regina Reserve, 18

Regina Riot, 140
Regina Roughriders, 147-8
Regina Rugby Club, 97
Regina Symphony Orchestra, 95, 148
Regina Theatre, 95
Regina Town Planning Association, 125
Regina Trades and Labour Council (RTLC), 71, 115, 116, 128, 140, 167
Regina Trading Company, 29, 57
Regina Transit System, 181
Regina Unemployed Workers' Council, 137
Regina Vics, 147
Regina Welfare Bureau, 140, 143
Regina-Moose Jaw Water District, 135
Relief Camps Workers' Union, 140
Rex Theatre, 95
Riel, Louis, 23, 37
Rink, Cornelius; as alderman, 84, 87-8, background, 87; mayoralty bids, 128, 139; as mayor, 139, 140, 143
Risberg, Swede, 147
Ritchie, Alvin Horace, 148
Ritter, Fred, 97
River Heights, 175
Robin Hood Mills, 61
Roman Catholic schools, 95
Roman Catholic Sisters of Charity (Grey Nuns), 89
Romanian Hall, 115
Romanian Greek Orthodox Church, 39, 66
Roseland Theatre, 95
Rosemont subdivision, 73, 175
Ross Industrial Park, 169
Ross, Malcolm, 83
Rotary Club, 125, 147
Royal Canadian Mounted Police (RCMP), 71, 79, 110, 140, 143, 188
Royal Flying Corps, 110
Royal North-West Mounted Police, 111
Royal Templars of Temperance, 51
rugby, 97
Rundschau, 35, 65
Rural Municipality of Sherwood, 175
Russia, immigrants from, 35
Ruttan, H. N., 43

Sacred Heart Academy, 95
Safeway Stores, 111

Salvation Army, 97
Sapiro, Aaron, 101
Saskatchewan; Golden Jubilee, 165
Saskatchewan Assessment Commission, 131
Saskatchewan Centre of the Arts, 180, 188
Saskatchewan Civil Service Association (SCSA), 97, 167
Saskatchewan Co-operative Credit Society, 153
Saskatchewan Co-operative Elevator Company, 58, 101
Saskatchewan Co-operative Wheat Producers Limited, 101
Saskatchewan Conference, 92
Saskatchewan Courier, 65
Saskatchewan Farmer-Labour Party, 146
Saskatchewan Government Employees' Association, 167
Saskatchewan Government Insurance Office, 153, 179
Saskatchewan Grain Growers' Association, 58
Saskatchewan Herald (Battleford), 12
Saskatchewan Housing Corporation, 178
Saskatchewan Indian Cultural College, 167
Saskatchewan Legislative Building, 58, 180
Saskatchewan Music Festival, 95
Saskatchewan Oil and Gas Corporation, 157
Saskatchewan Power Commission, 133
Saskatchewan Power Corporation (SPC), 157, 179, 183
Saskatchewan Roughriders, 188; ticket revenues, 188
Saskatchewan Telecommunications, 180
Saskatchewan Temperance Act, 115
Saskatchewan Water Supply Commission, 135
Saskatchewan Wheat Pool, 101, 102, 153
Scandinavian Club, 119
Scarth, W. B., 11, 17, 21
School Act; amendment of 1913, 67
Scott, D. L., 18
Scott, Walter, 47, 49, 57, 67, 74
Sears department store, 180
Second World War, 113, 123, 125, 135, 151, 159, 162, 165, 167, 169, 175, 181, 187
Sedley, 131
Settlement House, 115
Sharp, Bill, 159
Sheldon-Williams, Inglis, 149
Sherwood Co-operative Association, 111
Sherwood Credit Union, 153
Shevchenko, 66
Shoal Lake, (Manitoba), 29

Sifton, Clifford, 47
Robert Simpson Company, 101, 169, 178
Simpson-Hayes, Catherine, 52
Sing, Mack, 68
Smith, Donald A., 11
Smith, J. W, 84
soccer, 52; development of local leagues, 52
socialists, 131
Socony-Vacuum, 155
Sohio, 157
Solomon, George, 157
Sons of England, 95
Sons of Scotland, 52, 95; sports days, 52
"Soo Line", 21, 57
Souris, 61, 133
South Saskatchewan River, 133, 135, 181, 183
South-western Railway, 19
St. Andrew's Society, 52
St. Chad's Hostel, 92
Standard (London), 17
Stanley Park, 39, 74
Stapleford, E. W. 149
Stephen, George, 14, 18, 21, 33
Storey, Stan E., 79
Stoughton, 33
Strasbourg, 35
subdivisions, 73, 175, 177; residential expansion through, 177
Supreme Court of Canada, 71
Swift Current, 31, 155

Task Force on Indian and Métis Opportunity, 165
Taylor Field, 188
Telebus, 181
Territorial Bonspiel, 52
Territorial Council, 18
Territorial Exhibition of 1895, 25
Teutonia Club, 65
Teutonia Society, 113
Thatcher, Ross, 187
Tidewater, 157
Todd, Frederick G., 74, 79
Toothill, John, 140, 143
Touchwood Hills, 11
Town Planning and Rural Development Act, 125

Town Planning Commission, 173
Townsite Trustees, 25, 41, 47, 57
Training School for Teachers for Foreign Speaking Communities, 66, 115
Trans-Canada Airlines, 111
Trans-Canada Highway, 185
Trant, William, 97
Treaty No. 4, 11
Trianon Dance Palace, 119, 147
Turner Valley, 104
Turvery, Jack, 159
Tuxedo Park, 123, 169
Tuxedo Park Urban Renewal Scheme, 169

Ukraine, immigrants from, 35
Ukrainian Labour Farmer Temple Association, 115, 119
Ukrainian Social Democratic Party, 115
Ukrainians in Regina; use of language, 115; church, 119; cultural festival, 165
Union Government, 146
Union of Saskatchewan Municipalities, 62
Union School, 52
Union Station, 136
Unique Theatre, 95
United Brotherhood of Carpenters and Joiners, 71
United Church of Canada, 149
United Farmers of Canada, 146
University of Regina, 167, 180
University of Saskatchewan, 91-2, 149, 188; Board of Governors, 91-2
University Park, 177
Use-Districts, 125

Van Egmond, William G., 79
Van Horne, W. C., 12, 21
Vancouver Stock Exchange, 153
Vibank, 35
Victoria Hospital, 43, 89
Victoria Park, 66, 83, 95, 119, 180
Victoria Square, 14, 17, 39, 51, 52, 73, 79, 126
Victorian Order of Nurses, 43
Volksverein Deutsch Canadischer Katholiken, 65

Walker, C. P., 95
Walker, Helena, 139
Walsh Acres, 177
War Time Elections Act, 113

Ward One Ratepayers' Association, 87
Wartime Housing and Housing Enterprises Limited, 169, 173
Wascana Centre Authority, 180
Wascana Country Club, 87, 95
Wascana Creek, 12, 14, 52, 74, 83, 95, 173, 175, 177 see also Pile of Bones Creek
Wascana Lake, 62, 74, 84, 97, 110, 123, 125, 136, 173; CVA enclave, 187; electrical generating plant, 183; as focal point for inner city, 180
Wascana Park, 84, 110, 125, 188
Washington Park subdivision, 73
Watson, Dixie, 49
Welfare Bureau, 140
Westank Industries, 159
Western Canada Airways, 111
Western Canada Hockey League, 147, 188
Western Canada Summer Games, 180
Western Milling Company, 25
Westgate, R. J., 135
Wetmore Schools, 95
Wheat Board, 102
White Bear Lake, 135 see also Carlyle
Whitmore Park subdivision, 175, 177
Williams, C. C., 185, 187
Williams, J. K. R., 29
Williams, R. H., 29, 31, 57, 58, 79, 84, 97, 101, 147, 167
Willoughby, Charles H., 106
Willoughby, Morley, 106
A. E. Wilson Park, 180
Wilson, W. Knight, 148
Winnipeg, Board of Trade, 23
Wolseley, 25
Women's Christian Temperance Union, 51
Wood Mountain, 14, 23
Woodsworth, J. S., 67, 83, 97, 115
F. W. Woolworth Company, 111
World Grain Exhibition and Conference, 104, 136, 139
Wynne-Roberts, R. O., 89

Yellowhead Pass, 11
Yorkton, 57
Young, John M., 29
Young Men's Christian Association (YMCA), 51, 79, 97
Young Women's Christian Association (YWCA), 79, 97